EXTR
JOINT LOCKING
AND BREAKING

To my teachers, students, and friends in the martial arts:
thank you for helping me learn.

EXTREME JOINT LOCKING AND BREAKING

Restraint and Submission Techniques for the Street

Loren W. Christensen

PALADIN PRESS • BOULDER, COLORADO

Also by Loren W. Christensen:

Brutal Art of Ripping, Poking, and Pressing Vital Targets
Brutal Art of Ripping, Poking, and Pressing Vital Targets: The Video (video)
Deadly Force Encounters
Fighter's Guide to Hard-Core Heavy Bag Training (with Wim Demeere)
Fighter's Video Guide to Hard-Core Heavy Bag Training (video, with Wim Demeere)
Fighting Dirty (DVD)
Fighting in the Clinch
Fighting Power
Gangbangers
Hookers, Tricks, and Cops
Masters and Styles (DVD)
Restraint and Control Strategies (DVD)
Riot
Skid Row Beat
Speed Training
Speed Training: The Video (video)
Surviving a School Shooting
Surviving Workplace Violence
Vital Targets (video)
Warriors: Updated and Expanded

Extreme Joint Locking and Breaking:
Restraint and Submission Techniques for the Street
by Loren W. Christensen

Copyright © 2006 by Loren W. Christensen
ISBN 13: 978-1-58160-492-4
Printed in the United States of America

Published by Paladin Press, a division of Paladin Enterprises, Inc., Gunbarrel Tech Center, 7077 Winchester Circle Boulder, Colorado 80301 USA, +1.303.443.7250

Direct inquiries and/or orders to the above address.

PALADIN, PALADIN PRESS, and the "horse head" design are trademarks belonging to Paladin Enterprises and registered in United States Patent and Trademark Office.

All rights reserved. Except for use in a review, no portion of this book introduced into a retrieval system, or transmitted in any form without the express written permission of the publisher. The scanning, uploading, and distribution of this book by the Internet or any other means without the permission of the publisher is illegal and punishable by law. Please respect the author's rights and do not participate in any form of electronic piracy of copyrighted material.

Neither the author nor the publisher assumes any responsibility for the use or misuse of information contained in this book.

Visit our website at www.paladin-press.com

⌐FINGER TECHNIQUES⌐

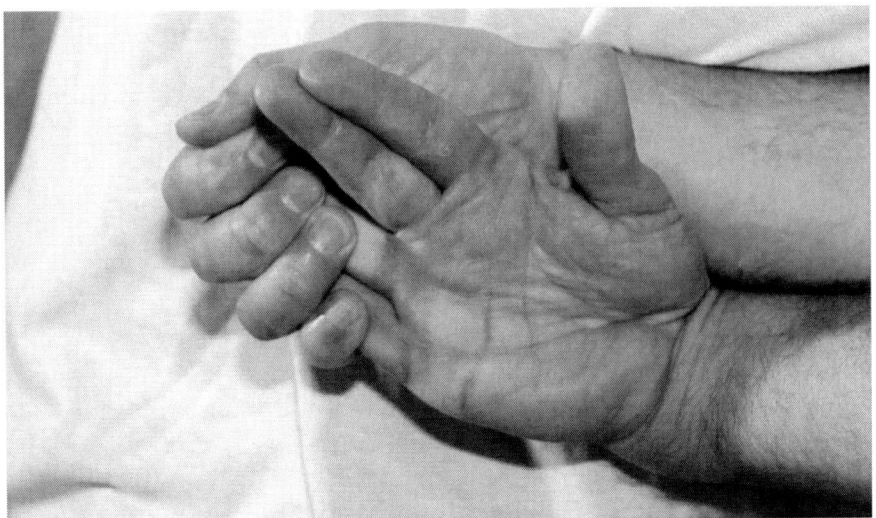

Variation 1
1. From the hand flex shown in step 2, slide your right hand across the back of your attacker's hand a bit and grasp his ring and little fingers.

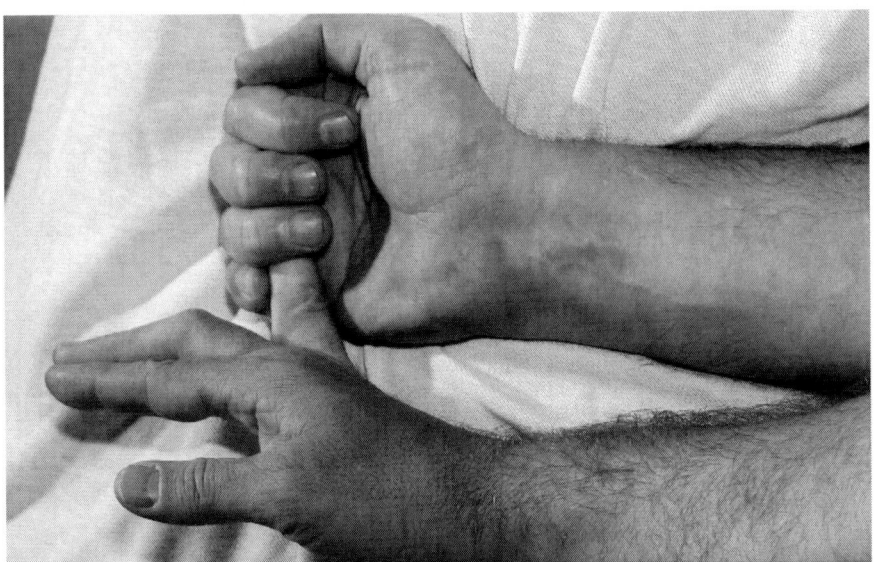

2. Rotate his hand so that it's palm down and then pull back on the fingers.

EXTREME JOINT LOCKING AND BREAKING

Keep his elbow pressed against your middle in both palm-up and palm-down positions.

If you forcefully move his fingers beyond their range in either position, you can cause severe internal injury. Be legally justified to use this force deliberately.

TECHNIQUE 2: HALF TWIST WITH FINGER JAM

If this move didn't hurt so intensely you would think it was just "a cute little technique." But hurt it does—and with a high potential for a break. It isn't terribly secure because, as you notice, you don't cover your attacker's grab hand with your free hand as is normally done when executing the wristlock portion of this technique. Instead, you drape your grabbed hand over the attacker's wrist and then jam his little finger with the thumb of your free hand. Take too long and you lose the moment. Do it fast and you save yourself from getting punched with his other hand.

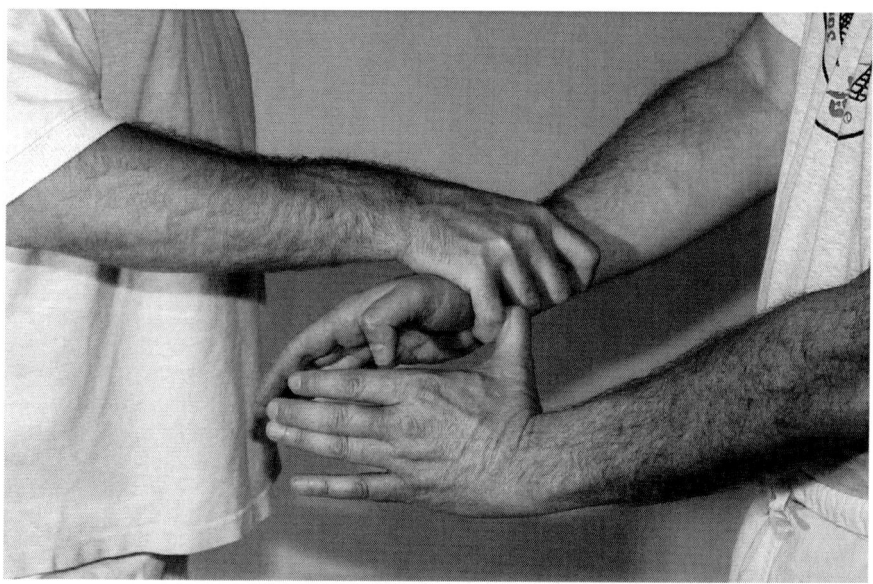

1. The attacker grabs your right wrist with his right hand. Immediately hook your left thumb under his little finger.

FINGER TECHNIQUES

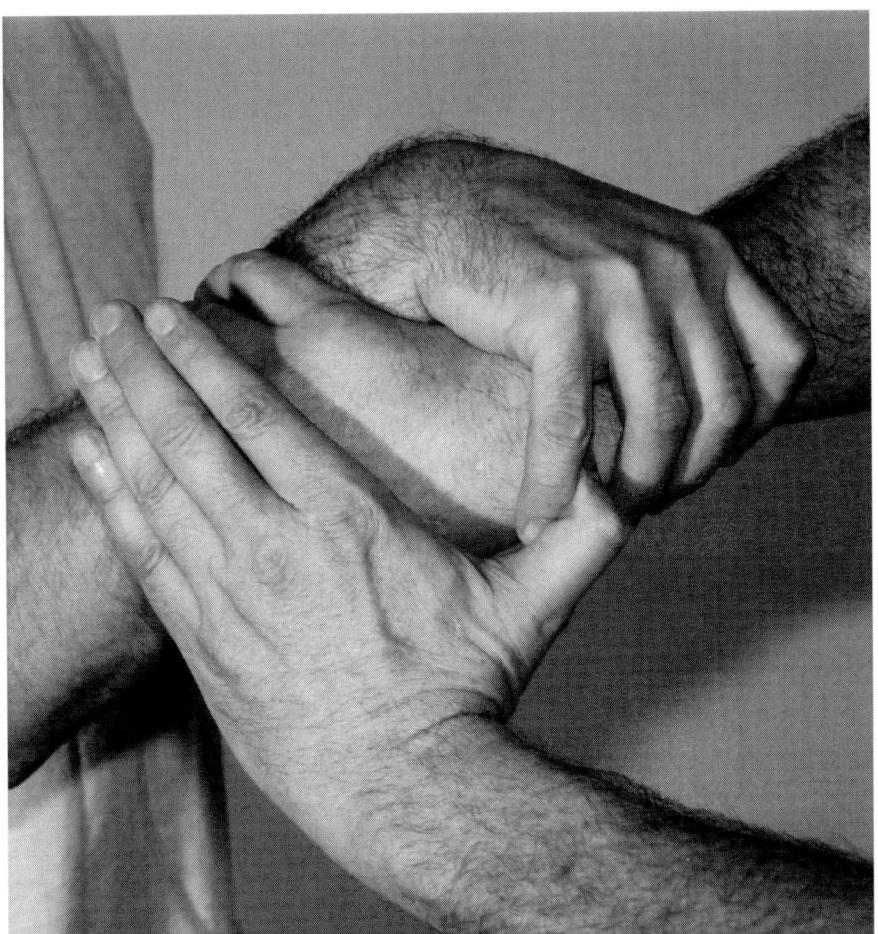

2. Simultaneous with your thumb hook, wrap your hand over the attacker's wrist as you push his little finger forward and slightly outward.

EXTREME JOINT LOCKING AND BREAKING

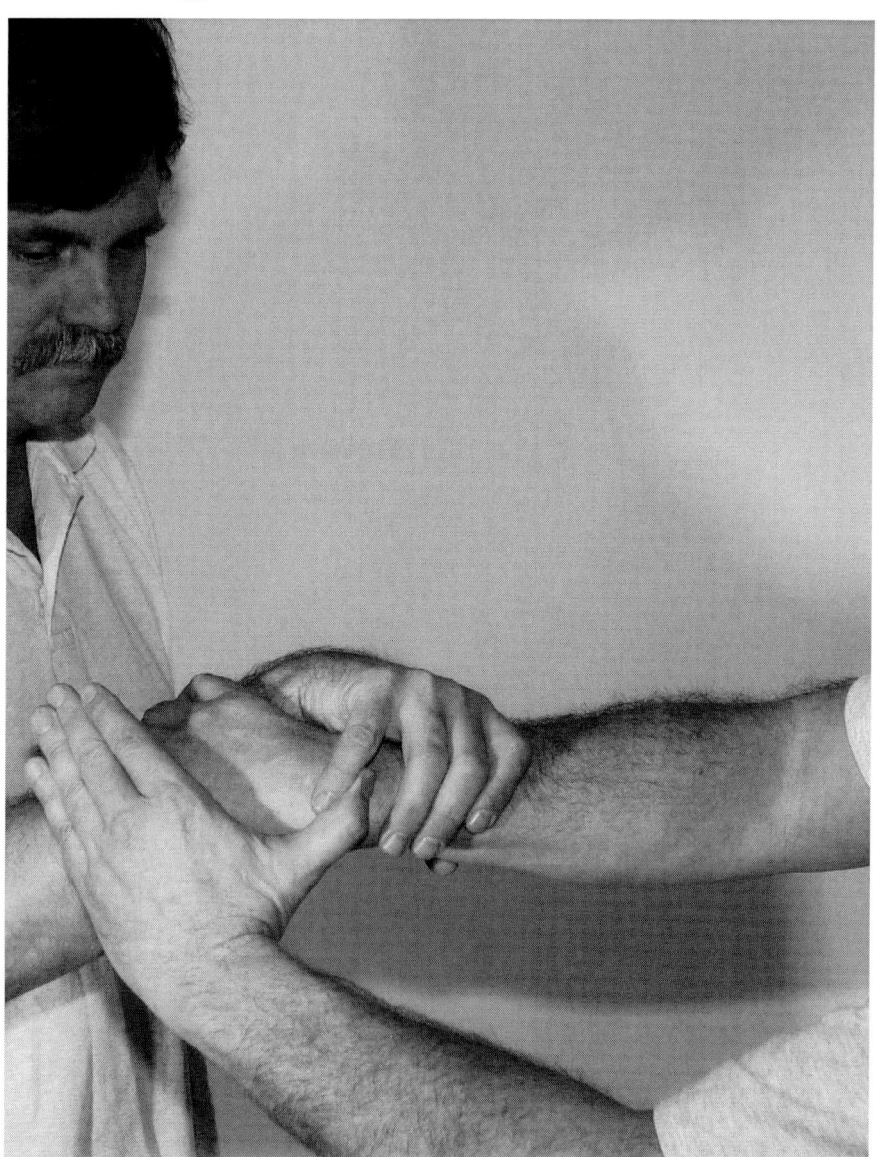

3. The attacker will feel a little pain in the little finger side of his wrist and a whole lot of pain in the finger. Should the attacker have a weapon in his other hand when he grabs you, ram his finger forward fast and hard.

FINGER TECHNIQUES

TECHNIQUE 3: FINGERS RIP

One of the qualities that make this technique so effective is that you can apply it easily from just about any position; you just need to be able to grab two of your attacker's fingers with both your hands and pull in opposite directions. This not only hurts and can cause serious structural damage to bones, tendons, muscles, and skin, it also has a powerful psychological impact. Just the thought of having one's fingers ripped apart will have most attackers crying, "I give up!" within seconds of the hold's being applied. The following are three situations in which to use it.

1. An attacker presses his palm against your chest to line you up for a punch with his other hand.

ᒪEXTREME JOINT LOCKING AND BREAKINGᴵ

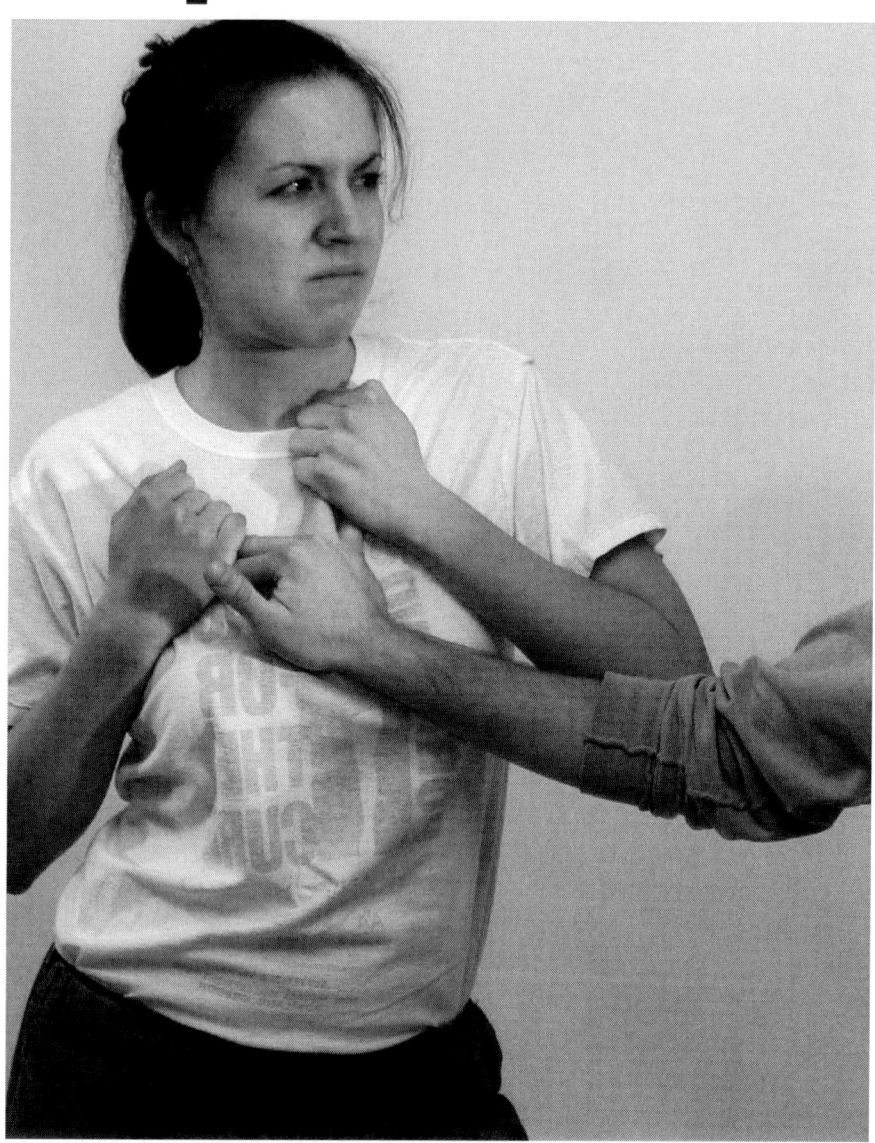

- Grab any finger with your left hand and any finger with your right and yank them apart. It's okay if in your haste you grab two fingers with one hand and one with the other, or two fingers in each hand. The primary rip occurs between the two fingers closest to each other.

⌐FINGER TECHNIQUES⌐

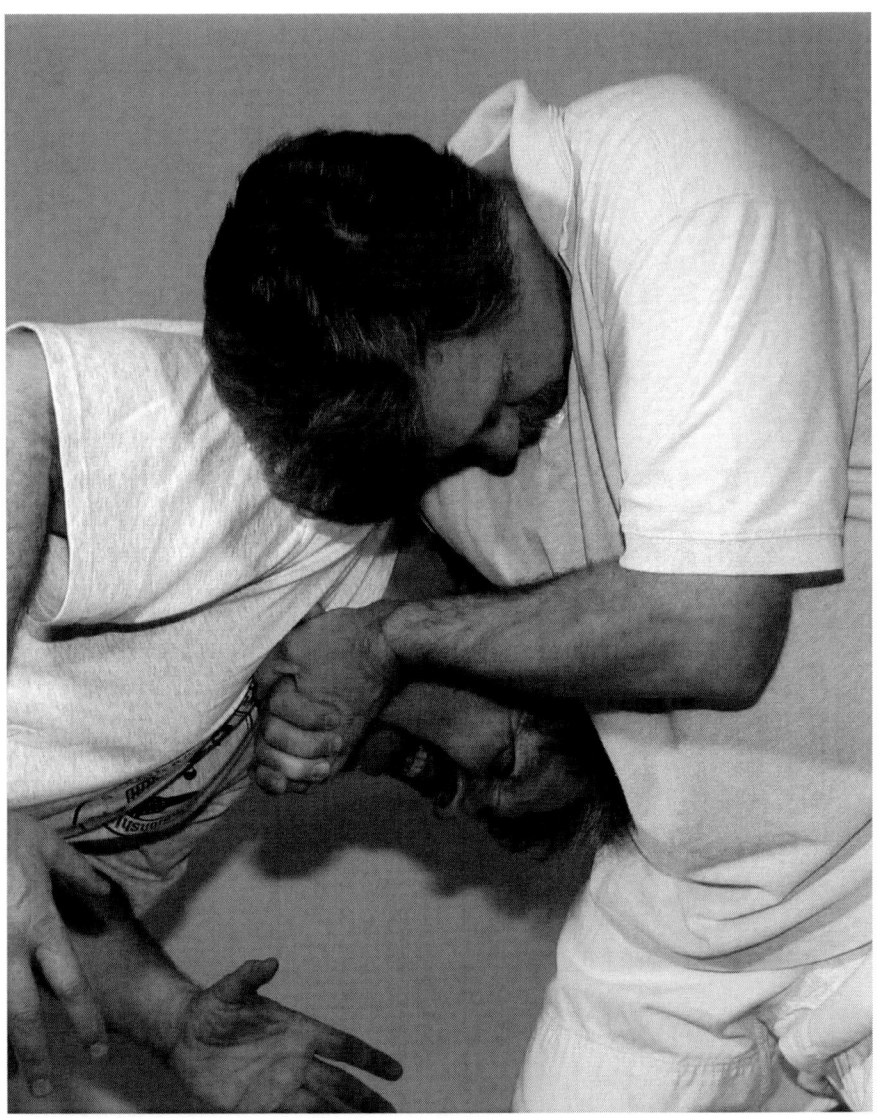

2. An attacker has applied a reverse headlock on you with his right arm.

EXTREME JOINT LOCKING AND BREAKING

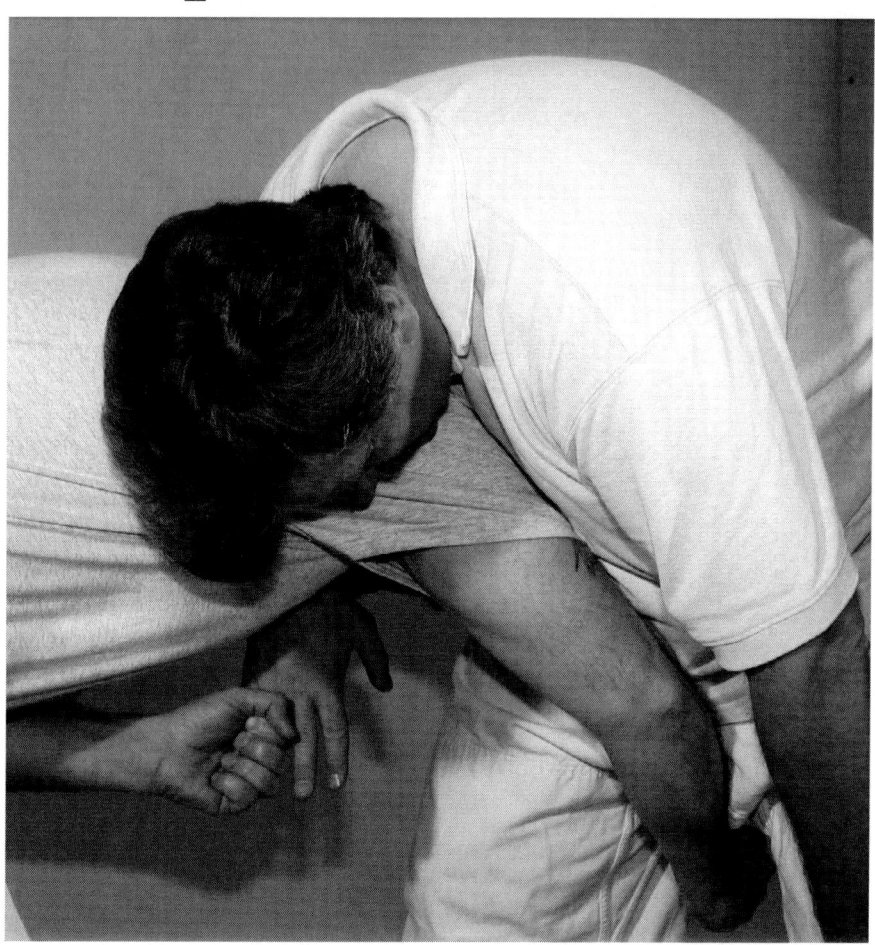

- Slam your right forearm up into his groin to get him to think about that spot for a moment as you reach for his hand with your left. Grab his little and ring fingers.

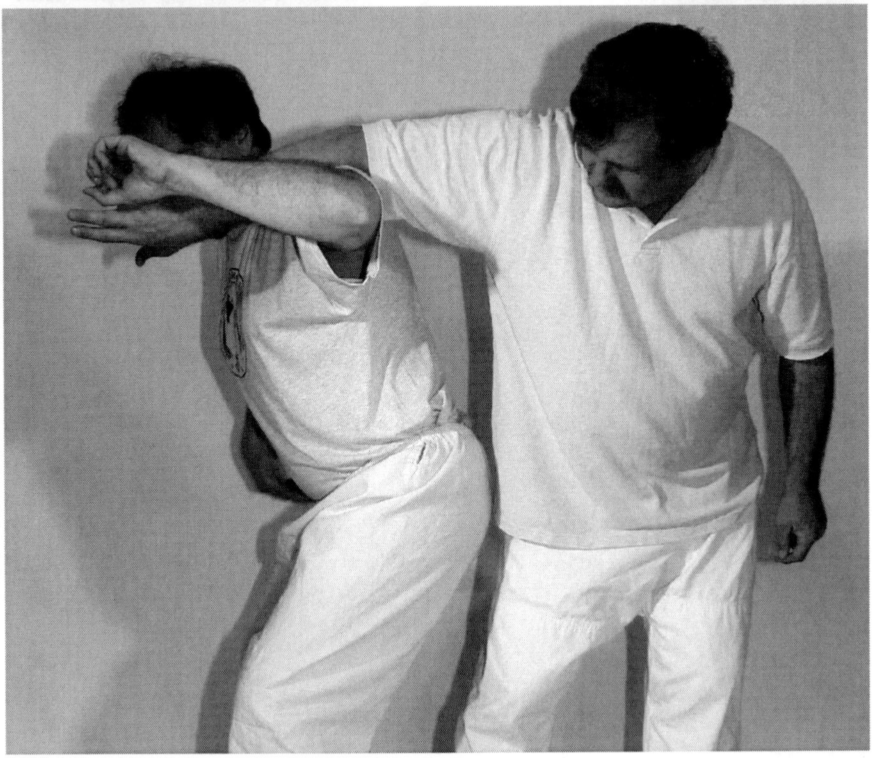

FINGER TECHNIQUES

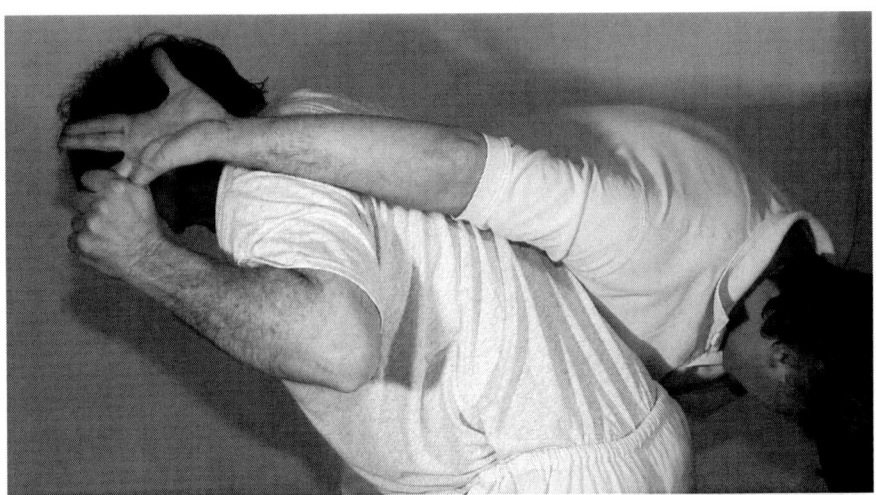

- As he wheezes from the groin shot, spin out of the hold while maintaining a tight grip on his two fingers.

EXTREME JOINT LOCKING AND BREAKING

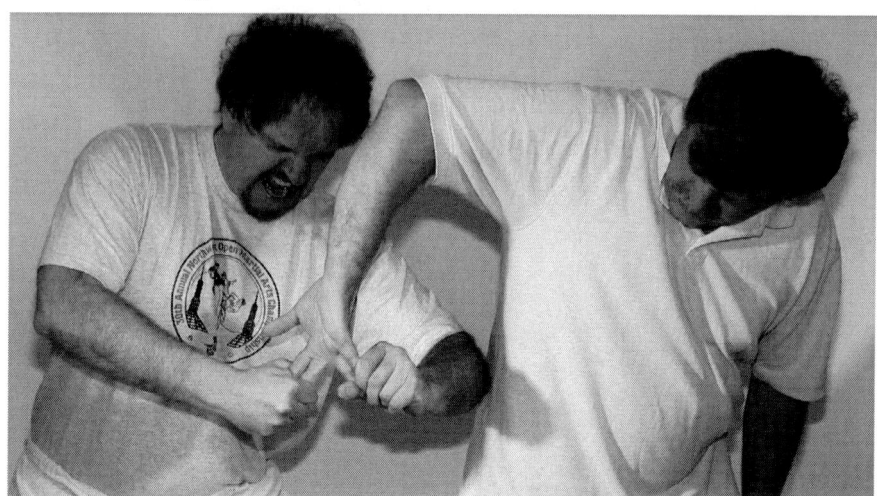

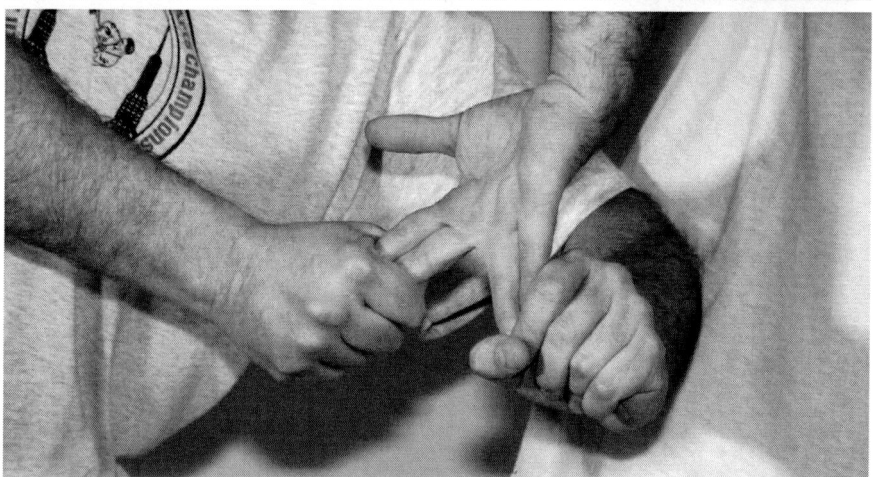

- As you come around to face the same direction as your attacker, grab his middle and index fingers with your other hand and move your hands apart to split his fingers until you get his cooperation.

Note that this is a variation of the bent-arm hand twist illustrated in the next chapter. All the elements are the same except you're not twisting his wrist to a great extent. Instead, you're tearing his fingers apart. If the situation warrants it, split his fingers with extreme prejudice.

⌐FINGER TECHNIQUES⌐

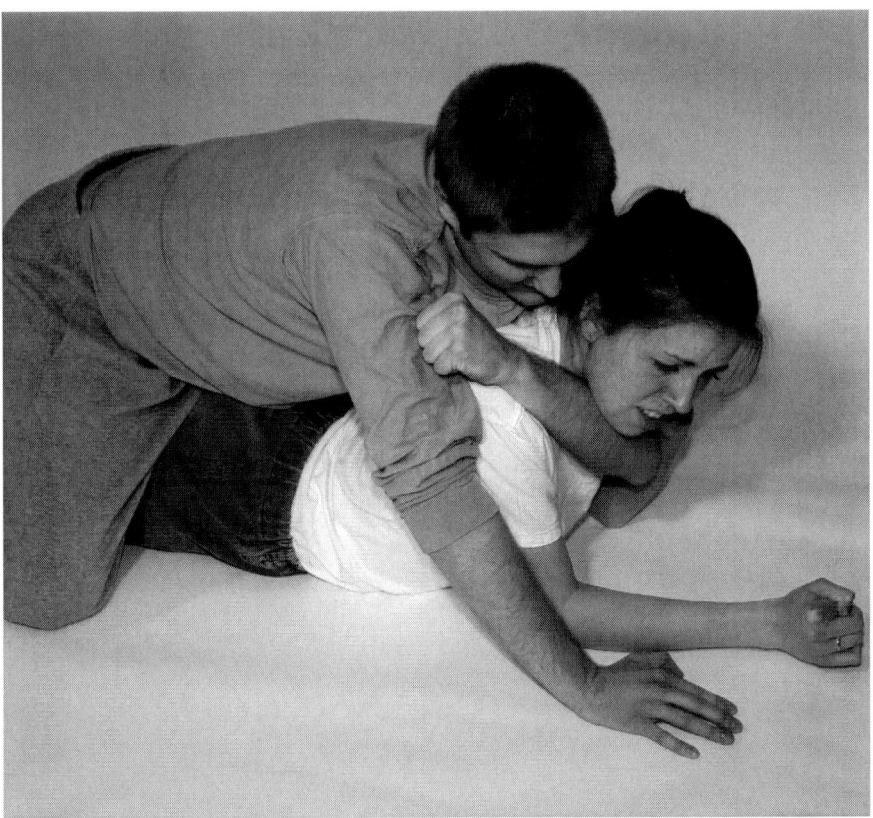

3. The fight isn't going your way. You're face down on the ground and the attacker is on your back going for a choke with his left arm as he supports himself on his right hand.

EXTREME JOINT LOCKING AND BREAKING

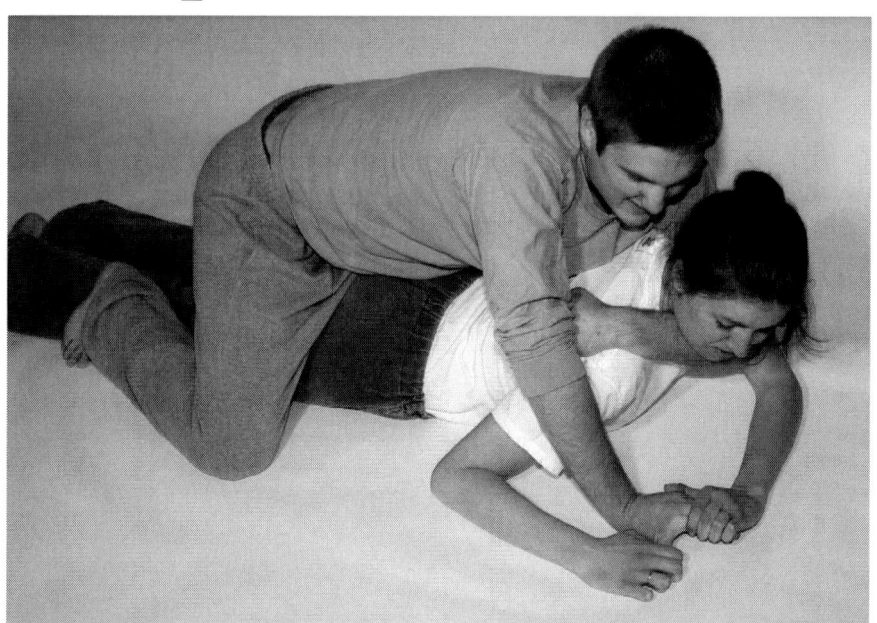

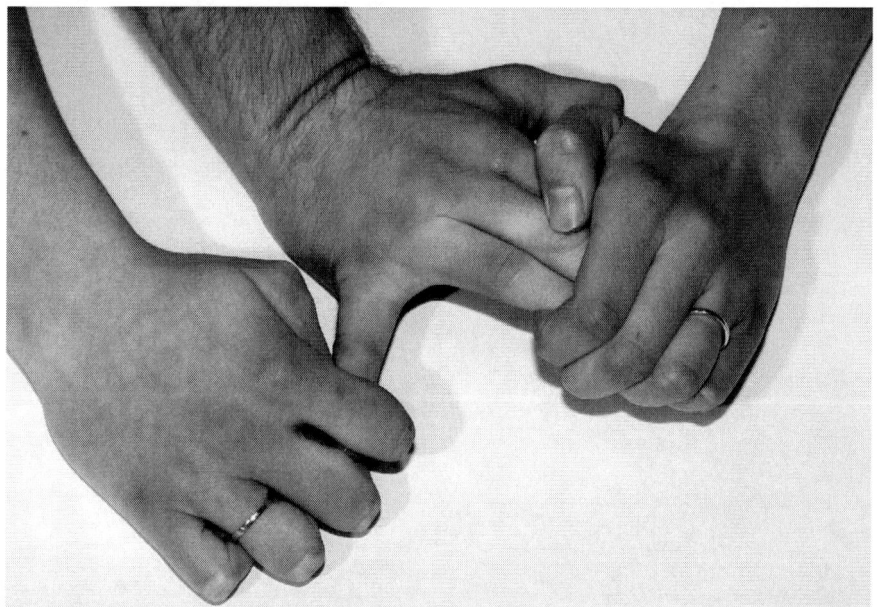

- Grab his ring finger with your left hand and his little finger with your right, and rip.

FINGER TECHNIQUES
"FINGER TIPS"

- The little finger is the easiest to break—push it back and then to the side. Do the same with the index finger. The ring and middle fingers should be pushed back.
- When you're in a hurry, grab whichever finger you can get.
- The element of surprise is important so that the attacker doesn't move his hand away from your grab.
- When the situation allows it, don't let go of the finger after you have broken it. Yank it forward, back, and in little circles to underscore the pain.

CHAPTER 2
wrist techniques

I learned quickly on the mean streets that some people can tolerate that bread-and-butter of all police control holds: the wristlock. Alcohol, drugs, and over-the-top rage blunts pain for many people. You don't think drugs are that powerful? Consider a man high on PCP who deliberately pressed his palm into a red-hot skillet and fried it like a patty of beef. Another man, high on the same drug, ripped his own teeth out, one by one, with a pair of pliers.

I ran across another type once, a guy with a mind-set that he wasn't going to feel anything I did to him. He was an outlaw biker, and I was told later that the ability to tolerate pain was part of his gang's creed. I had the guy pressed against a wall, his arm behind his back as I applied a standard police wrist flex. He kept turning his head and looking at me without expression or any indication that my technique hurt him. I increased the pressure harder and harder, but still his flat, emotionless face just looked at me. When he began to squirm in an effort to defeat my hold, I slammed it on full force. Where there should have been resistance in the muscles and tendons of his wrist there was a sudden release of tension that coin-

EXTREME JOINT LOCKING AND BREAKING

THE WRIST AS A TARGET

Fracture

A wrist fracture most often occurs from a fall or when a sudden force pushes the hand backward, forward, or laterally beyond its normal range of movement. Most often the fracture is of the forearm radius bone where it connects at the wrist. When this bone is broken, it's common to have pain, swelling, and deformity in the joint.

Sprain

A sprain occurs when the ligaments (the bands of tissue that control which direction joints can bend) are stretched. A minor wrist sprain usually doesn't swell, so if there is swelling it's likely the wrist is broken.

---

cided with an audible popping sound. I had broken his wrist. There was a slight flicker of realization on the biker's face, and then his blank stare returned. I let go of the broken limb, grabbed his other hand and applied the same technique to that wrist. He began cooperating then, probably because he didn't want two broken wrists.

All pain compliance techniques work *most* of the time, which means none of them work *all* the time. If you discover that a pain compliance technique isn't doing the job, you can choose between two options: segue into another technique, or, if the situation warrants it, use the one you have to inflict extreme damage.

WRIST TECHNIQUES
TECHNIQUE 1: OUTSIDE WRIST TWIST

This wrist twist technique usually doesn't hurt unless it's executed with tremendous snap. Even a gentle twist will force an attacker off balance and send him to the ground, but it's hard to be gentle when you think you're about to look at the cruel end of a gun.

Such was the case when, as a cop, I applied this technique on a guy who threatened to shoot me. I had just pulled him out of a burning car, in which he was fistfighting with another drunk. Oblivious to the fact that I had just saved both their lives, the guy in question threatened to shoot me. When he thrust his hand under his jacket, I quickly grabbed his forearm, sidestepped away in the event he had secured a gun, slid my hand down over the back of his hand—which was empty—and executed an outside-wrist-twist takedown that couldn't have been more perfect. The next day he complained to Internal Affairs that I had struck his wrist—which had swollen to twice its normal size—with my gun. Since he didn't follow through with the complaint, the case was dropped, and I never learned the extent of his wrist injury.

Let's look at how you can apply the twist after you have taken your attacker down, as well as at a move you can make if the attacker still hasn't released the weapon.

EXTREME JOINT LOCKING AND BREAKING

1. An attacker brandishes a screwdriver and demands your money. Even if he doesn't tell you to do so, raise your hands so that you can position them close to the weapon.

WRIST TECHNIQUES

2. As quick as a blink, grab the weapon hand and push it away from you.

EXTREME JOINT LOCKING AND BREAKING

3. Grab with your other hand and execute the takedown.

WRIST TECHNIQUES

4. Drop your knee into his ribs to take his breath away.

EXTREME JOINT LOCKING AND BREAKING

5. Brace your knee against the inside of his elbow and twist his hand outward. His wrist receives the full intensity of the twist because your knee prevents his elbow from moving. Most often this forces the attacker's hand open and causes the weapon to drop. If he has a high tolerance for pain and you feel that the situation warrants extreme force, jam his hand hard into the twist until the joint sprains or breaks and the knife falls free.

WRIST TECHNIQUES

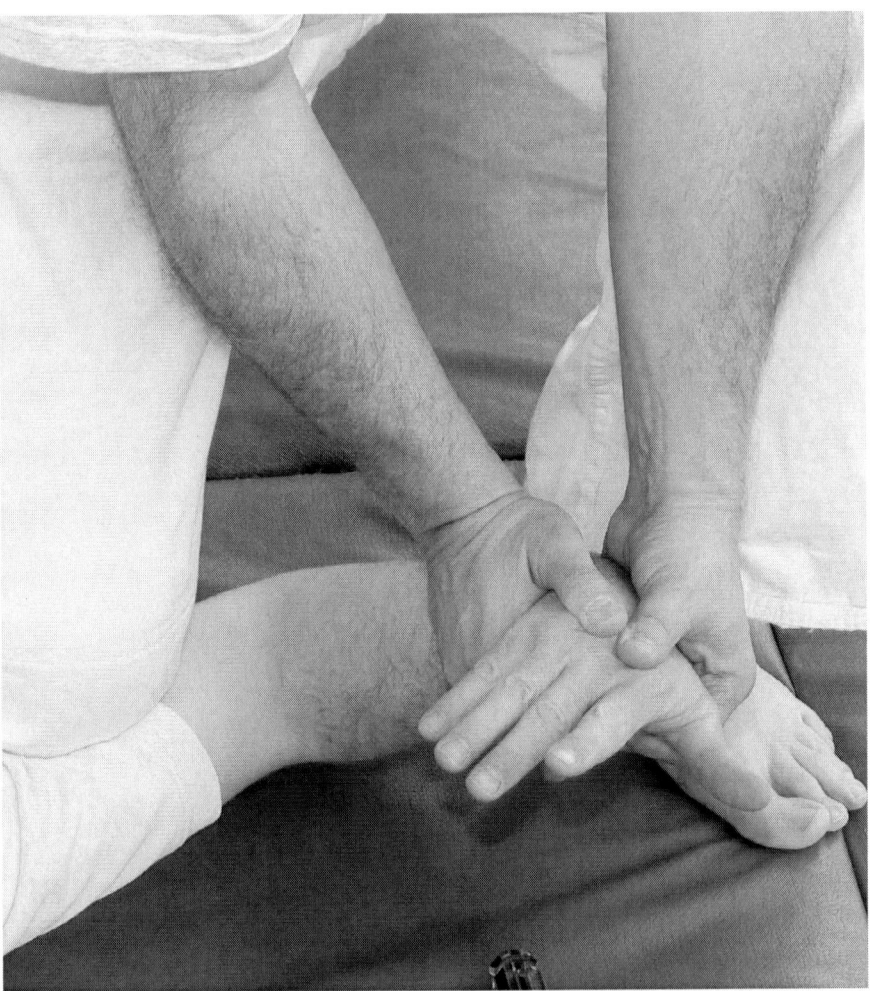

6. If you aren't justified to break his wrist but would like to deliver a little more pain, press your knee into his tender biceps and saw your knee back and forth a little as you continue to twist his hand.

EXTREME JOINT LOCKING AND BREAKING

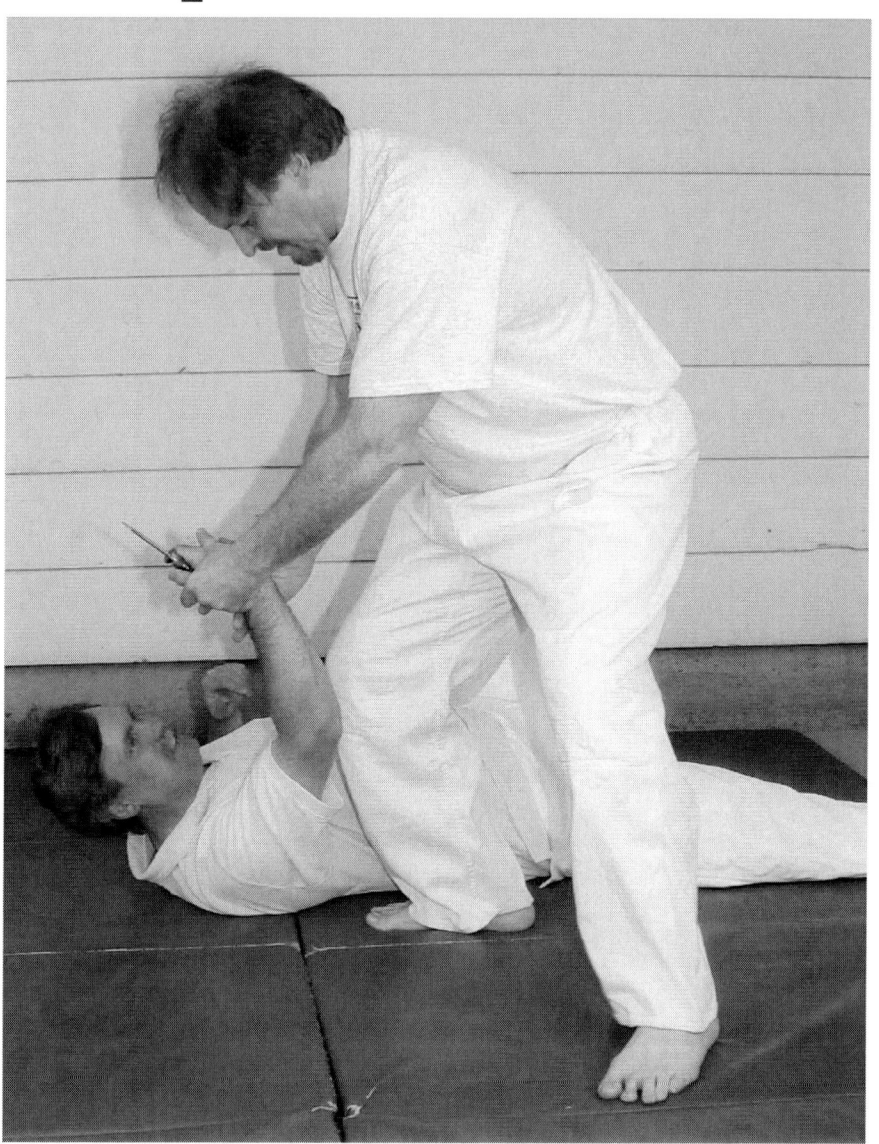

Variation 1
You have executed steps 1 through 6, but the subject still hasn't released the weapon.

WRIST TECHNIQUES

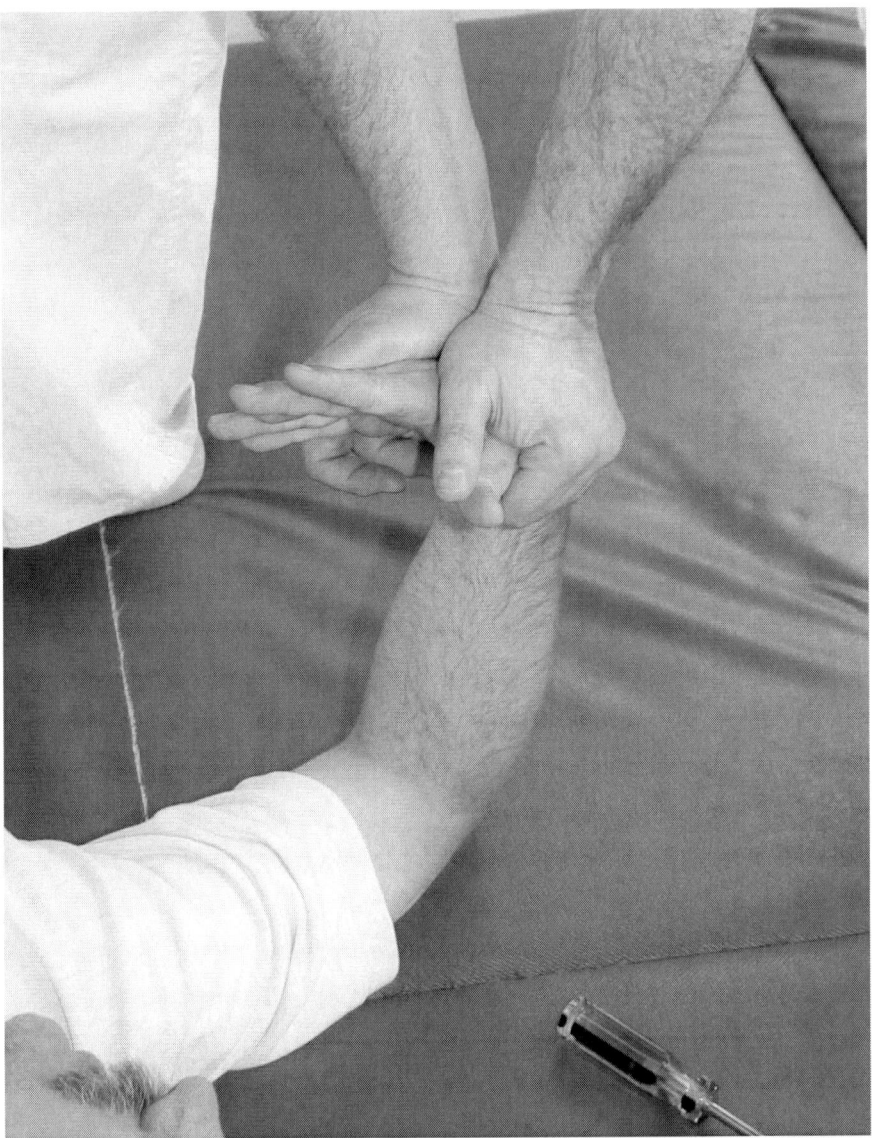

1. Ram his vertical forearm downward while flexing his wrist downward. Use the heels of your hands to drive your weight into the back of his hand and the stretched tendons of his bent wrist. This has the potential to cause serious damage, so be sure that your actions are justified.

EXTREME JOINT LOCKING AND BREAKING

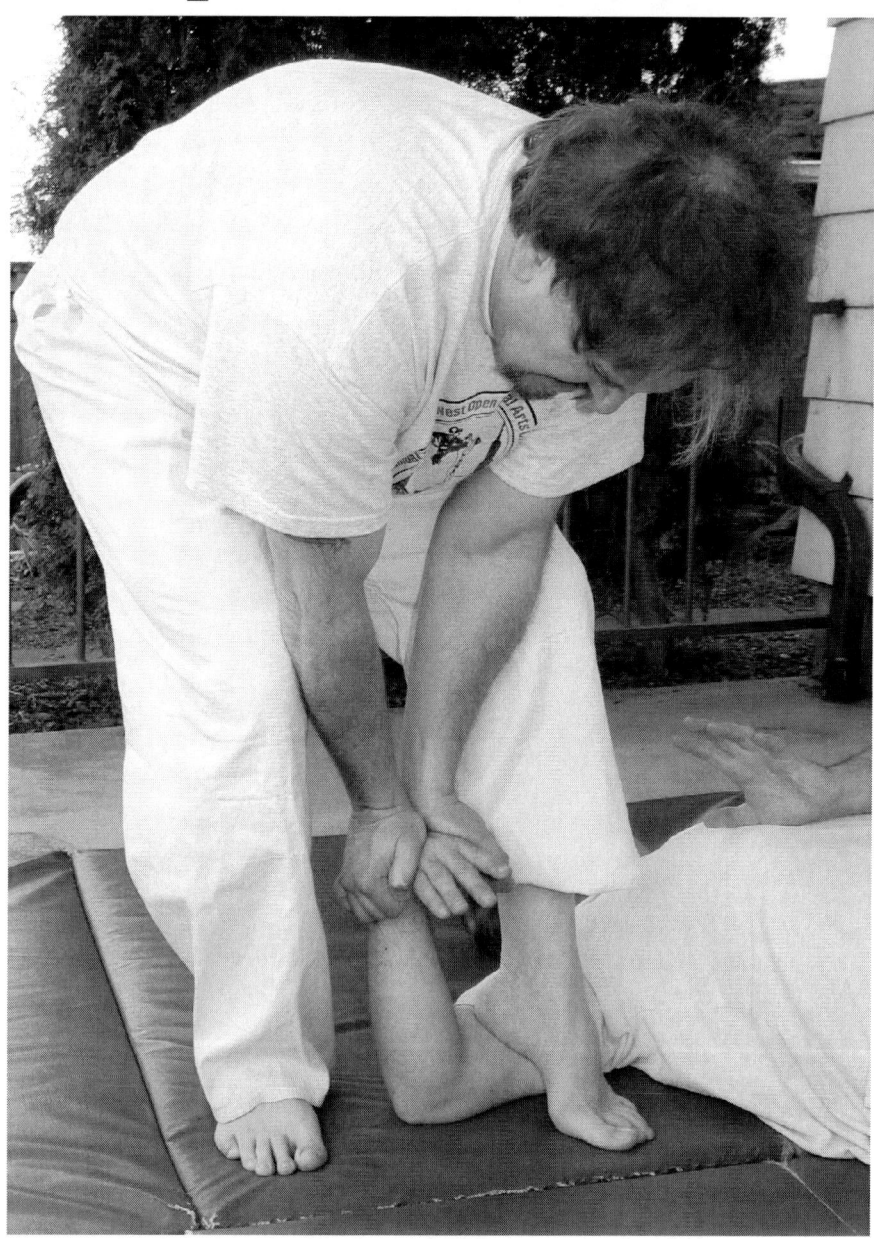

2. If you aren't justified to break his wrist but you would like to deliver a little more pain, press your heel into his tender biceps.

WRIST TECHNIQUES
TECHNIQUE 2: BENT-ARM HAND TWIST

Police agencies often recommend using this popular wrist twist as a pain-compliance hold. Officers use it to extract suspects from cars, as a come-along hold to move unwanted people a short distance, and as the first step in one method of handcuffing. Although I've come across people who could tolerate this twist, most will spring up onto their tiptoes and do a funny little pain dance when it is applied.

Here is how a friend described what happened to his wrist when a training partner applied the hold with "too much zeal":

> *The ulna popped out, subluxing away from its connection to the bones of the hand. This caused a locking of the wrist so that I couldn't supinate it. I popped it back in and taped it tightly, and it was mostly okay until about three years ago. Now it goes out a lot more often. I also have some arthritis where the ulna connects to the elbow. I attribute this to trauma/instability brought on by the lock.*

There are a number of ways to inflict extra pain with this twist. Here is a powerful one that can be done in most positions in which you apply the bent-arm twist. Let's look at doing it when the attacker is leaning.

EXTREME JOINT LOCKING AND BREAKING

1. As you pass by a bully, he extends his arm to block you.

WRIST TECHNIQUES

2. Grab his wrist with your left hand and rotate it.

EXTREME JOINT LOCKING AND BREAKING

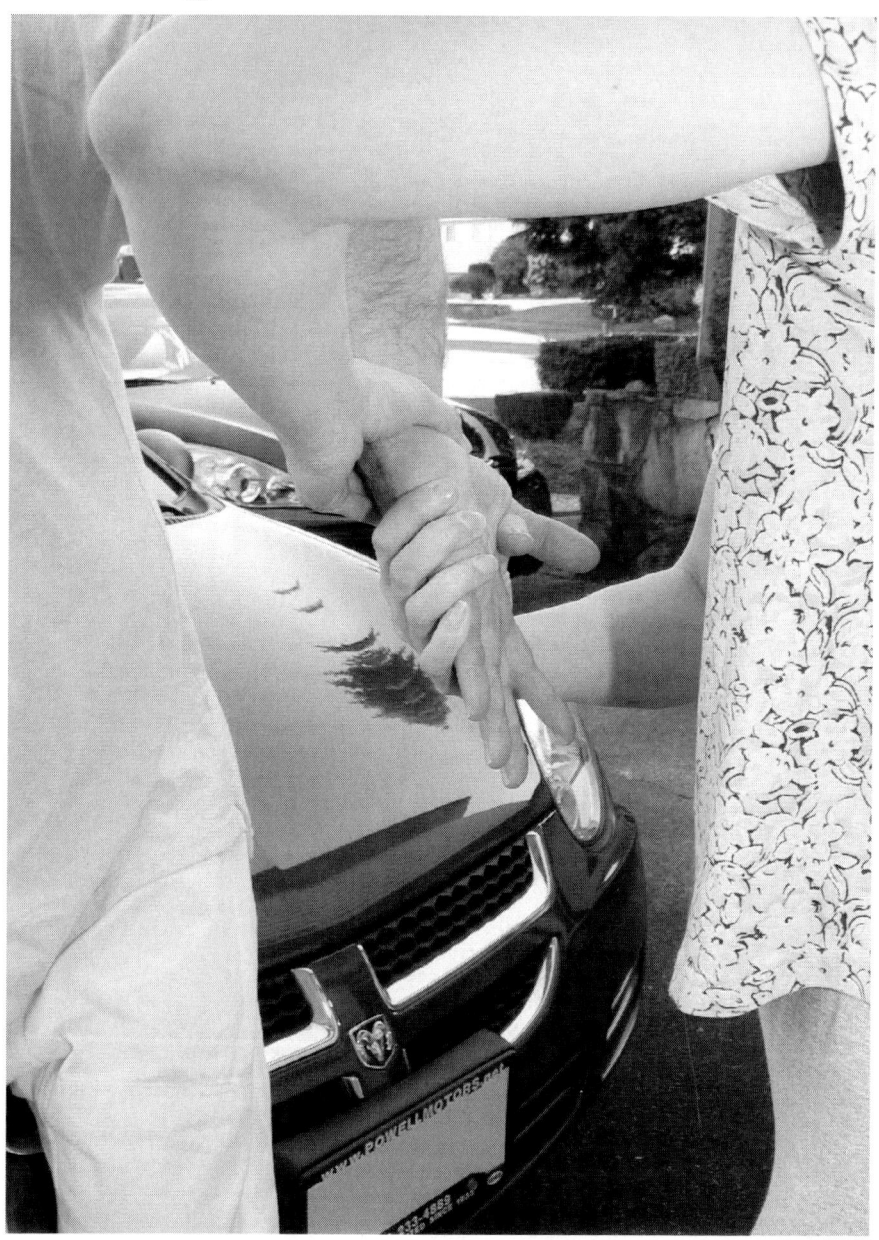

3. Wrap the four fingers of your right hand around the heel side of his hand.

WRIST TECHNIQUES

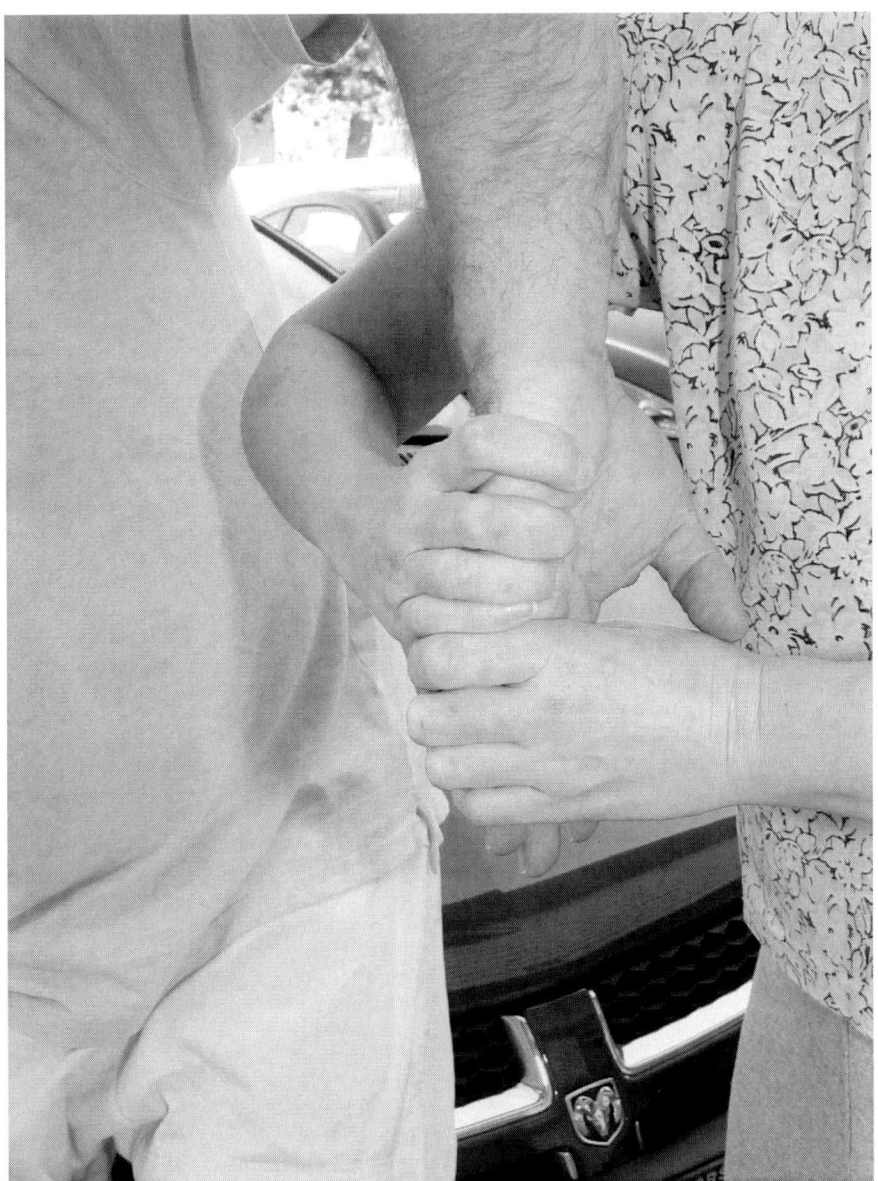

4. Turn his hand a little more so you can grab his fingers with your left hand and then push his arm up so that it's bent about 90 degrees. Twist his hand so that yours turns toward him while keeping his hand about 18 inches from

EXTREME JOINT LOCKING AND BREAKING

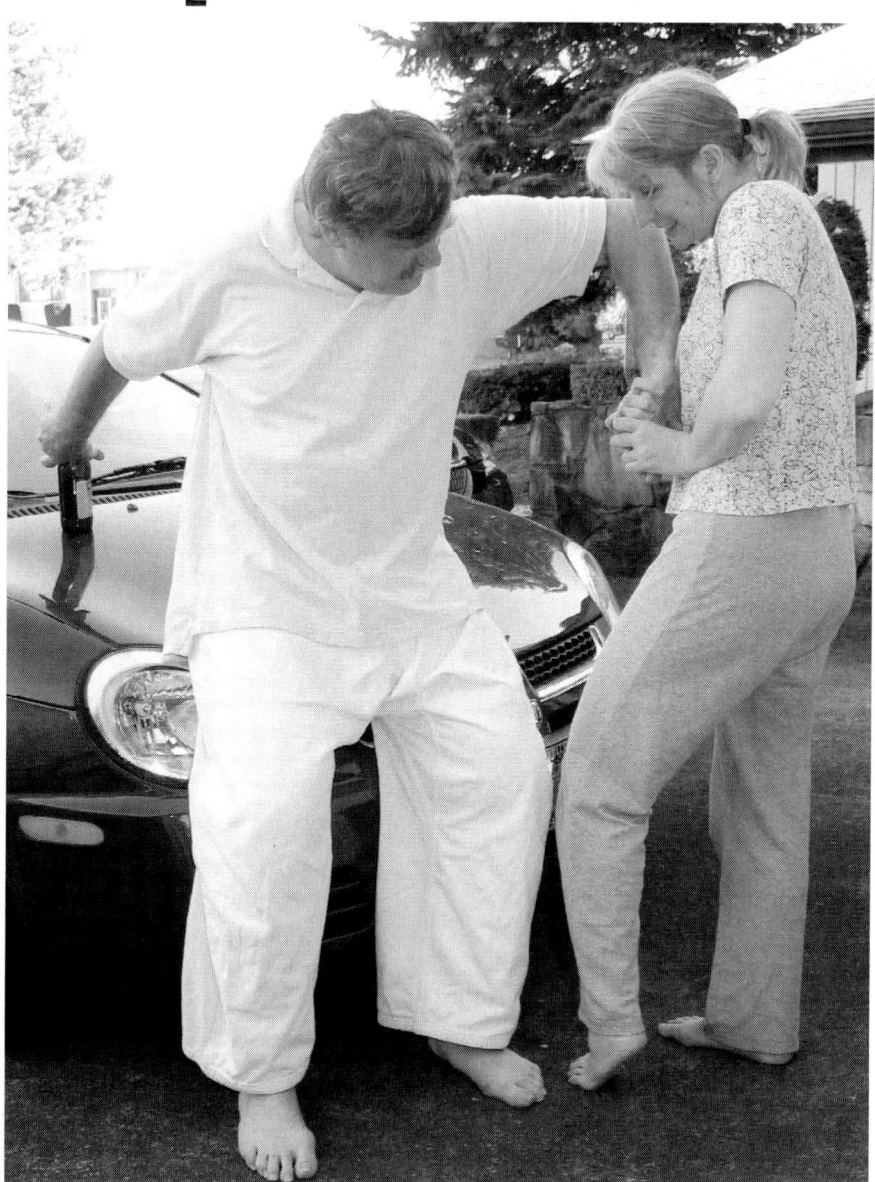

his side. When he reaches for a bottle with his free hand, step inward with your left foot. This uses the power of your body to twist his hand violently. Don't let his arm move so that all of the torque impacts his wrist joint.

WRIST TECHNIQUES
TECHNIQUE 3: SHEARING

This technique is subtle and blisteringly painful. What looks like a simple armbar is indeed an armbar but with a shearing action to the wrist that feels as if bone dust should be drifting to the floor like sifted flour. It's versatile too. You can apply it just about anytime you have your attacker's straight arm at your disposal. If the situation calls for extreme damage to the wrist, you can do it easily without altering your position.

EXTREME JOINT LOCKING AND BREAKING

1. Your attacker throws a right punch, which you sweep block with your left hand.

WRIST TECHNIQUES

2. Catch his wrist with your right hand and press 1 inch above his elbow with your forearm.

EXTREME JOINT LOCKING AND BREAKING

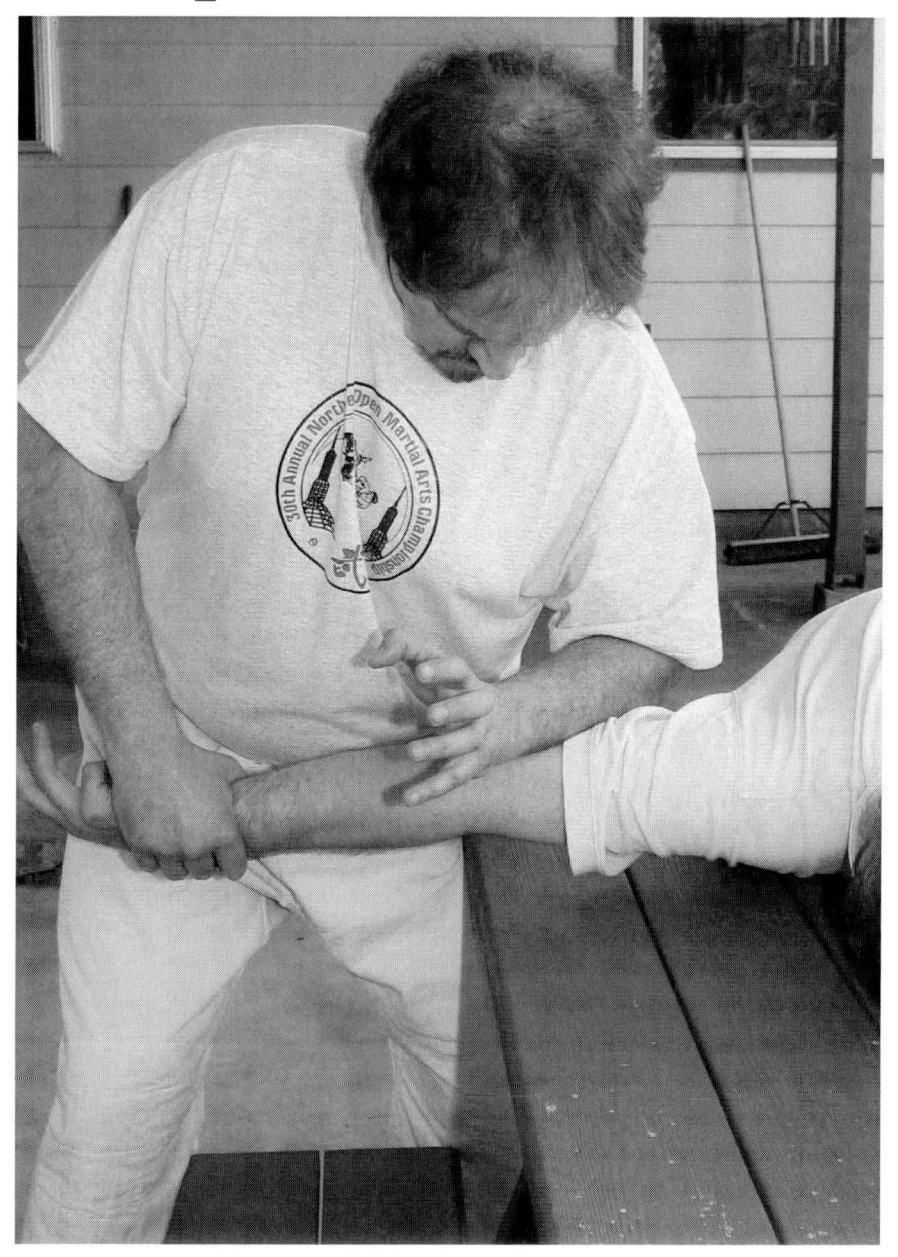

3. Slam him onto a table and lean your weight just above his elbow joint.

WRIST TECHNIQUES

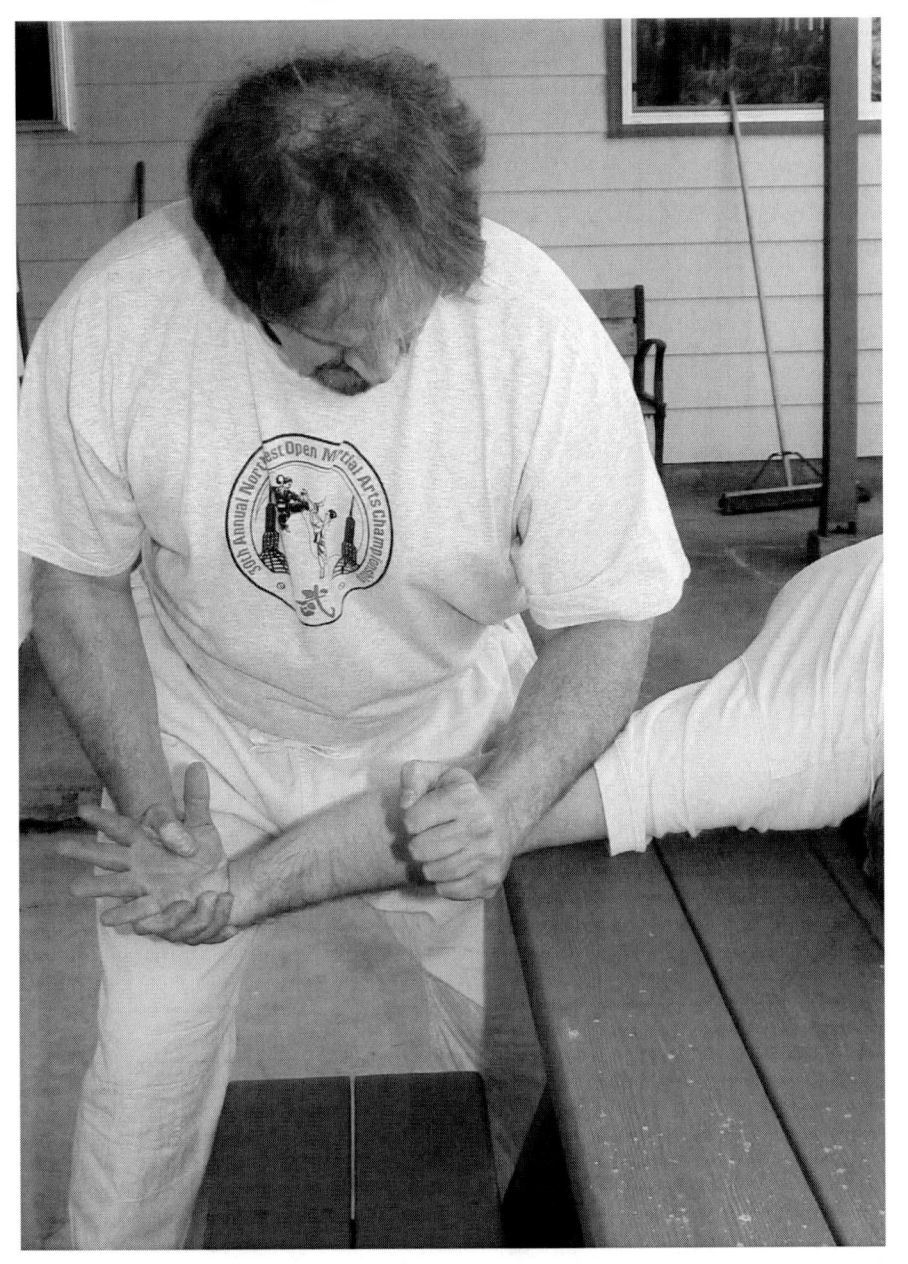

4. Quickly regrip your right hand so that your palm covers the back of his.

EXTREME JOINT LOCKING AND BREAKING

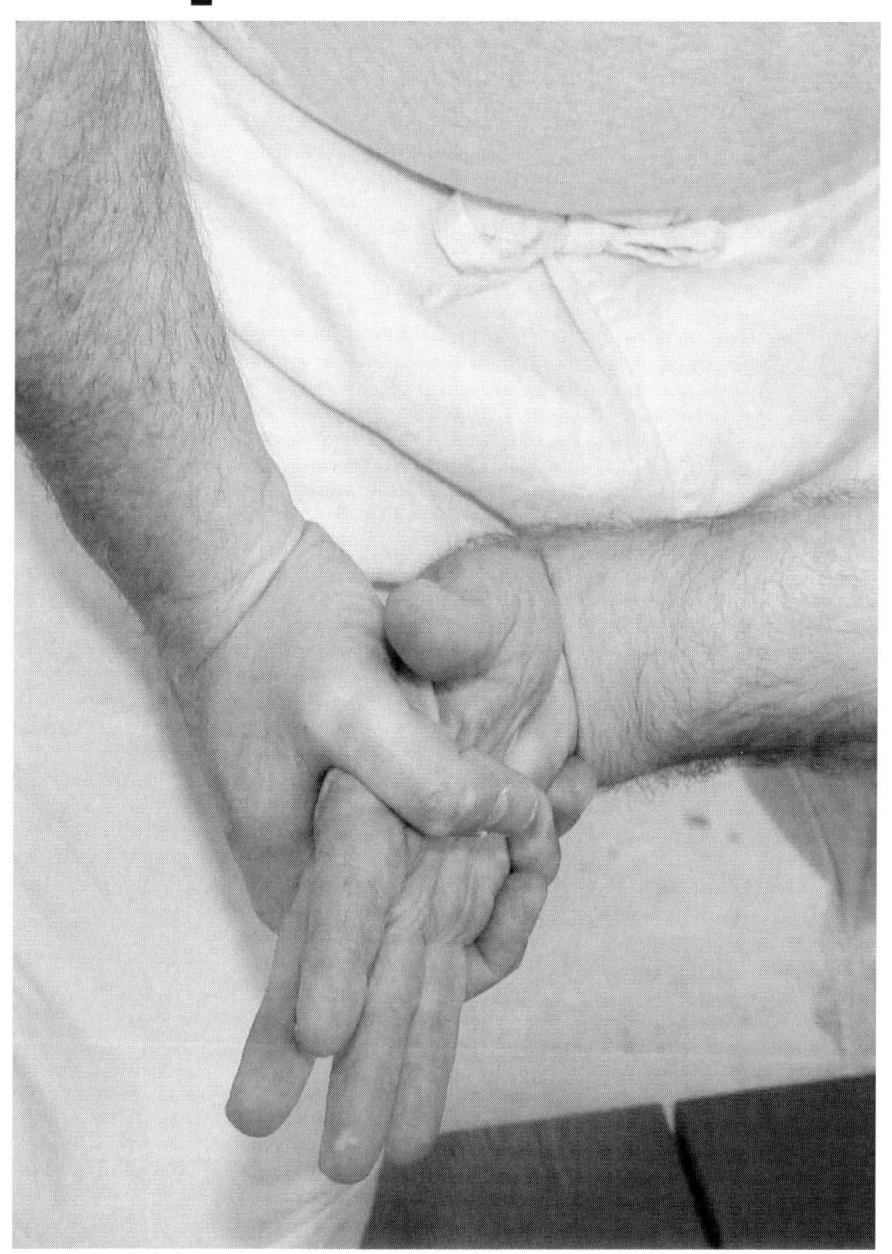

5. To shear the joint, rotate his hand as if to pour water from his index finger.

WRIST TECHNIQUES

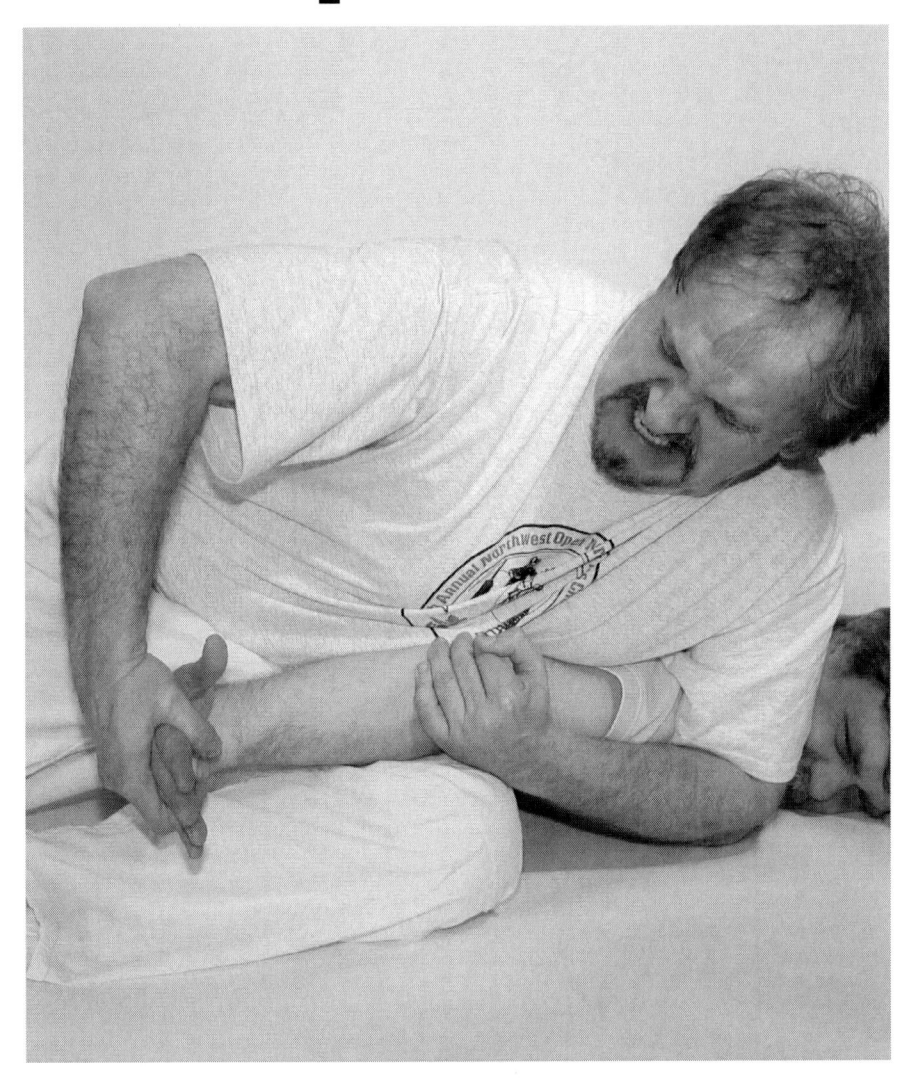

Variation 1
1. Either you have taken the attacker down with an armbar, or in the course of grappling with him on the ground you find yourself in this position. Lean on him to prevent him from moving and then draw your left knee forward to brace his arm over it. Shear his wrist by rotating his fingers downward.

⌐EXTREME JOINT LOCKING AND BREAKING⌐

Variation 2
1. Use the shearing motion to force a person from a seated position.

Should the situation in any of these variations call for extreme force—the subject is starting to muscle out of the technique and has a weapon in his other hand—rotate his hand into the shear with great force.

CHAPTER 3
elbow techniques

Elbow locks are among the most common winning techniques in submission-type fighting events. The instant any one of a long list of elbow locks is slapped on an opponent, he usually taps out in a hurry, even if he towers 6 feet 6 inches and weighs as much as two bodybuilders. The reason is simple: elbow locks deliver an awful pain that shoots throughout the arm, triggers the nausea reflex, and then brings on mental images of multiple ineffective arm surgeries that leave the limb stiff as a rod for the rest of one's life.

Okay, that's a little over the top, but not by much.

As a cop, I found that elbow techniques worked when all else failed. They worked well when leverage was needed, and they were almost always foolproof in eliciting cooperation when pain—always a powerful motivator—was needed. Let's look at some ways to apply acute agony using elbow locks and, if necessary, joint destruction.

TECHNIQUE 1:
OVER-THE-SHOULDER HYPEREXTENSION

I hate this technique. It gives me the creeps

EXTREME JOINT LOCKING AND BREAKING

THE ELBOW AS A TARGET

The elbow joint is made up of the humerus bone in the upper arm and the radius and ulna bones in the forearm. Where they meet in the middle makes up the single joint capsule. The structure of the joint prevents the arm from moving backward, so when it's forced past its natural range (which varies from person to person), it hurts. Specifically, when pressure is applied against the elbow while the wrist is restrained, the humerus moves forward while the ulna moves backward.

Dislocation and Break

When the pressure is extreme or slammed on with great force, the elbow will dislocate or break and cause additional trauma to the muscles, tendons, and nerves. Most likely, an attacker will be unable to use that arm, and the pain will be so acute that he will be distracted from doing anything else.

even to see it being done on someone else. I've received a couple of serious hyperextended elbows over the years, and they remain sensitive to even a minimum amount of pressure. This technique, with just the slightest bit of effort, places tremendous force against a locked elbow joint. With a little more pressure, the joint can easily be injured.

A friend once used the over-the-shoulder hyperextension to break an attacker's elbow. He tells it this way:

> *First, I blocked a punch to my face with an outer fan/knife hand block. Then I delivered a snap punch to his ribs to stun him a little before I took a two-handed grip on his wrist, rolled his arm up and over, and then broke his elbow over my shoulder. Then, maintaining the grip on his wrist, I moved under and out to sidekick his knee. The combination of broken elbow and injured knee made him pass out.*

Here is the classic way to get into the hold.

ELBOW TECHNIQUES

1. When the attacker reaches for your throat, block it with a quick two-arm sweep.

EXTREME JOINT LOCKING AND BREAKING

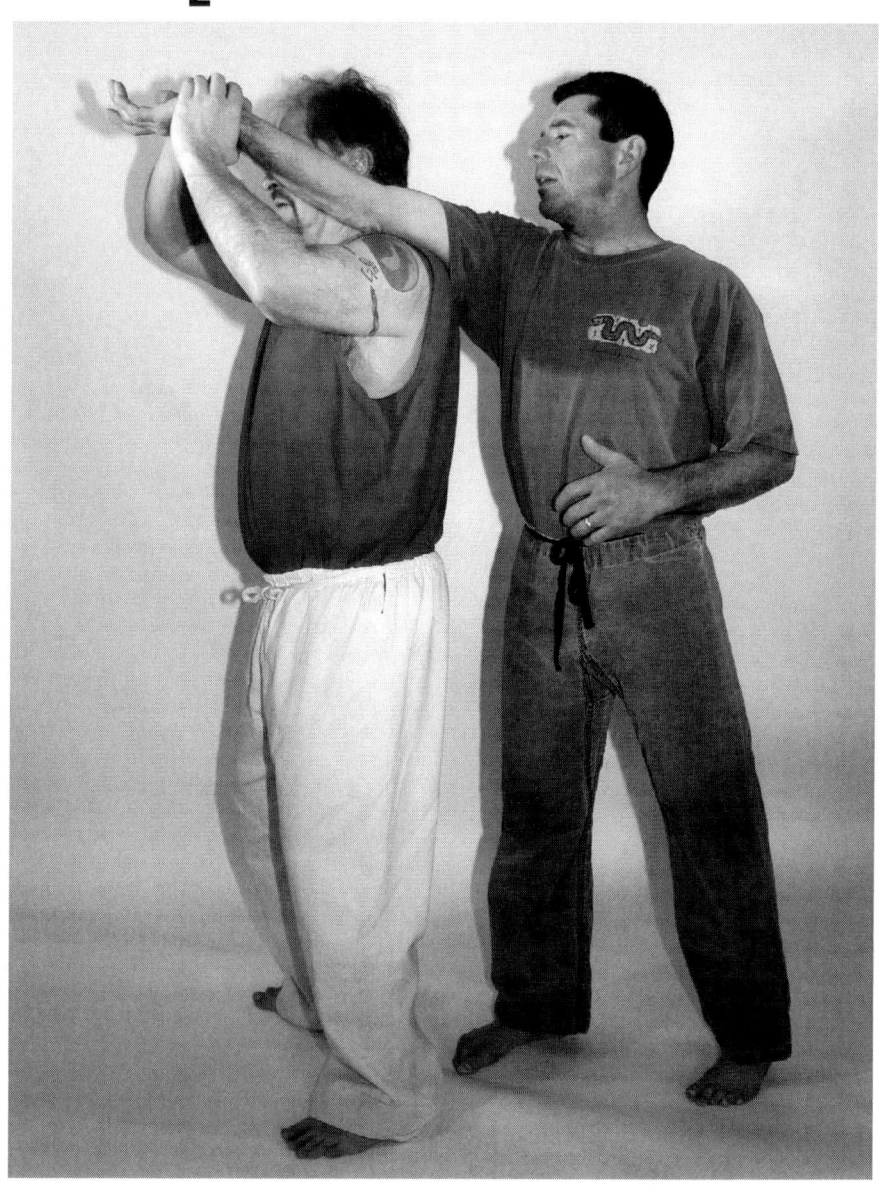

2. Secure his wrist with both hands and lift his arm up and over your shoulder, with his palm up. If it's his right arm, place it on your left shoulder, and vice versa. This makes it difficult for him to reach you with his free hand.

ELBOW TECHNIQUES

3. Pull down sharply on his arm as you thrust your hips back and straighten your legs.

⌐EXTREME JOINT LOCKING AND BREAKING⌐

4. If the situation warrants extreme force, jerk his arm down hard on your shoulder and repeat three or four times.

ELBOW TECHNIQUES
TECHNIQUE 2: ELBOW POP GET-ALONG

This can be used when you want someone to move away from you or you want to make a point that you're not to be hassled. As a cop, I used this often as a way to "encourage" a rooted person to get moving. There is no control factor here, just a quick shot of pain.

1. Grab the attacker's wrist as before.

▙EXTREME JOINT LOCKING AND BREAKING▜

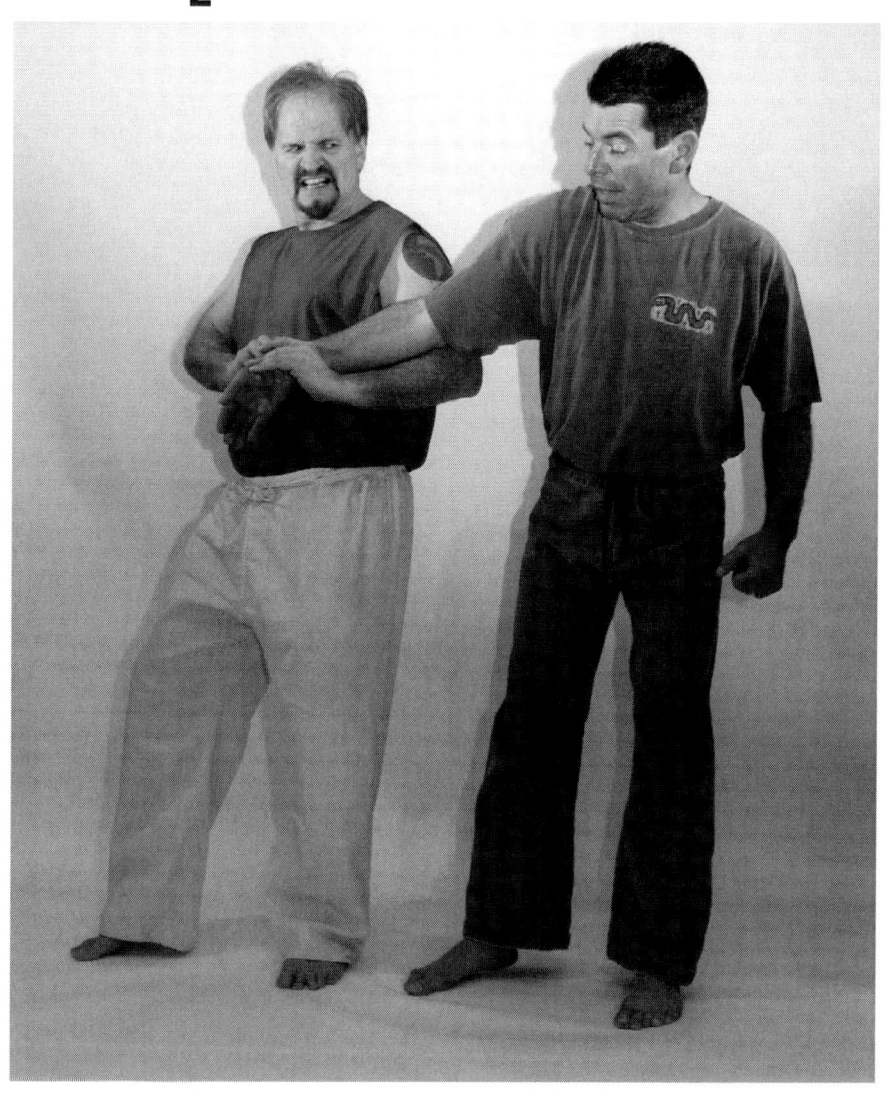

2. As you yank his arm toward you, rotate your left side sharply so that your upper arm hits his elbow joint as you pull back on his wrist a little. Even when doing this hard, you probably won't break the joint, but you will traumatize it.

You can now push him away, pop his elbow a couple more times with your arm, or run away.

⌐ELBOW TECHNIQUES⌐

TECHNIQUE 3: PRONE ARMBAR BRACE

This technique can be seen in many grappling books and submission fighting contests of every ilk. It's so popular because it works from a variety of setups. It can be used to effect tremendous pain, restraint, and, if warranted, structural damage.

If you're already fighting on the ground, this is a good technique to maneuver into. Or you can execute a takedown on your attacker and then follow him to the ground. Now, some people might argue that it's never a good idea to deliberately go down, while others feel completely comfortable doing so. If you are of the latter school, be alert for your attacker's friends, who just might kick you all the way to the next block.

EXTREME JOINT LOCKING AND BREAKING

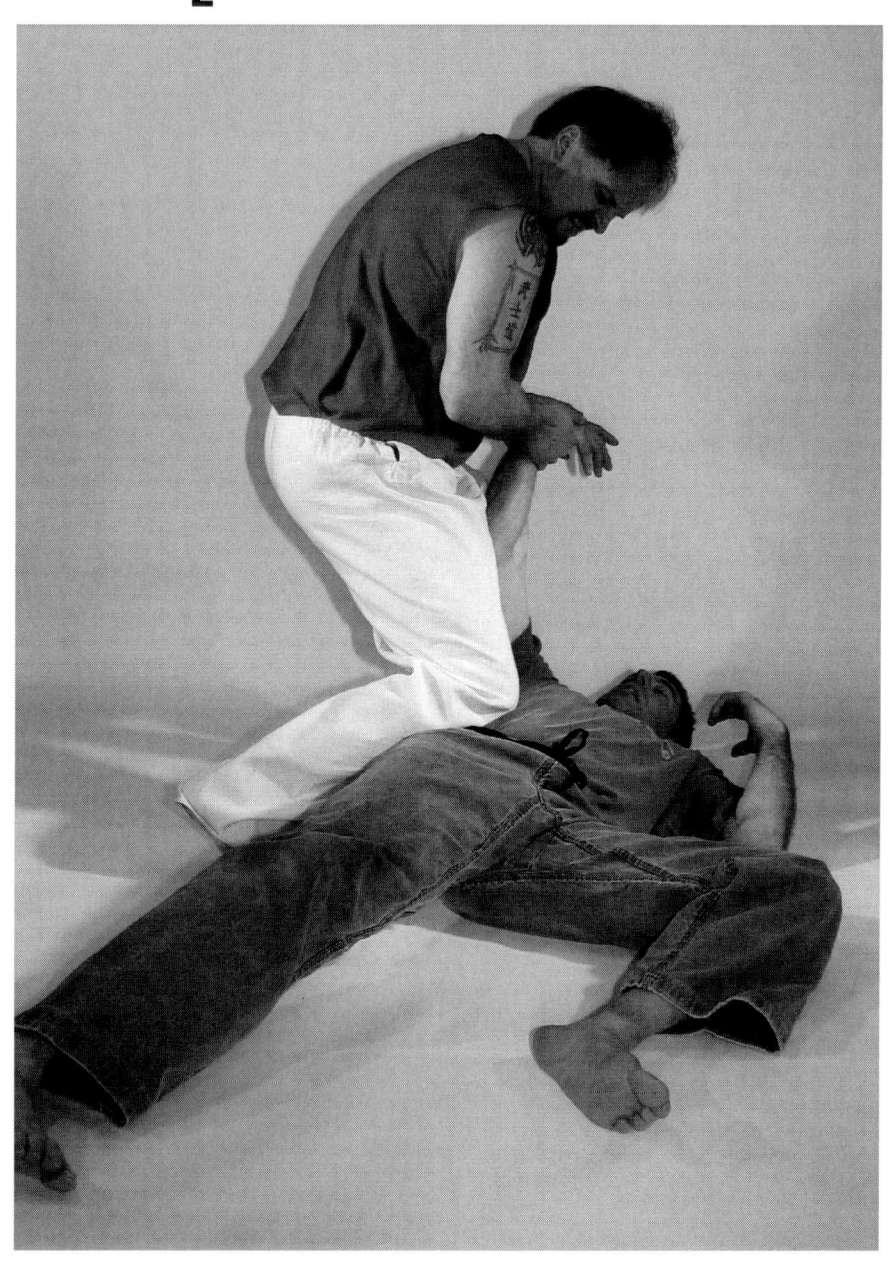

1. You have dumped your attacker to the floor. As soon as he lands on his back, drop your knee into his ribs.

ELBOW TECHNIQUES

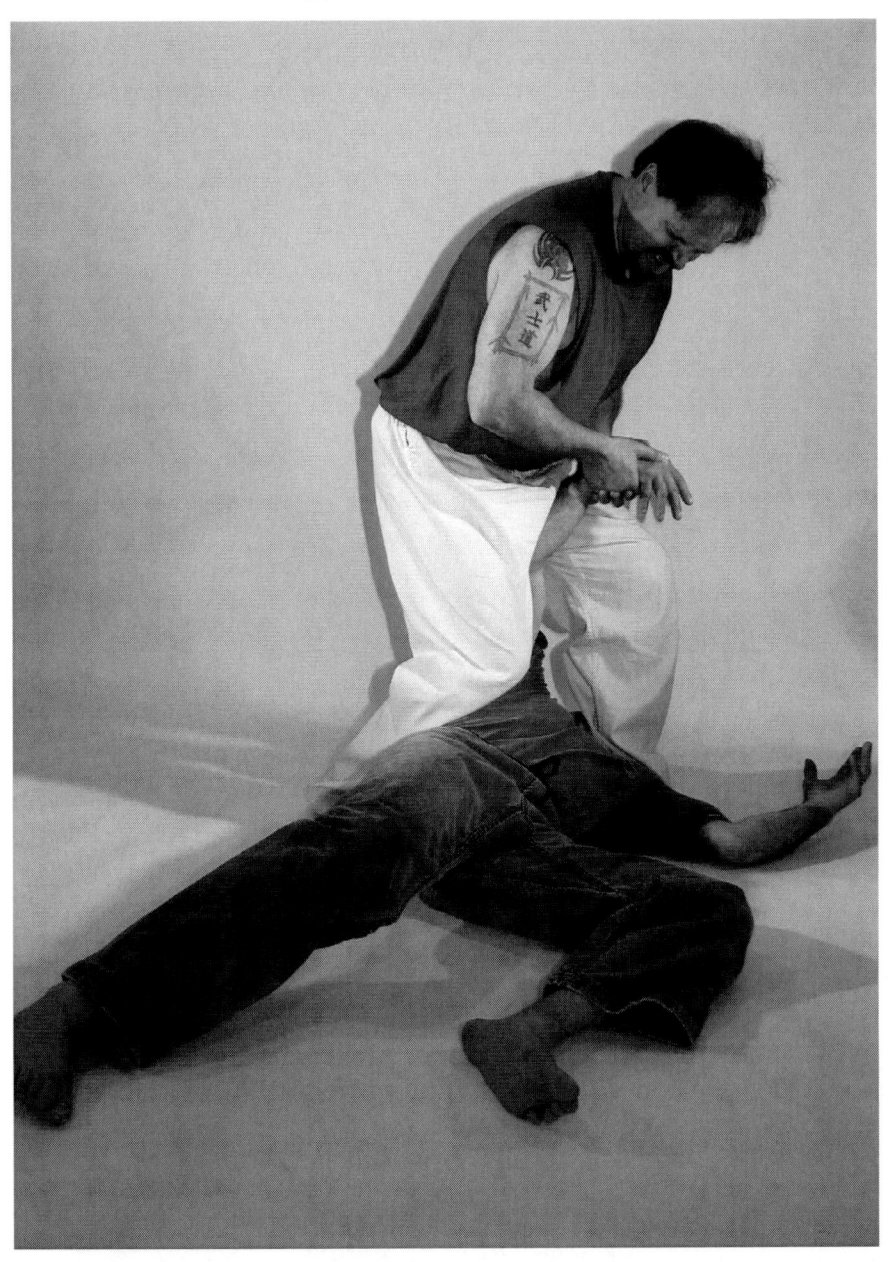

2. Jerk him up onto his side and knee-drop him again to knock the wind out of him.

EXTREME JOINT LOCKING AND BREAKING

3. Step over his head with your left foot (if the situation warrants it, allow your foot to scrape down his face). Sit down close to his shoulder (a common error is to sit too far away), tucking his elbow into your abdomen. Use your forearm to pull his arm in tight.

ELBOW TECHNIQUES

4. Lean back to straighten his arm and squeeze your legs together to control his shoulder. His elbow is across your upper inner thigh. Make sure the thumb side of his hand is pointing upward so that it's hard for him to curl his arm as you pull down with both of your hands.

EXTREME JOINT LOCKING AND BREAKING

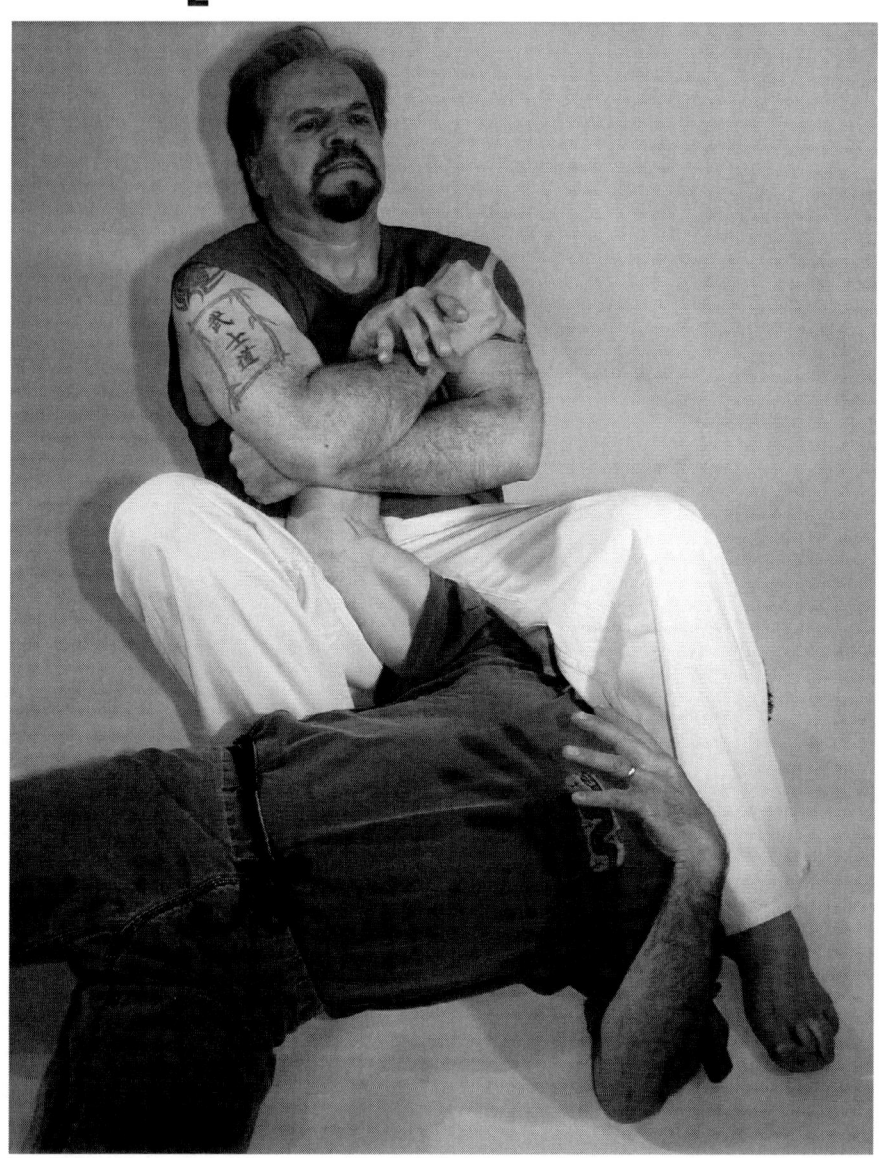

5. If your attacker is especially strong, cross your forearms over his and use the power of your upper body to pull downward. To cause extreme pain and possible joint injury, bridge your hips up as you pull his arm down.

ELBOW TECHNIQUES

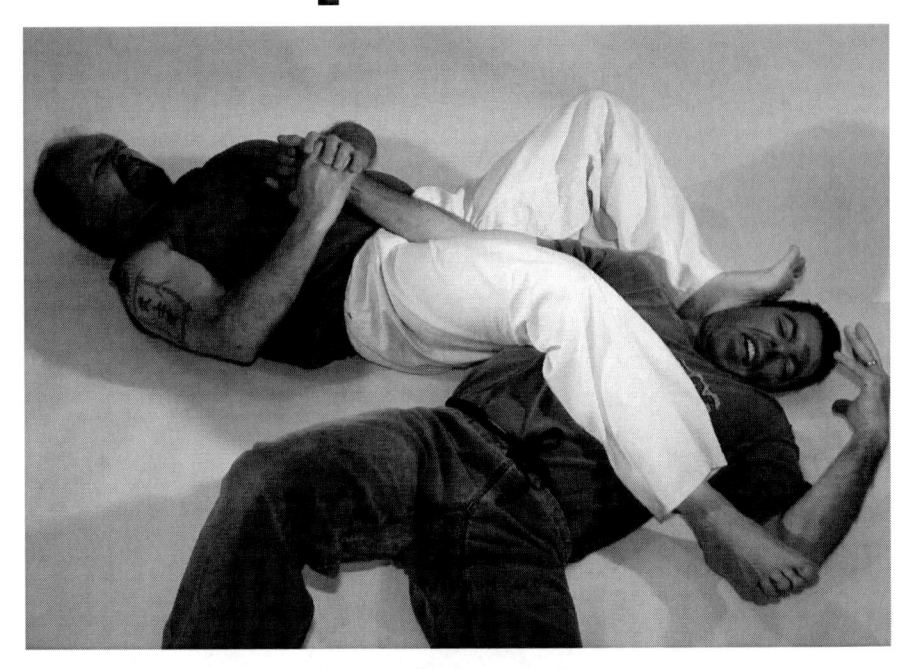

Variation 1

Slip your right leg over his upper body to ensure that he can't wiggle away. Use your left foot to stomp his head and then push it painfully to the side.

TECHNIQUE 4: OPPONENT ON SIDE ELBOW LOCK

When you take someone down onto his back with a wrist technique, it's best to get him over onto his belly as quickly as possible so that he has fewer weapons to use against you.

Life doesn't always go your way, however. Maybe you didn't execute the technique well, and you fell to one knee alongside him. Before you can get up, he rolls toward you and launches a punch at your face with his far arm. Here is a powerful plan B that will save the day for you. Let's begin with a takedown.

EXTREME JOINT LOCKING AND BREAKING

1. Execute a rear-shoulder-tuck takedown on the attacker.

ELBOW TECHNIQUES

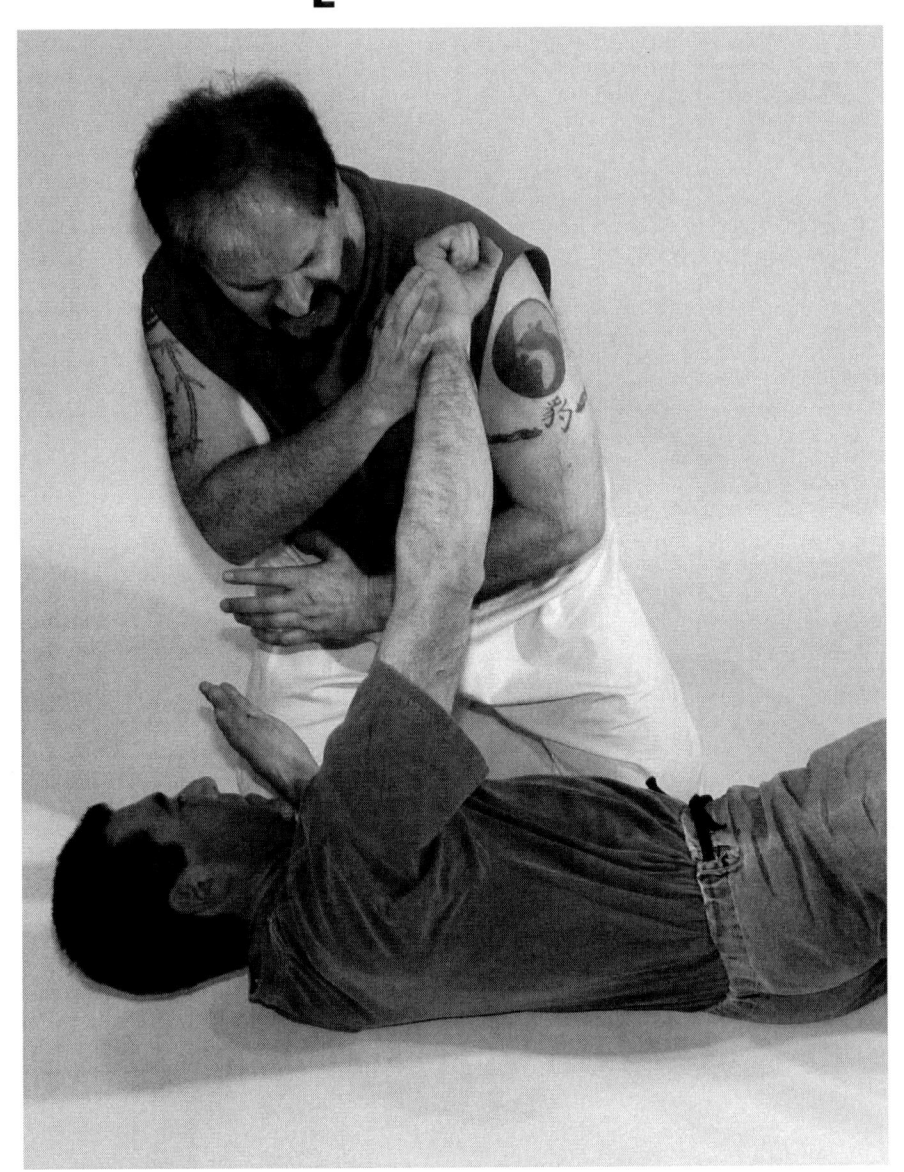

2. For whatever reason, you lose your balance and fall next to the left side of his head. Before you can recover, he twists toward you and launches a right punch. Sweep-block the punch with your right hand and guide it toward your left shoulder.

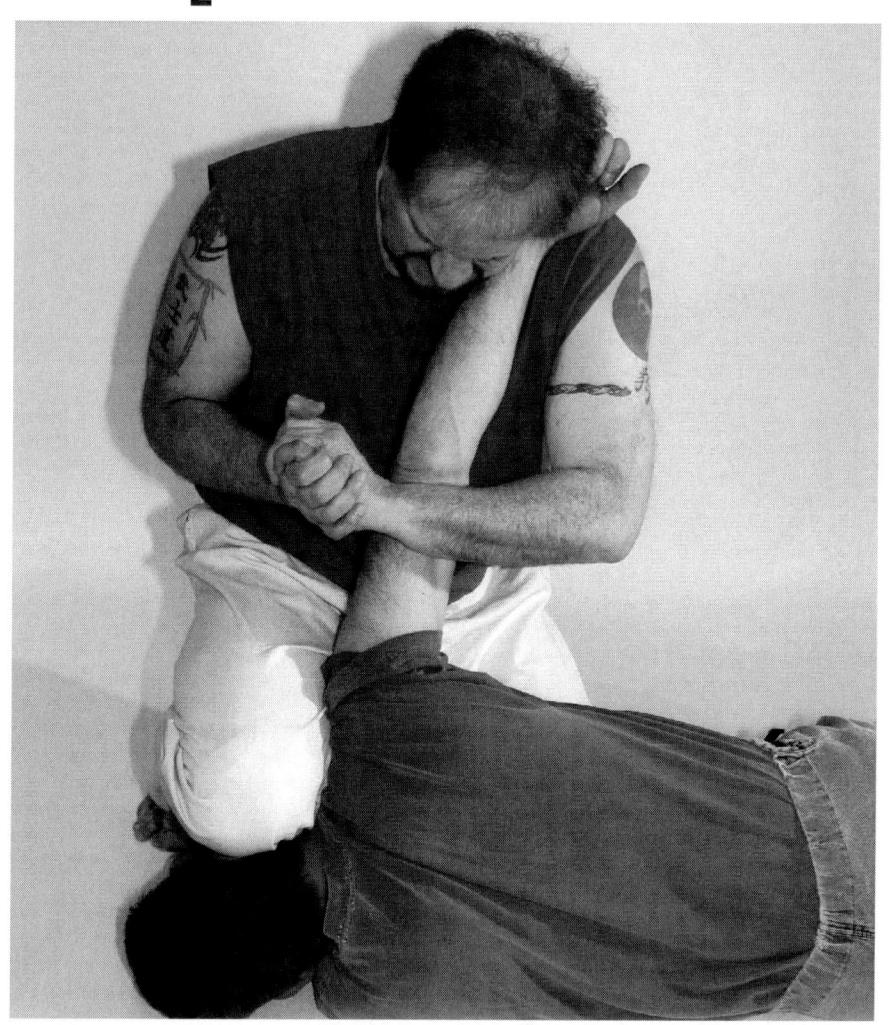

3. His wrist is pressed into your shoulder, creating a bridge at his elbow. To tighten the hold even more, pin his hand/wrist between your head and shoulder and use both hands to pull his elbow joint toward you. Your left knee presses against his chest or abdomen as your right knee leans on his head to prevent him from getting up. To underscore the pain, forcefully rub his ulna nerve (an inch above his elbow on the shoulder side) with the sharp edges of your wrists or use the option explained in step 4.

ELBOW TECHNIQUES

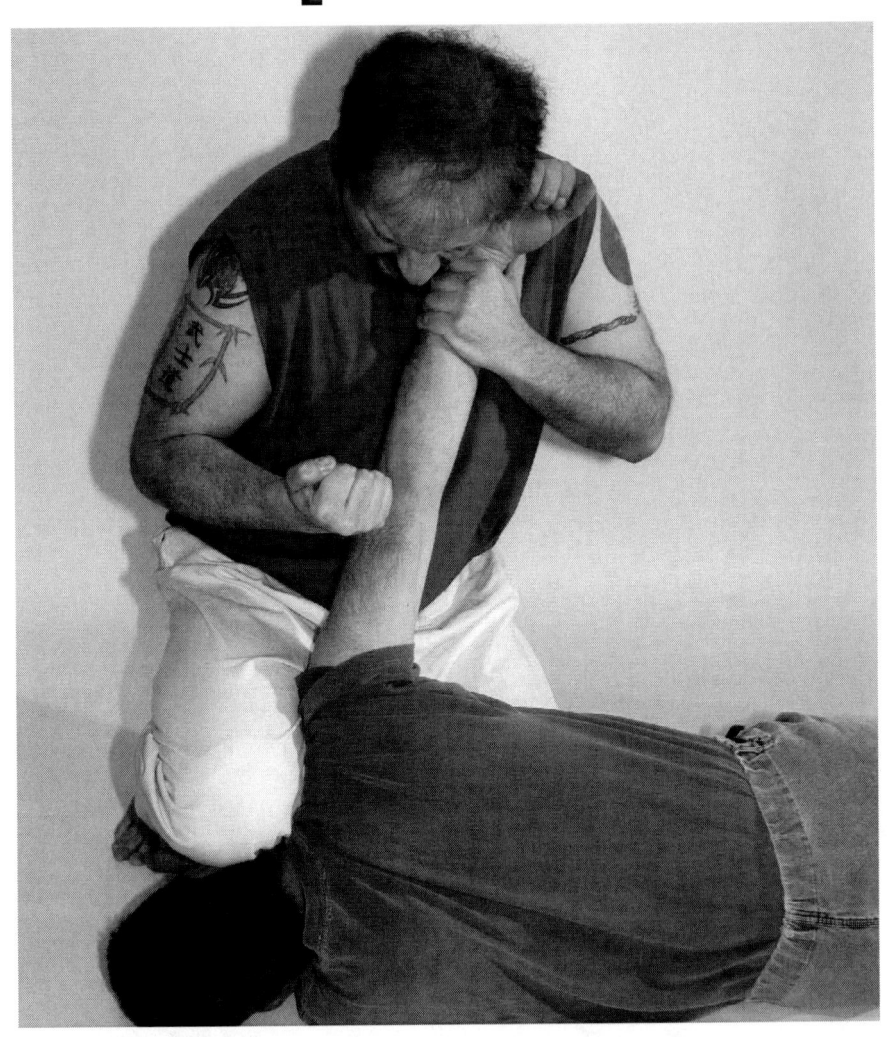

4. Should the situation warrant extreme force, slide one hand up his arm a few inches to secure it in place and then smash his elbow joint with your other fist.

⌈EXTREME JOINT LOCKING AND BREAKING⌉
TECHNIQUE 5: UPSIDE DOWN ARMBAR

Usually you execute this elbow lock when the opponent is on top of you and between your legs, a position known in training as "being in your guard." Let's relate this to the street.

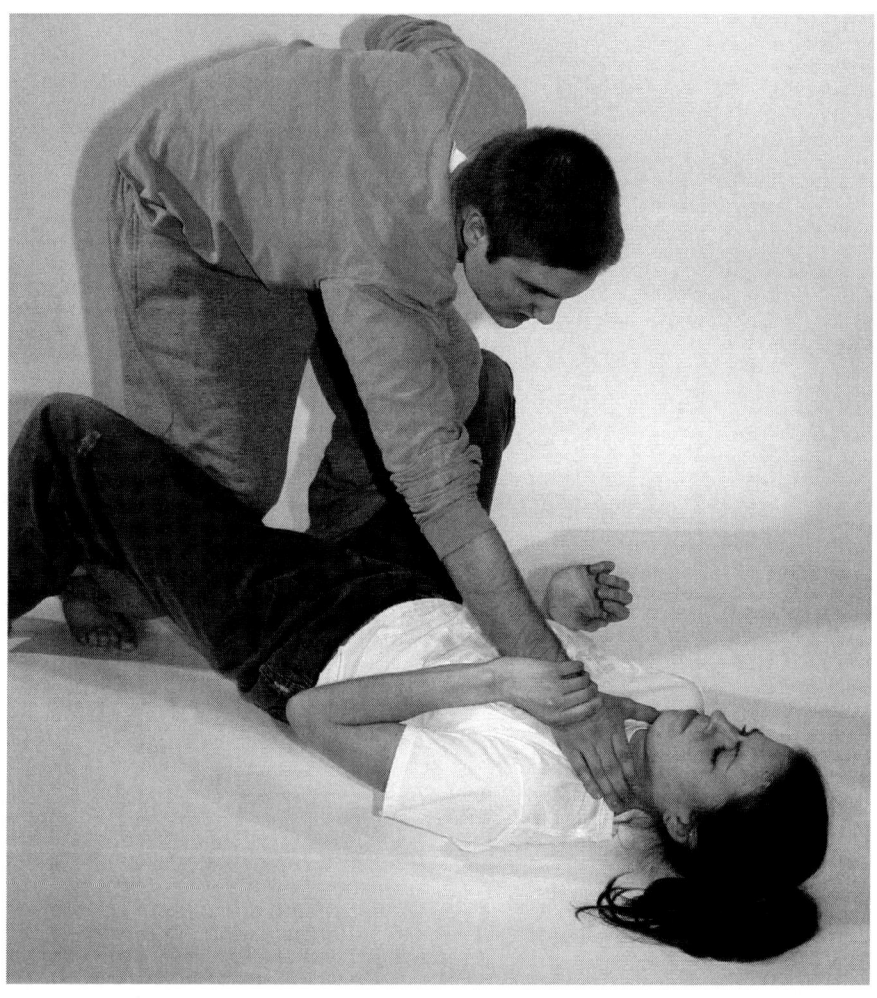

1. Your attacker has knocked you down, or you have slipped and fallen on your back in front of him. He smells blood and charges between your legs with his right arm extended to punch or grab you.

ELBOW TECHNIQUES

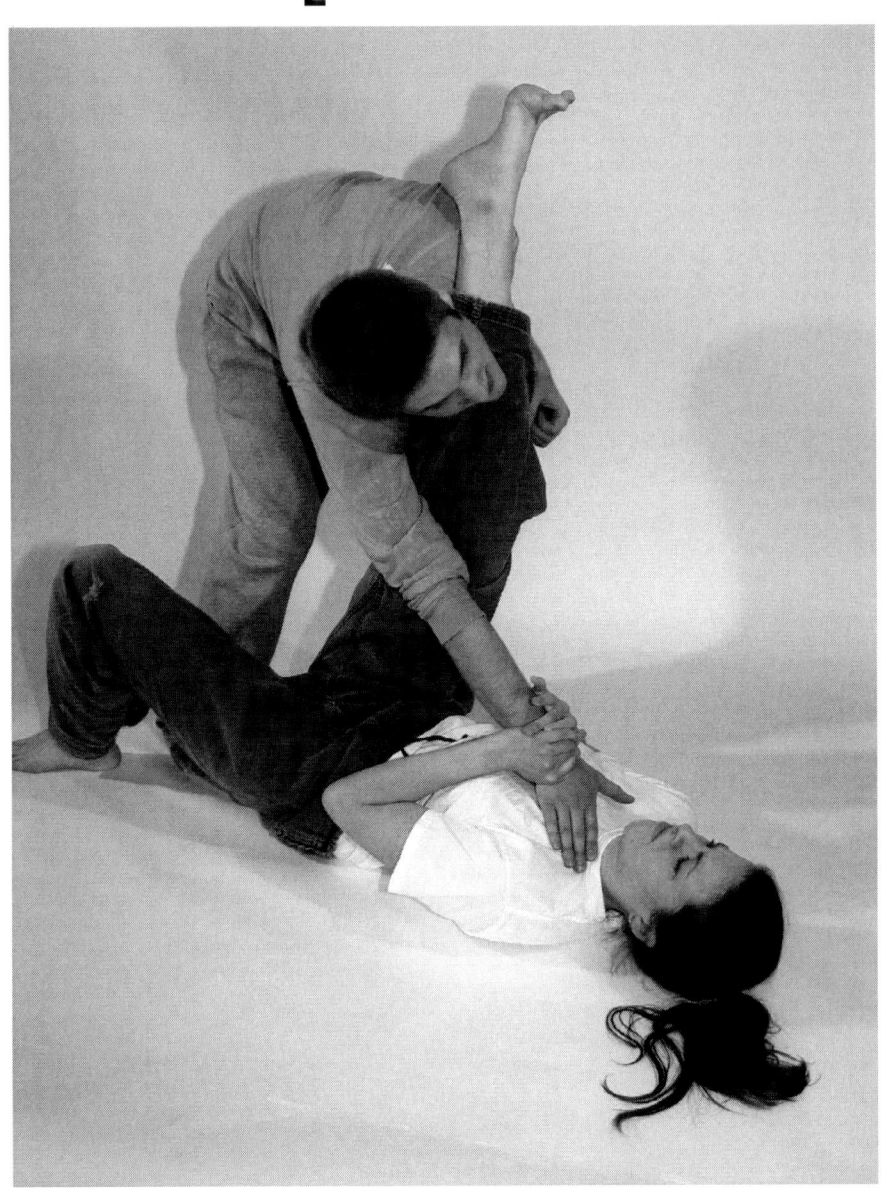

2. Grab his wrist with both hands and thrust your right foot toward his face. Your objective is to wrap your leg around his neck, but if the situation is grave, take a chunk out of his cheek with your heel as it passes by.

EXTREME JOINT LOCKING AND BREAKING

3. Shoot your left foot up the outside of his right arm and on the other side of his head (take another chunk of his face as needed). Execute a figure four around the attacker's head and push his straight arm so that his locked elbow is hyperextended against your thigh. Push your hips up to increase the pressure.

ELBOW TECHNIQUES

If he moves forward, your combined weight will hyperextend your neck. Lift your hips higher to increase his elbow pain and shout at him to back up. It's amazing how many people follow verbal commands when experiencing pain. If he obeys and moves back a little, you get relief from the pain in your neck and, to his chagrin, he gets more pain in his elbow. If he doesn't move back and you feel justified to use greater force to protect your neck, slam your hips hard into his locked elbow joint as you press his arm hard against your leg.

CHAPTER 4
shoulder techniques

Talk to 10 martial artists and nine of them will have bad shoulders. While it does go with the territory, knowing that doesn't make it hurt any less. A shoulder "problem" can range from a dull ache to an inability to move it—and perhaps the arm hanging from it and the head just above it. That is what makes it a good target in self-defense: give your attacker a problem in his shoulder, and he feels it from his head to his fingertips; give it to him suddenly and with tremendous force, and you take his attacking arm out of commission, maybe for a long time.

TECHNIQUE 1: POLICE STRAIGHT ARM

This is a powerful prone control hold used by many police agencies. It consists of four primary pain factors that never failed me on the street, but I'm going to give you a fifth level of pain in the event your situation suddenly turns bleak.

EXTREME JOINT LOCKING AND BREAKING

THE SHOULDER AS A TARGET

The shoulder consists of two primary bones: the humerus (the upper arm bone) and the scapula (shoulder blade). The shoulder joint is a ball and socket between the humerus and scapula. Cartilage cushions the joint, and ligaments connect the shoulder bones. The bones are connected to the surrounding muscles by tendons.

Dislocation

It's possible to dislocate the shoulder joint forward, backward, or downward. A partial dislocation means the humerus head is partially out of the socket; a complete dislocation means it's all the way out. Both cause tremendous pain.

Rotator Cuff Tears

The rotator cuff is made up of the muscles and tendons that surround the top of the upper arm bone to hold it in the shoulder joint. A rotator cuff injury can occur from a bad fall or violent torque on the joint, or by forcing it far beyond its natural range of movement.

Break

The shoulder blade is quite mobile and enjoys lots of protection from surrounding muscles, but it can break from an awkward fall or when forced beyond its range. This can be enormously painful and is usually accompanied by swelling around the shoulder. Most important, the attacker's arm is made useless.

⌐ **SHOULDER TECHNIQUES** ⌐

1. Use the attacker's hair to dump him on his belly. Point your elbows down for maximum strength.

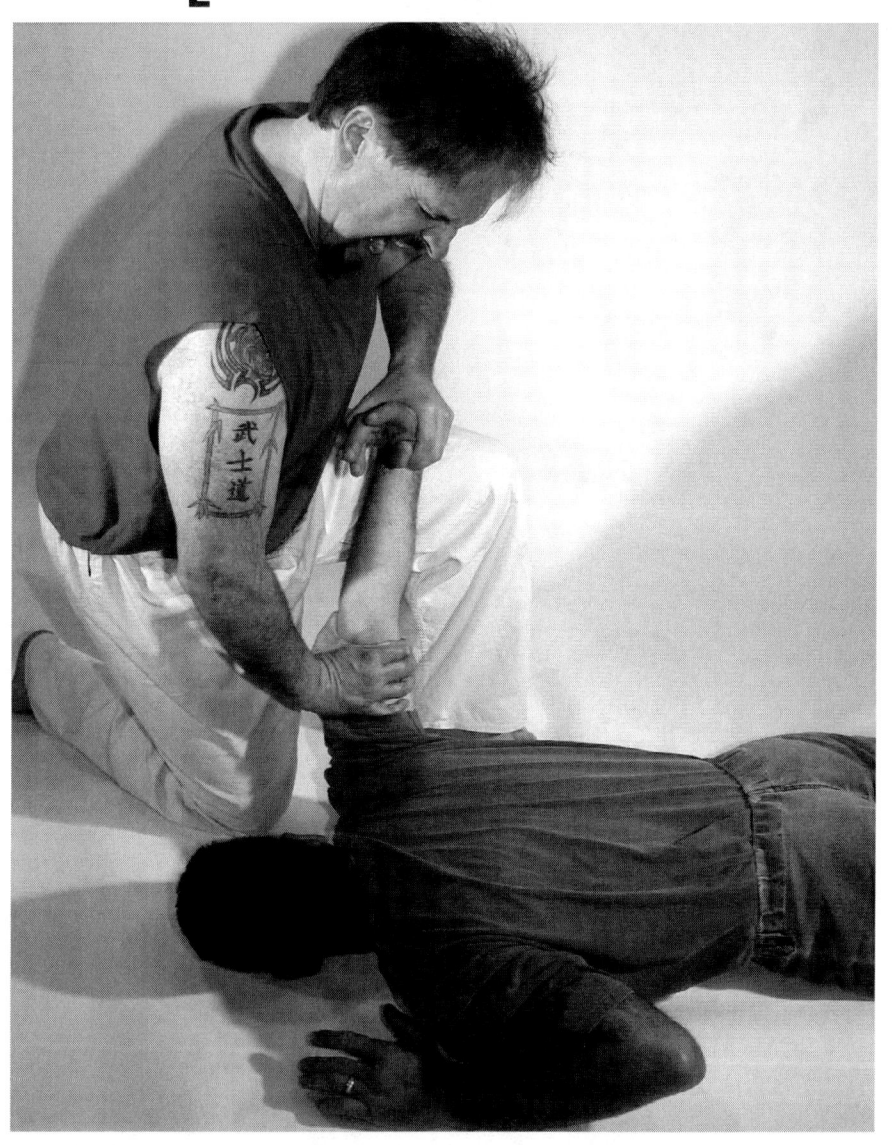

2. Kneel at his head and hold his upraised arm as shown. Apply pain by the following methods:
- Pushing down on the back of his hand
- Hyperextending his locked elbow
- Jamming his arm down into the joint
- Pushing his arm toward his head

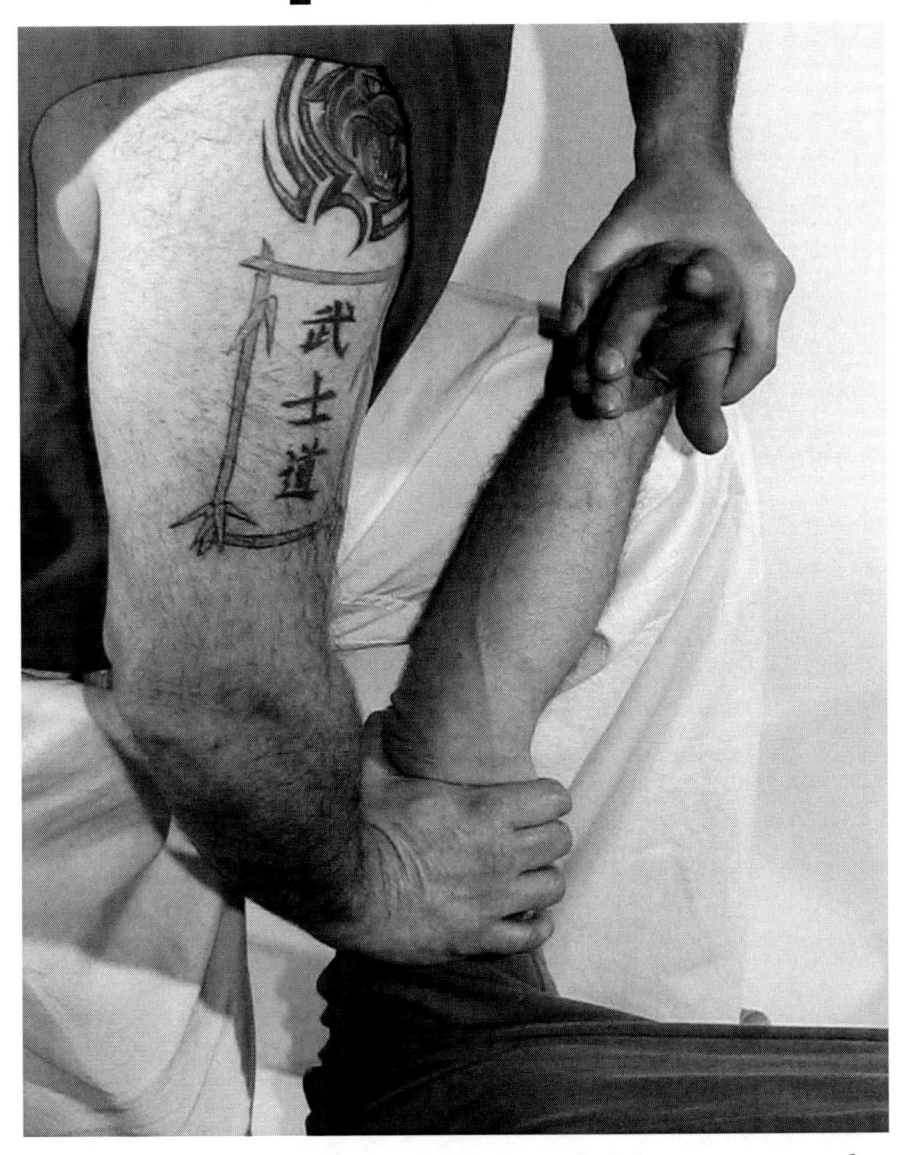

3. Although this is excruciatingly painful, a person under the influence of a brain-numbing intoxicant might tolerate it. Should he start to squirm out of your hold or reach with his free hand for a weapon on his person, ram his arm toward his head to inflict a trail of internal damage.

EXTREME JOINT LOCKING AND BREAKING

TECHNIQUE 2: PRONE BENT-ARM SHOULDER LOCK

As a copper, I used this technique and its variations many times and never had it fail to get a confession. Just kidding about the confession, but it did do a magnificent job of controlling unruly people while handcuffing them.

I have bad shoulders today as a result of this lock. As a defensive tactics instructor on the police department for 25 years, I often volunteered to play the bad guy in arrest scenarios. Too many rookies applying techniques with too much zeal eventually tenderized my shoulders so that today I need to bow out whenever the class works on shoulder locks. Whether my problem is a result of one exceptionally hard application or dozens of lesser ones over the years, I don't know. I do know that I have seen many suspects, as well as martial arts students, injured from one hard application of this technique. And since it takes only 20 percent of your strength to inflict pain, it's easy to see how 50 or 60 percent could cause serious injury to the shoulder joint and all its connective tissue.

SHOULDER TECHNIQUES

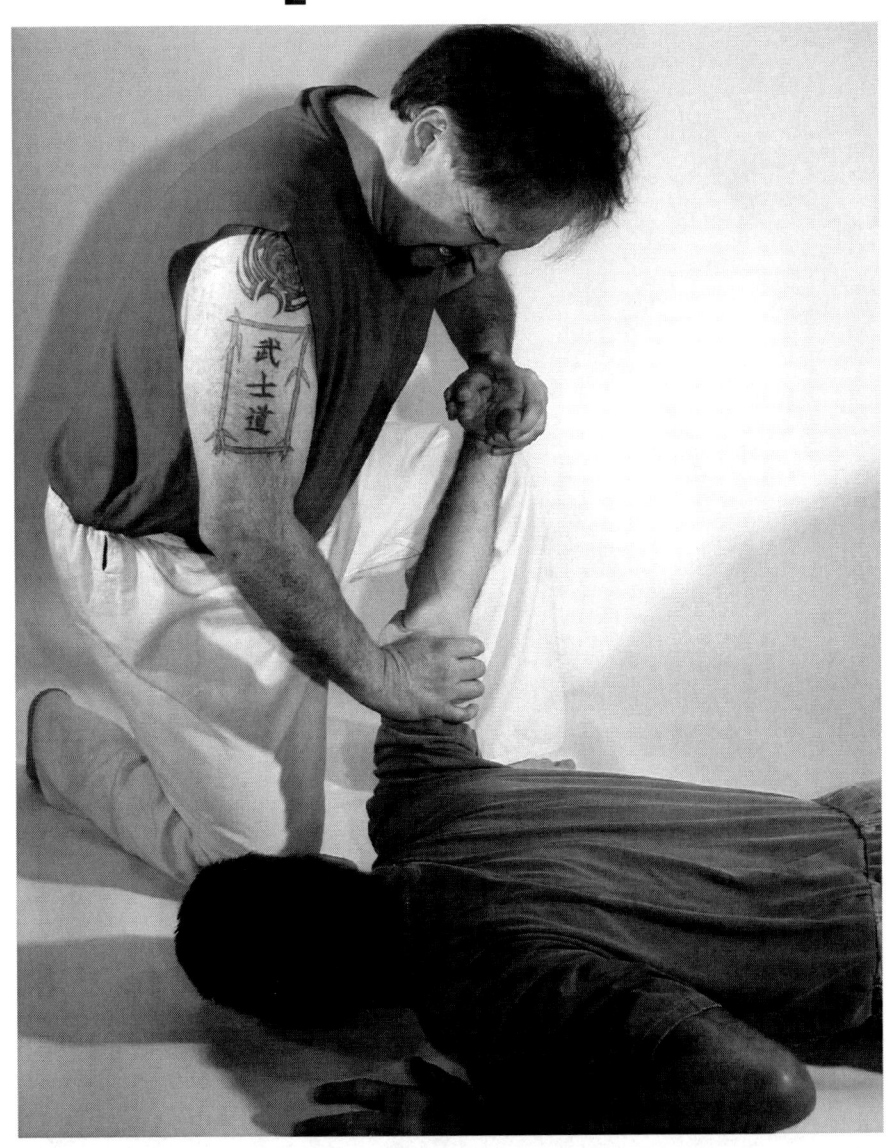

1. You're kneeling by the attacker's right shoulder, holding his upright arm as in the last technique. You want to move his arm to his lower back to handcuff him or to move into another technique.

EXTREME JOINT LOCKING AND BREAKING

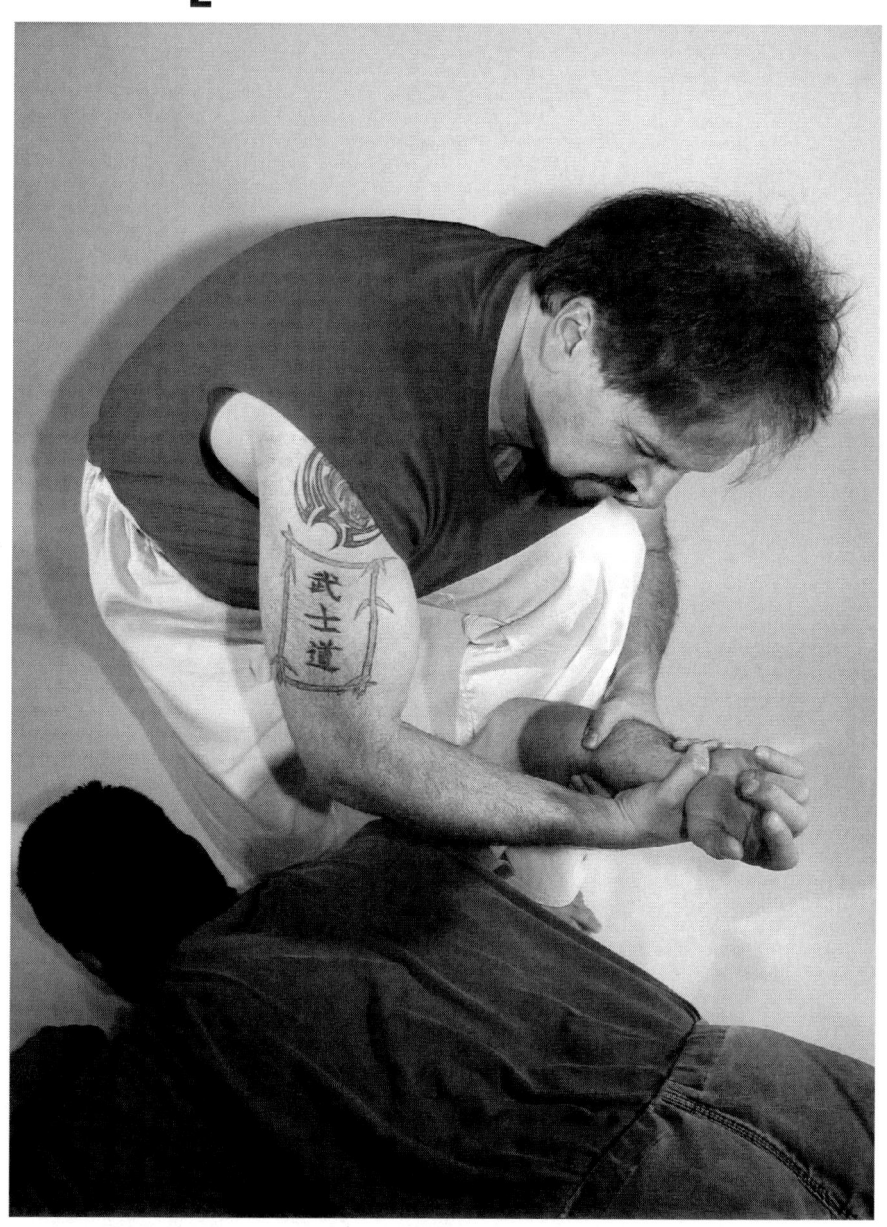

2. Switch hands by grasping his wrist with your right hand and his elbow with your left.

┌ SHOULDER TECHNIQUES ┐

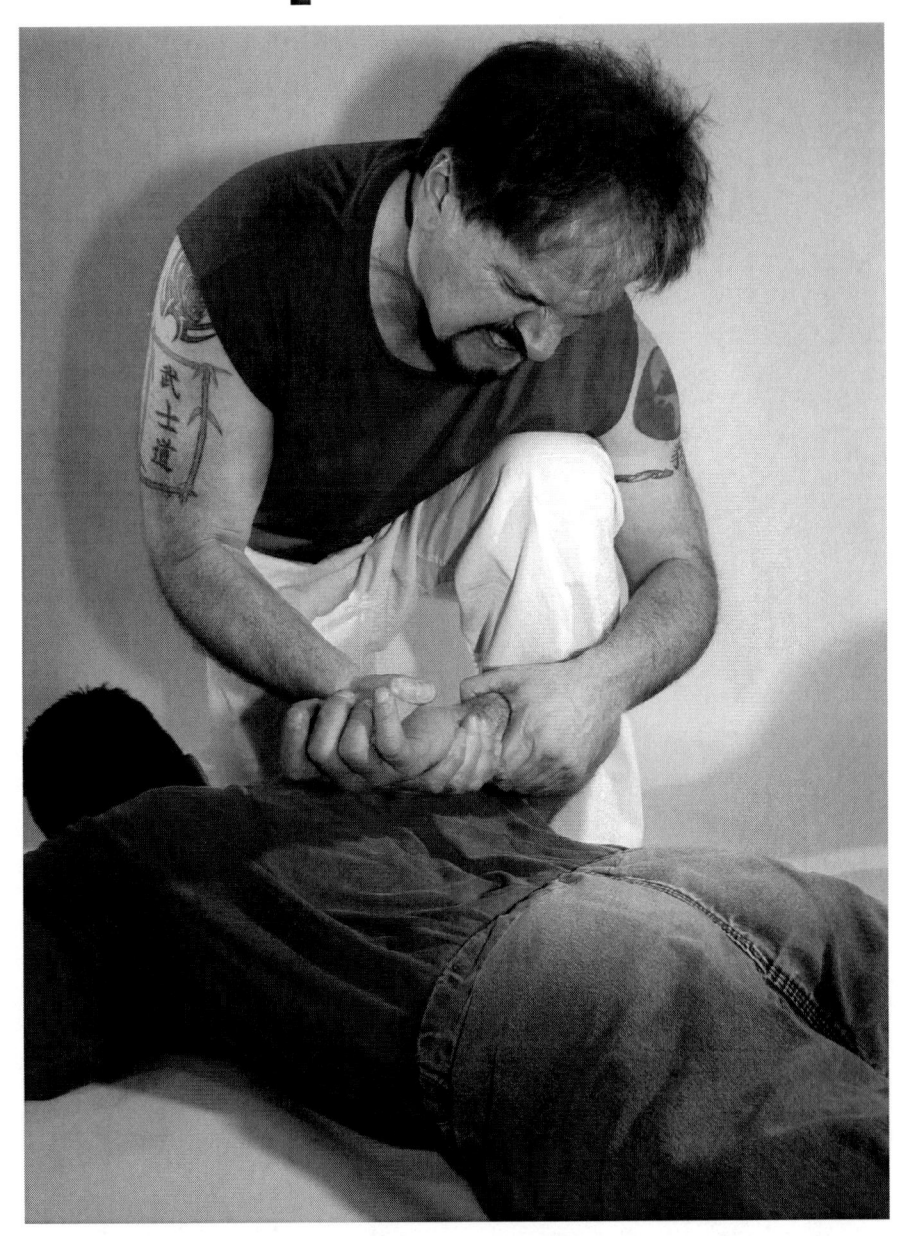

3. Swing his arm down to his lower back, but hold it off the surface to maintain constant tension. Push your left shin against his upper arm to lock him into place.

EXTREME JOINT LOCKING AND BREAKING

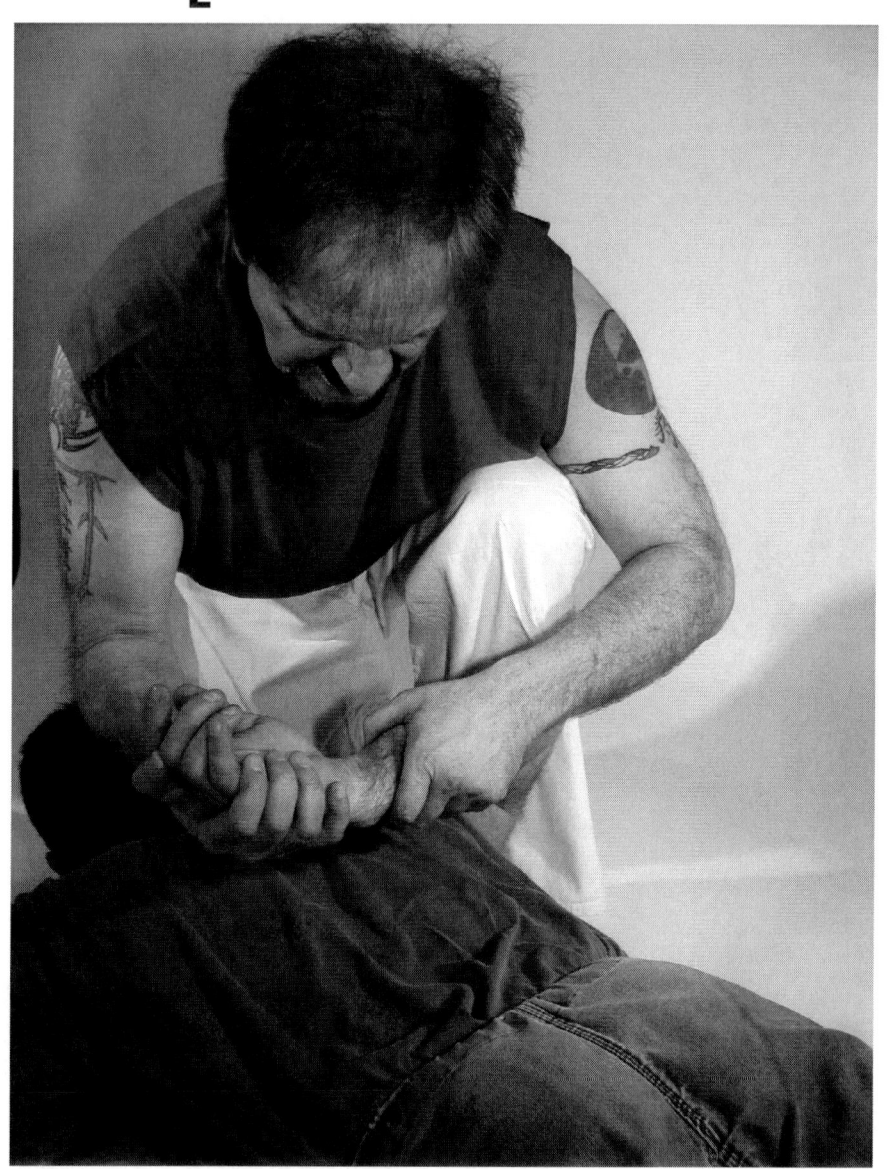

4. To apply greater pain, lift his arm higher as you pull his hand toward his opposite shoulder. If he tolerates this and begins reaching for a weapon with his other hand, you can jerk his arm up hard and toward his shoulder, which is likely to cause internal shoulder damage.

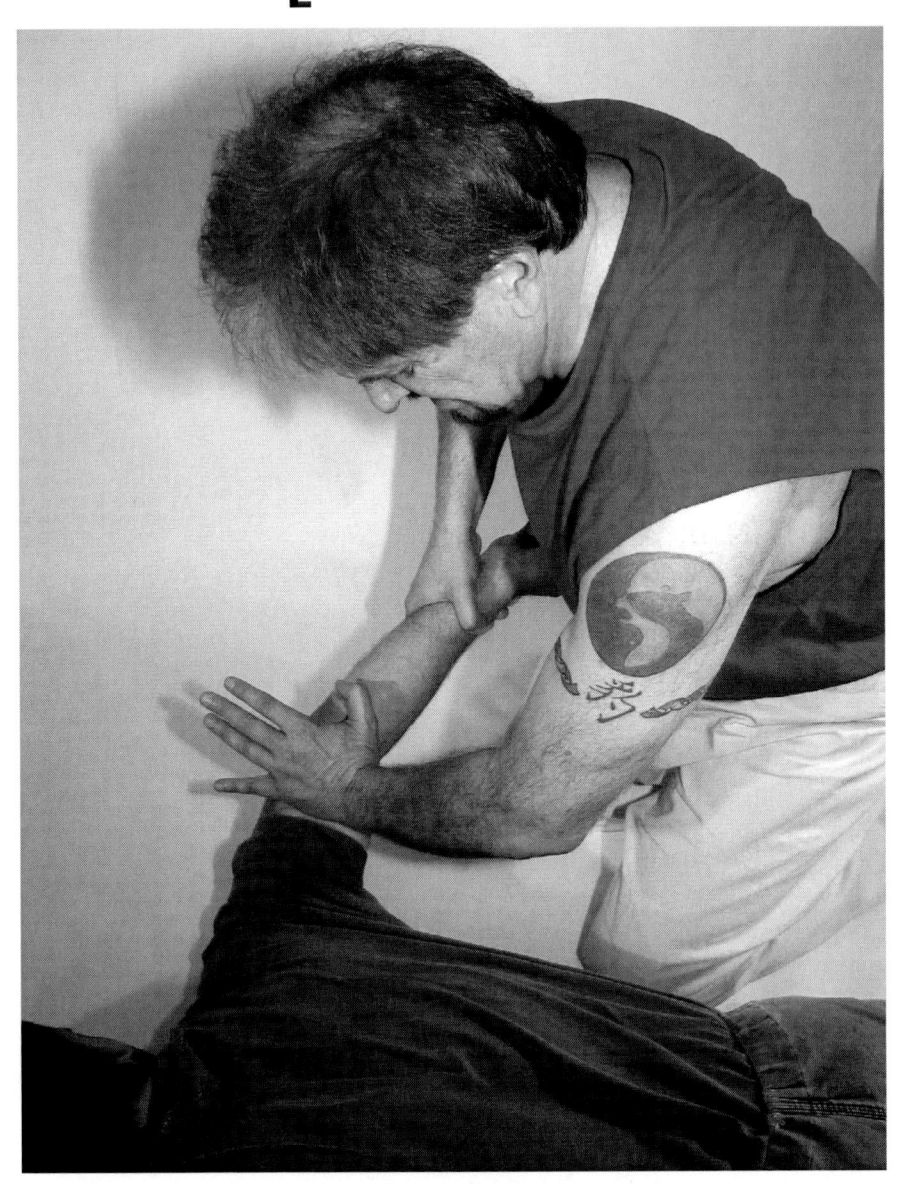

L SHOULDER TECHNIQUES ⌐

Variation 1
1. In the process of taking an attacker down, say with an armbar as pictured, you lose your balance and drop onto your knees beside him.

EXTREME JOINT LOCKING AND BREAKING

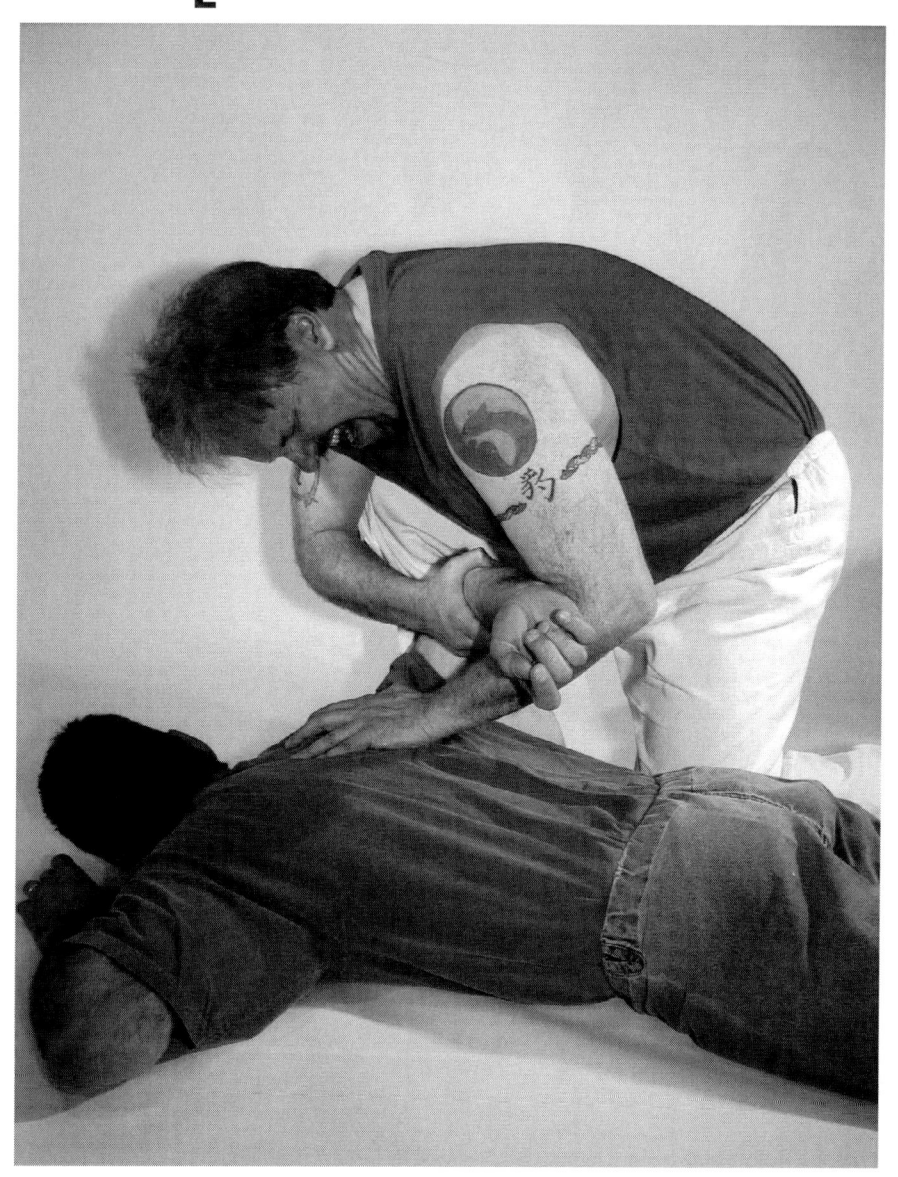

2. Immediately force his arm behind him with your right hand as you place the palm of your left hand on his mid-back. Keep control of his elbow as you use your left arm as a prying tool, forcing his arm and shoulder into the pain zone.

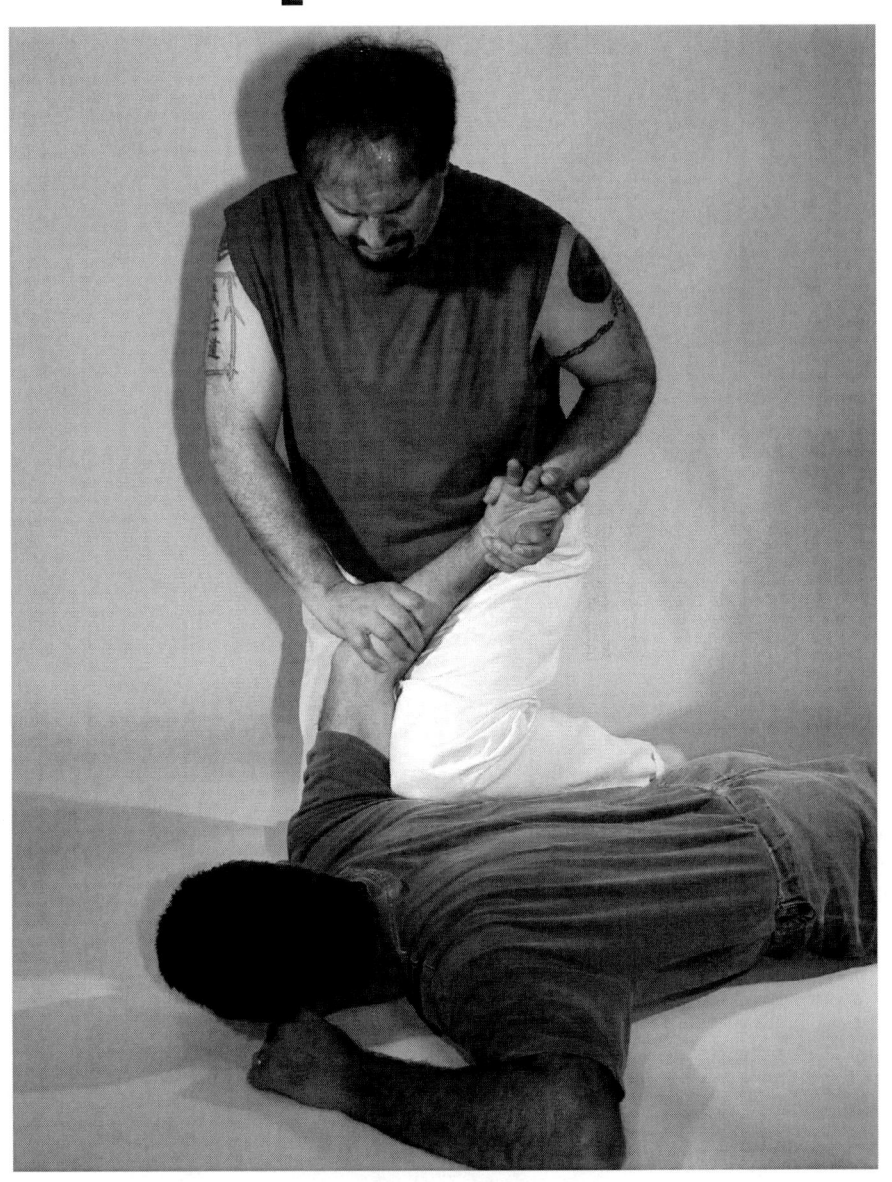

⌐SHOULDER TECHNIQUES¬

Variation 2
1. As you take the attacker down, drop beside him, with your knee in his armpit and his arm on your thigh.

EXTREME JOINT LOCKING AND BREAKING

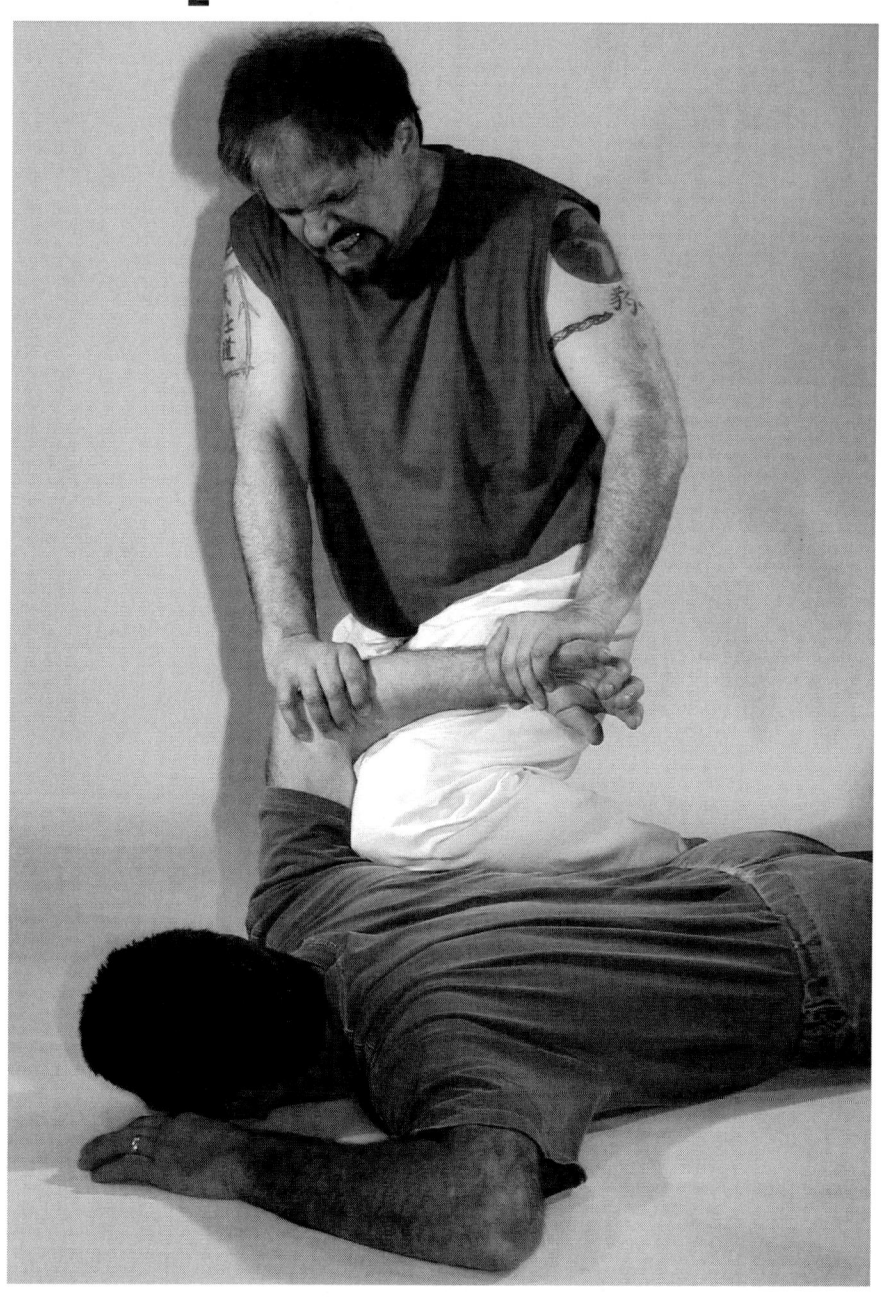

2. Push his arm down your thigh and listen to him squeal.

SHOULDER TECHNIQUES
TECHNIQUE 3: SHOULDER LOCK WITH KICKOUT

Although this is easy to apply, you must take advantage of a small window of opportunity because it requires your attacker's arm to be straight and stiff. **CAUTION**: Notice in the next to last photo of this sequence that I begin to kick my leg out in preparation to drop to the floor. Even this position puts painful pressure on my partner's shoulder. The last photo in this sequence, on the floor, is posed because even if I had taken my training partner down slowly I might have injured his shoulder joint. Be careful in practice. Simulate the takedown.

1. An attacker attempts to grab your shoulder with his left hand so he can hit you with a weapon in his right hand. Sweep his grab with your left palm as you begin to lift your right arm for the trap.

EXTREME JOINT LOCKING AND BREAKING

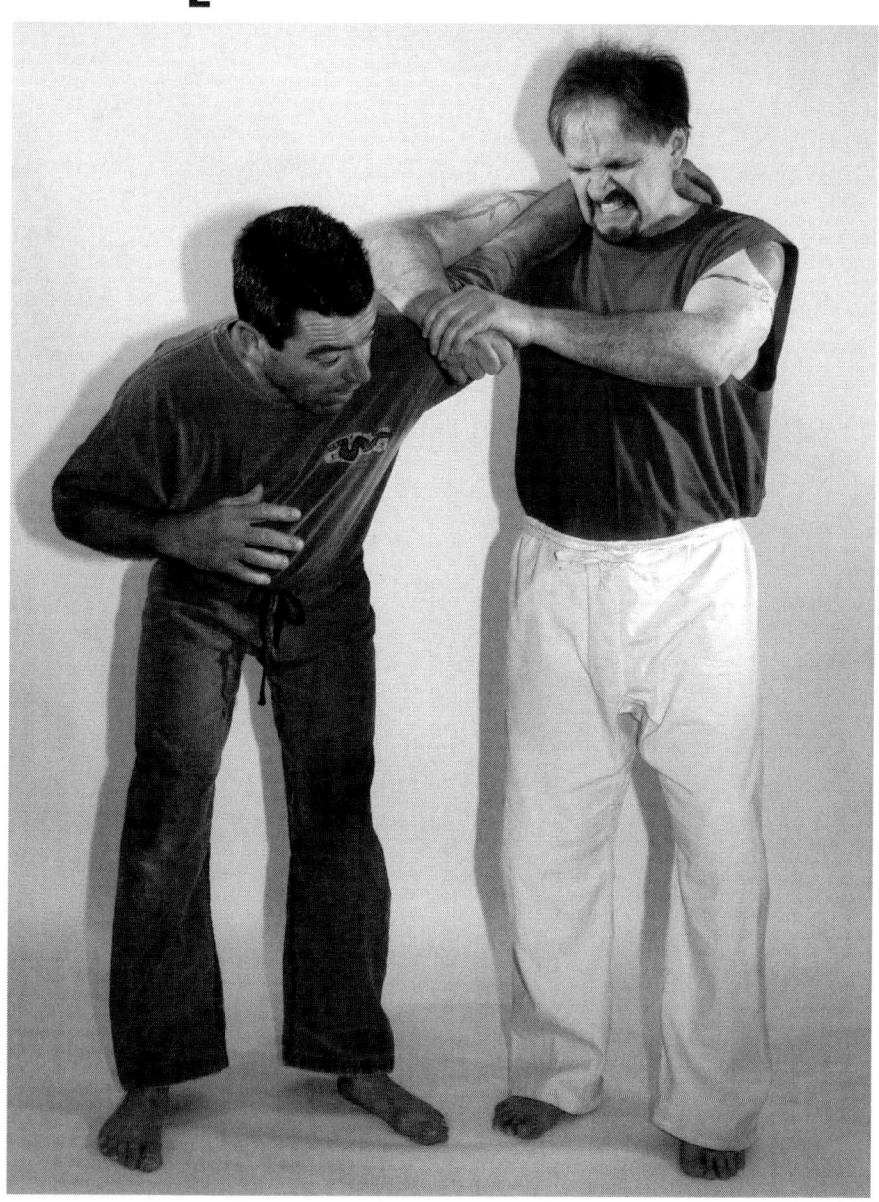

2. Use your left hand to trap his hand and wrist next to your head as you wrap your arm over the side of his shoulder.

SHOULDER TECHNIQUES

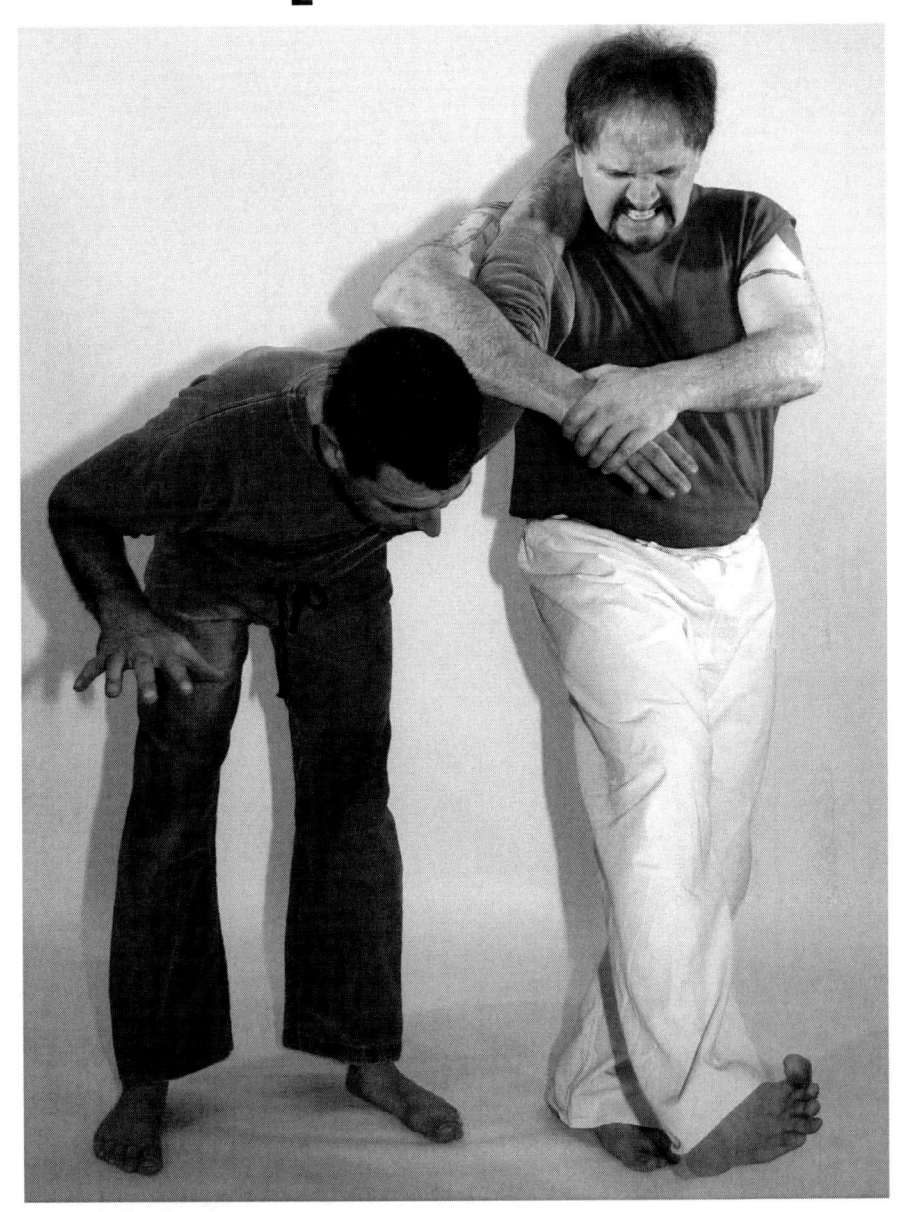

3. Use your right arm to bend him over. Grab your right hand with your left for added strength. Keep your body straight to maintain the lock on his shoulder and his hand next to your head. Kick your right leg forward.

⌐EXTREME JOINT LOCKING AND BREAKING⌐

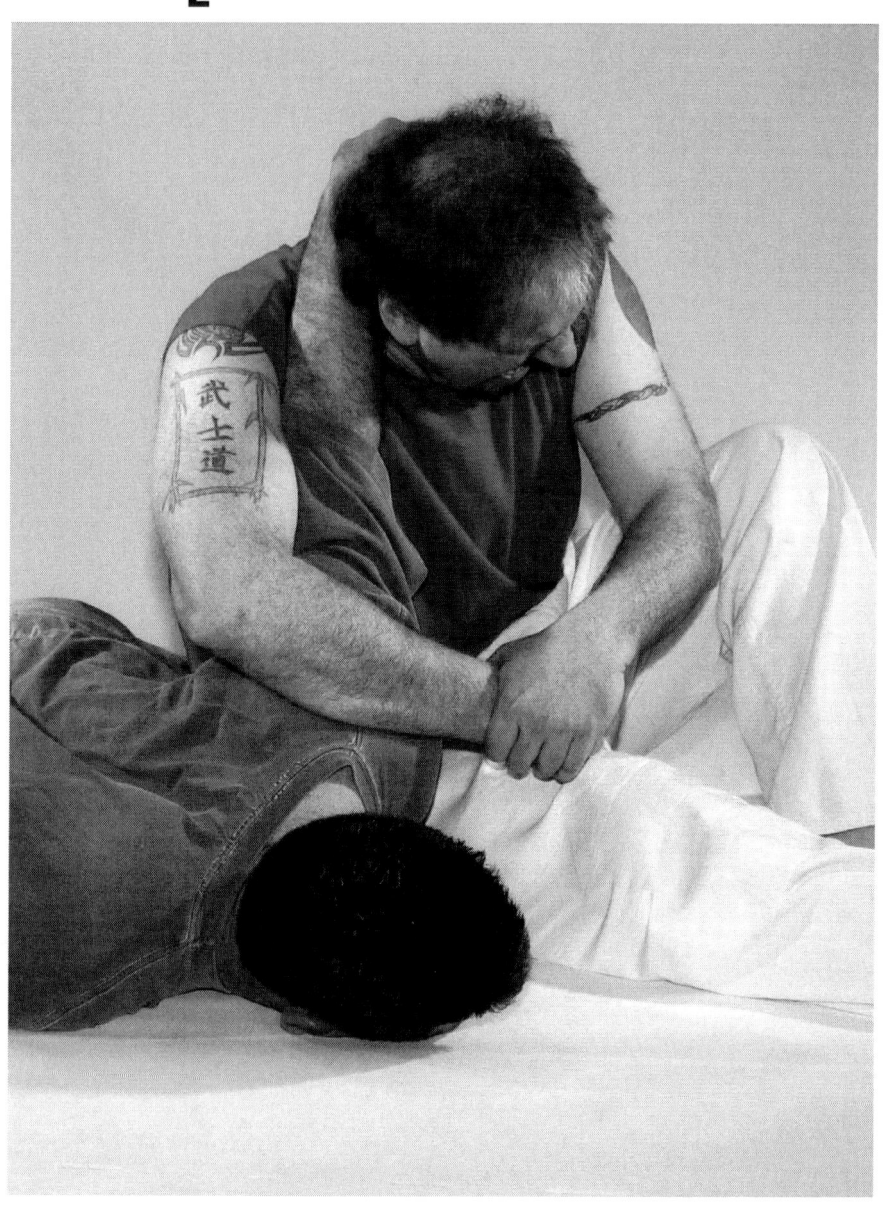

4. Drop onto your hip to blow out his shoulder. **CAUTION:** Don't execute this last step in practice because doing so will likely injure your partner's shoulder. This photo is *for illustrative purposes only.*

SHOULDER TECHNIQUES
TECHNIQUE 4:
SHOULDER LOCK, WRISTLOCK, AND SIT DOWN

This is similar to the last technique, though some fighters find it easier to apply. When a friend of mine was jumped on the street, he used it to break his attacker's clavicle. Actually, he broke the man's wrist, too, because he had a good wristlock on him at the same time. My friend says that the only variation in this case was that in his adrenaline rush he jerked the man's arm straight up as he applied the lock. Hmm, maybe he has something there. Try it both ways and see which you prefer.

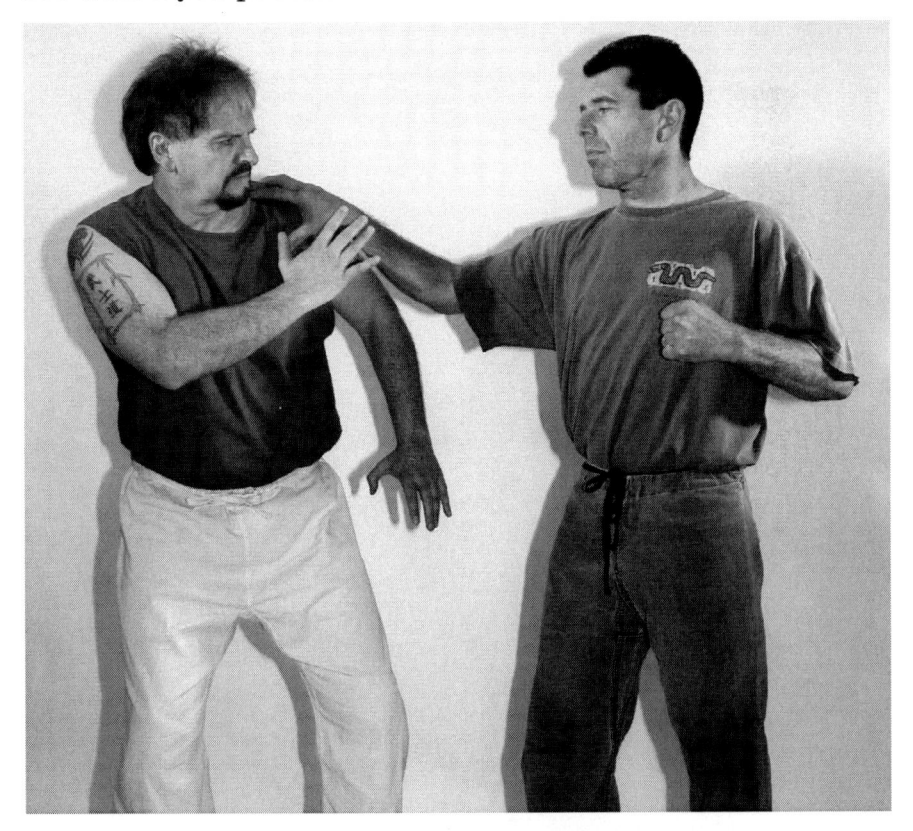

1. An attacker grabs at your left shoulder with his right hand.

EXTREME JOINT LOCKING AND BREAKING

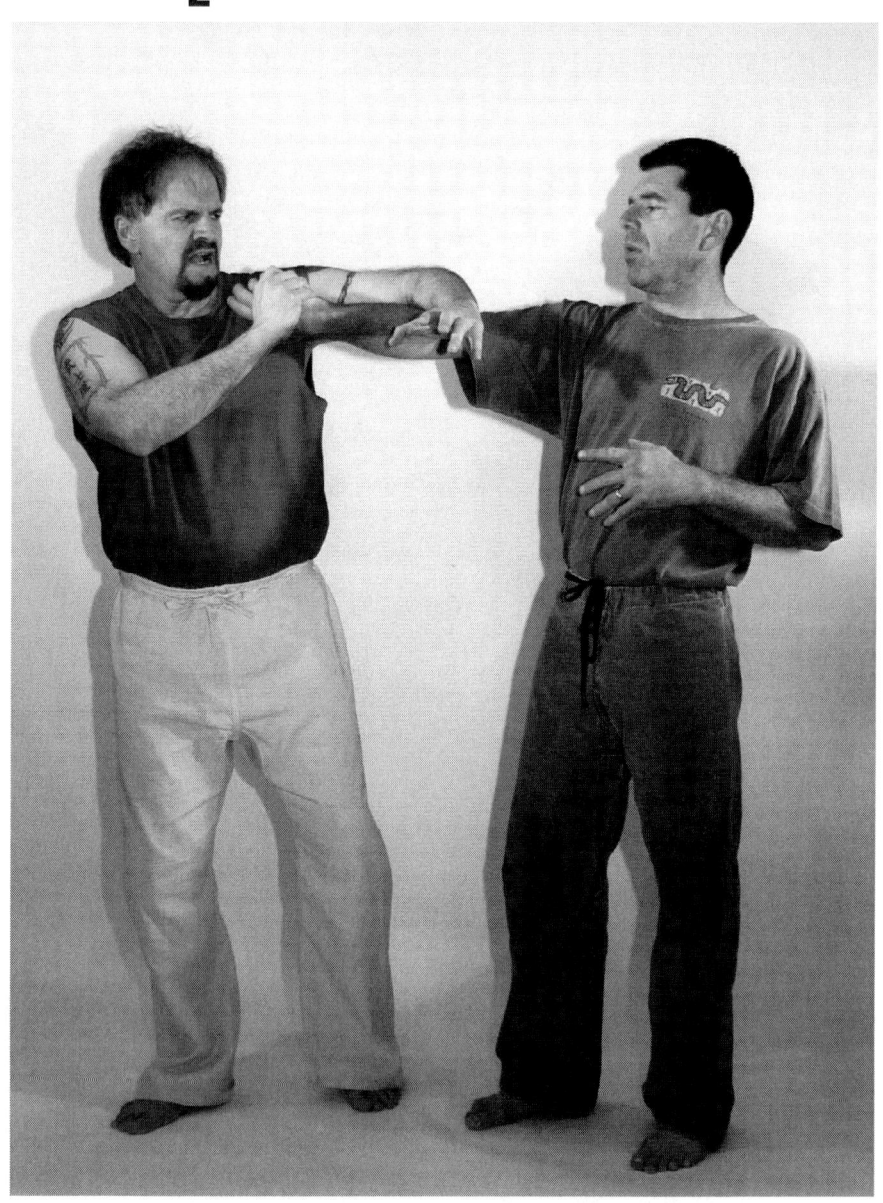

2. Reach across with your right hand and peel it off (if he grips your clothing, kick him in the groin) and begin to shoot your left arm over his upper arm.

⌐SHOULDER TECHNIQUES¬

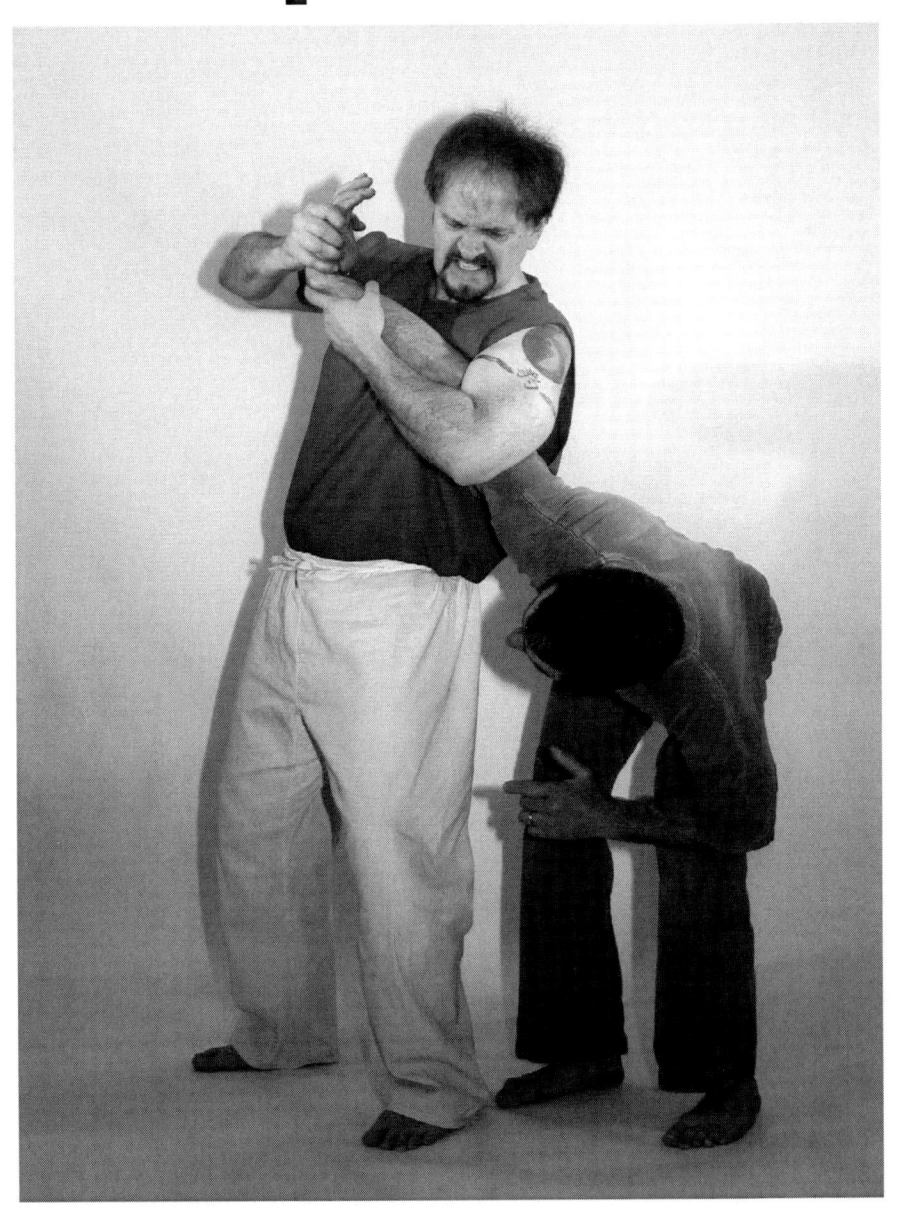

3. Wing your left elbow in tight to pin his arm, and grip his forearm with your left hand.

EXTREME JOINT LOCKING AND BREAKING

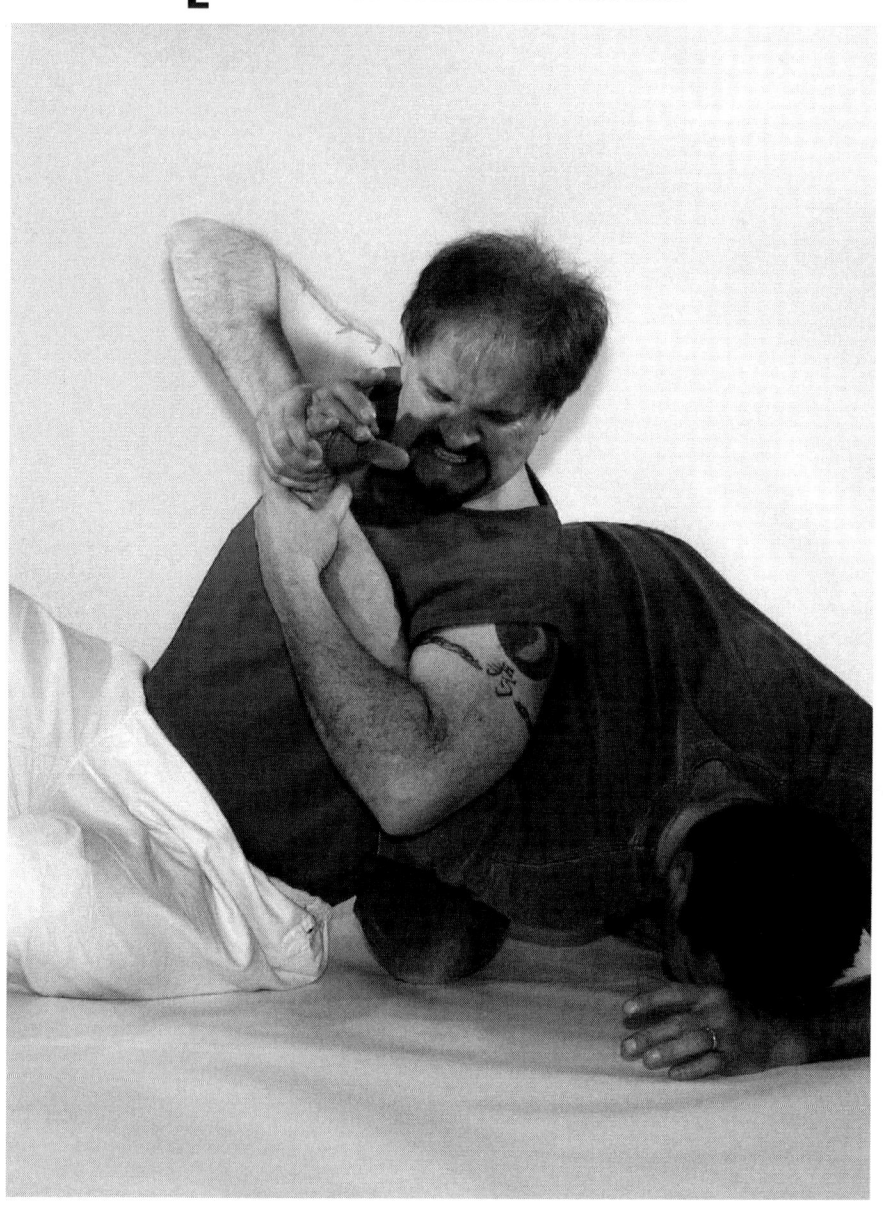

4. If the situation warrants greater bone-breaking force, drop onto your rear.

┗ SHOULDER TECHNIQUES ┓

TECHNIQUE 5: SHOULDER CRANK

This crank is a particularly good one should you be injured or ill because it takes so little strength to get your attacker to cry "uncle" or "mama." In class it generally has your opponent tapping the mat quickly even though you have applied only 10 to 20 percent of your strength.

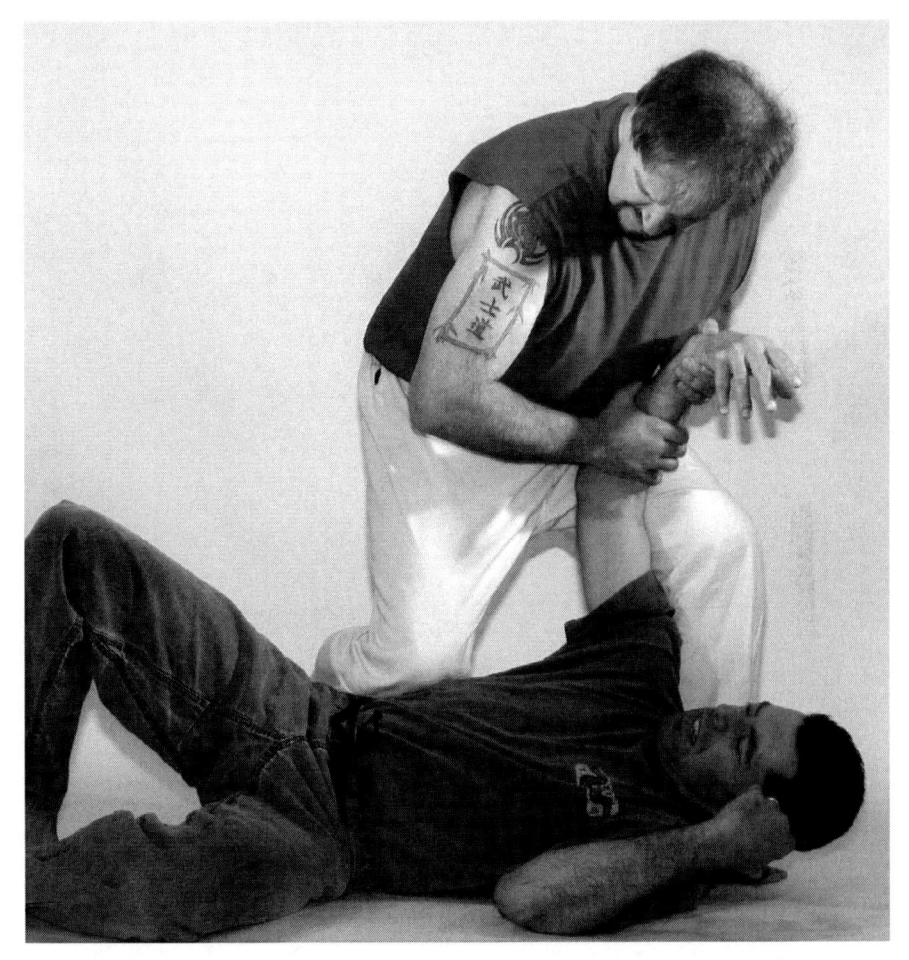

1. You have dumped your attacker on the floor. Hold on to his right arm and drop your knee into his lower ribs to knock the wind out of him.

EXTREME JOINT LOCKING AND BREAKING

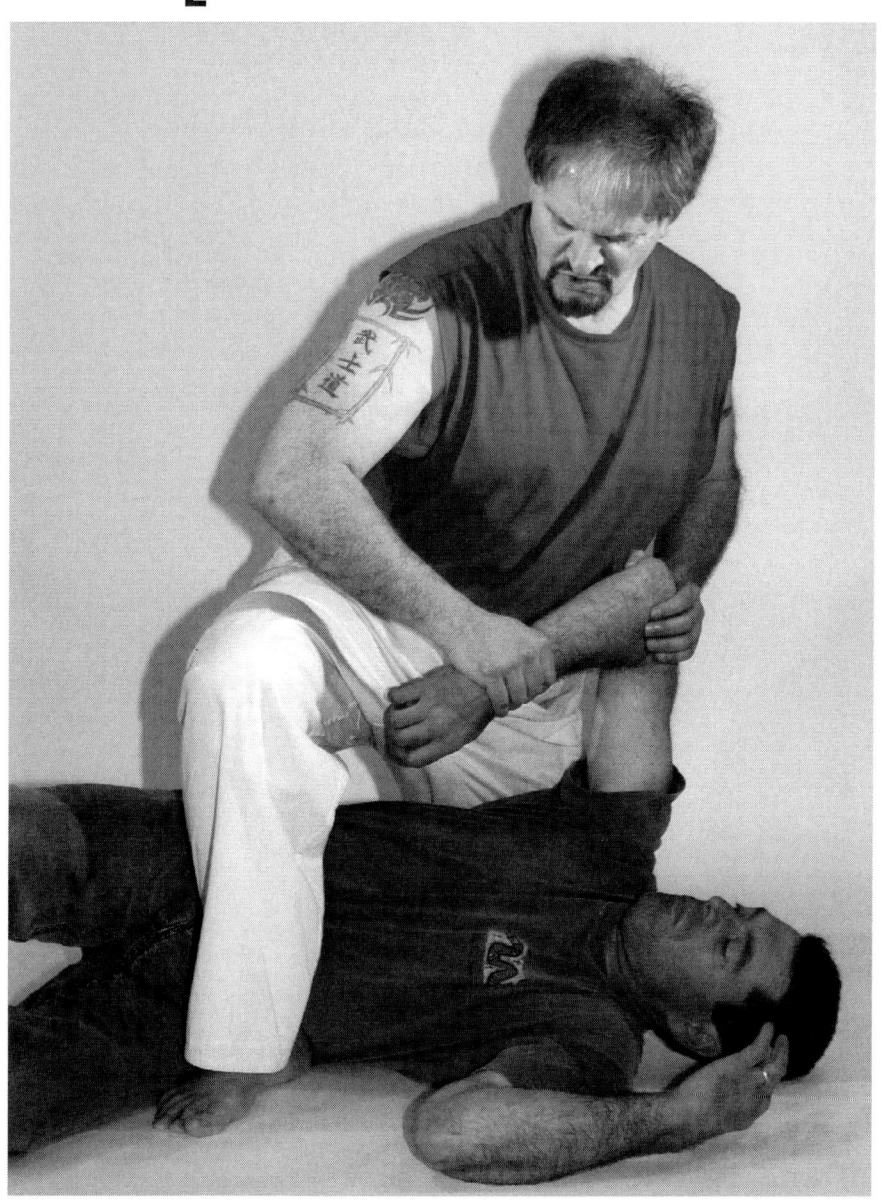

2. In this version, the attacker's arm is bent with his hand near his legs. Step over his chest with your right foot. Press your calf closely to his body to prevent him from scooting away when you begin to crank.

SHOULDER TECHNIQUES

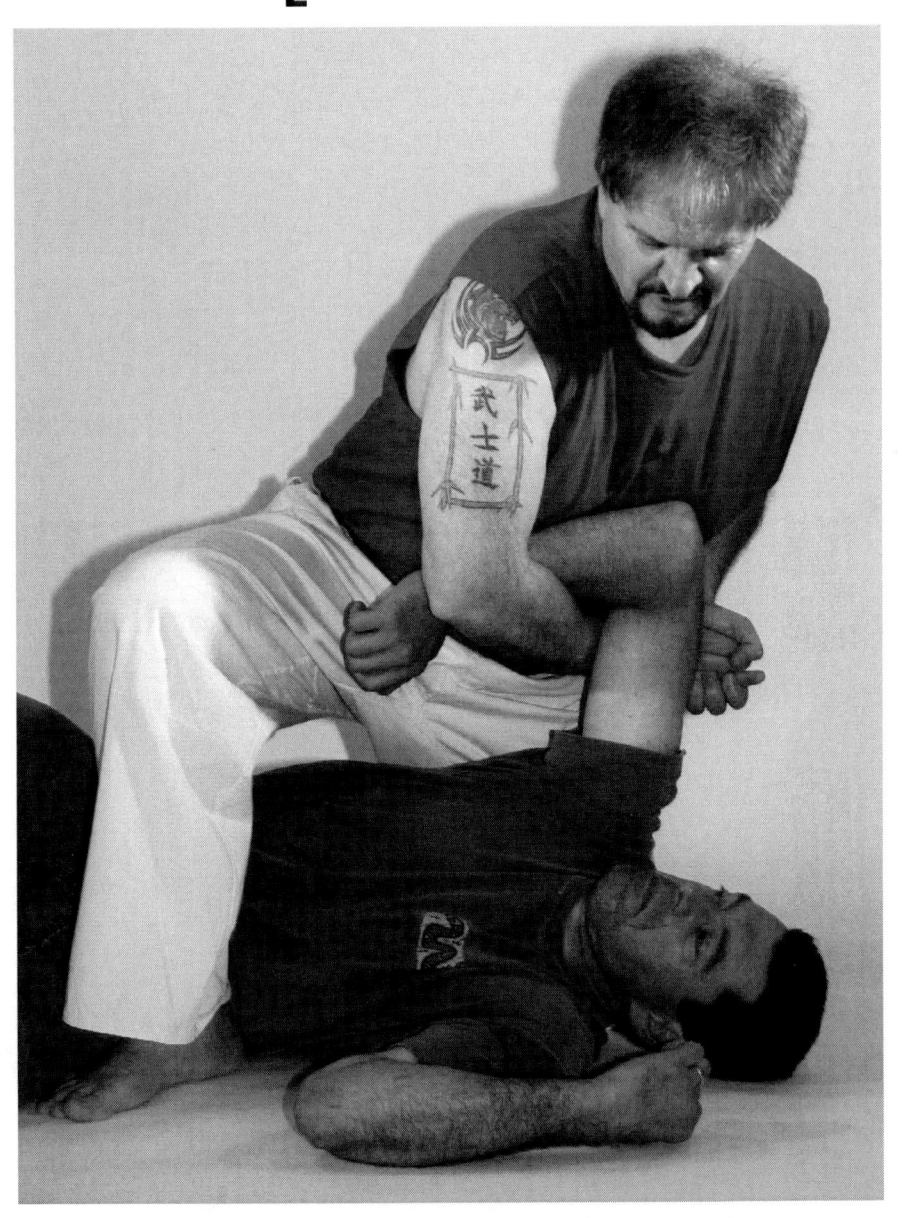

3. Begin to insert your right arm under his upraised upper arm. See if you can place your left knee on his head. The attacker's hand is near his head.

EXTREME JOINT LOCKING AND BREAKING

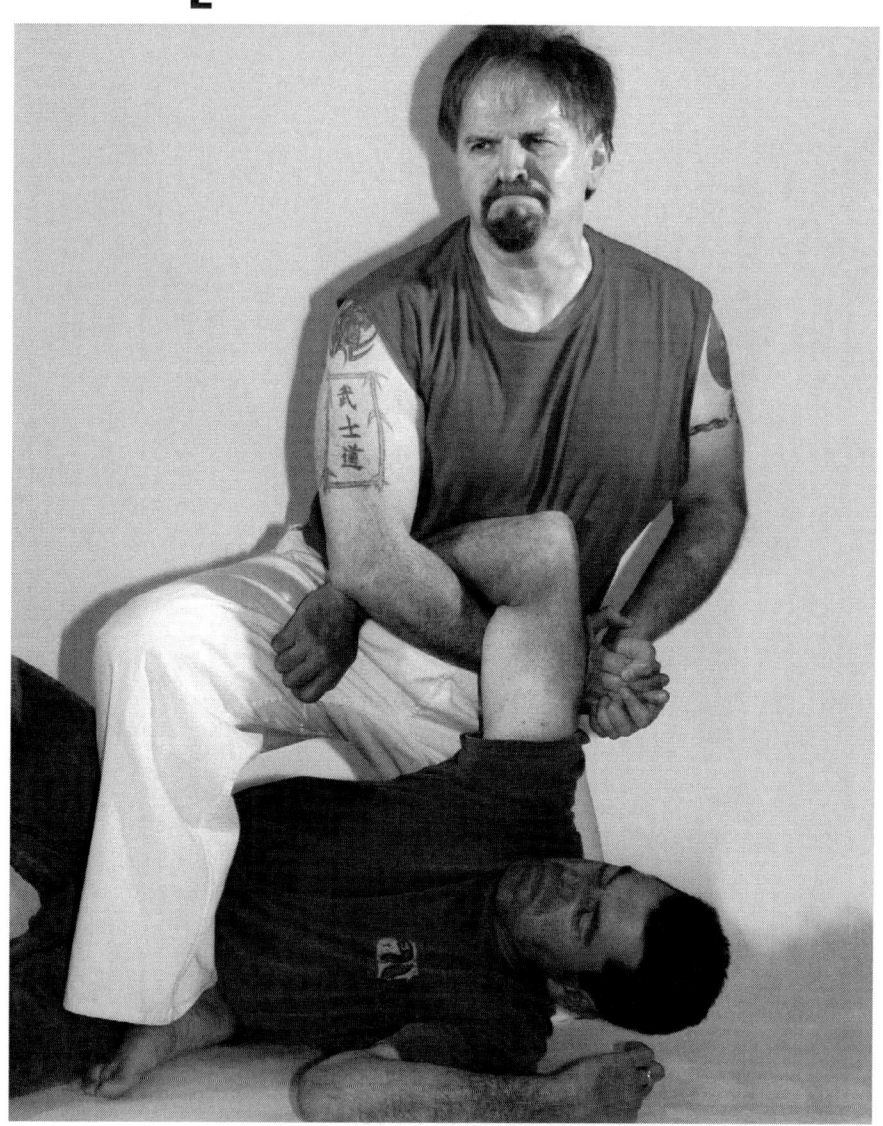

4. Clasp hands and push with your left so that your forearm moves outward like a crowbar to inflict great pain on his shoulder. Straighten your back as much as possible. To move beyond simply inflicting pain to causing internal damage in his shoulder, use your left hand to slam your right hand and arm outward.

SHOULDER TECHNIQUES

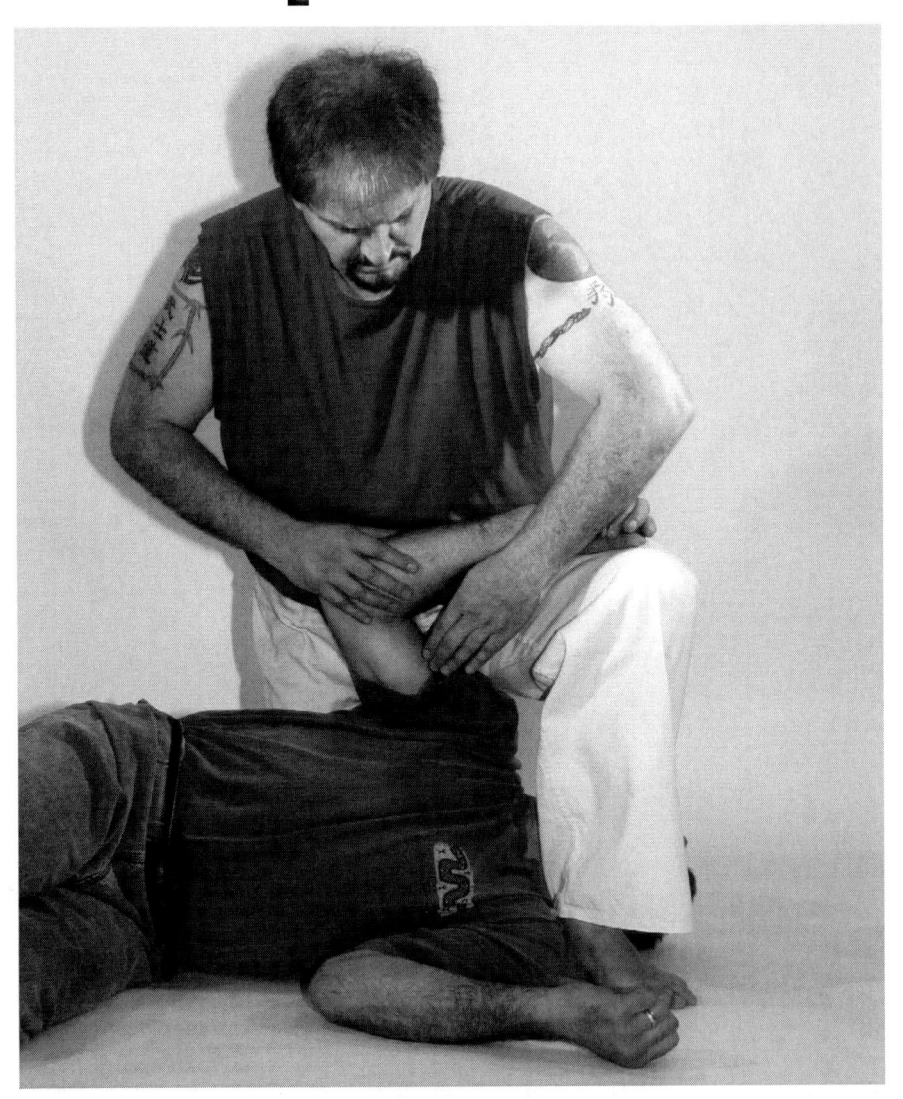

Variation 1

In this variation, the attacker's arm is bent with his hand near his head. It's the same crank except that nearly all the steps are reversed.

1. Begin to insert your left arm as you step over his head with your left foot. Grind your heel down his face if needed.

EXTREME JOINT LOCKING AND BREAKING

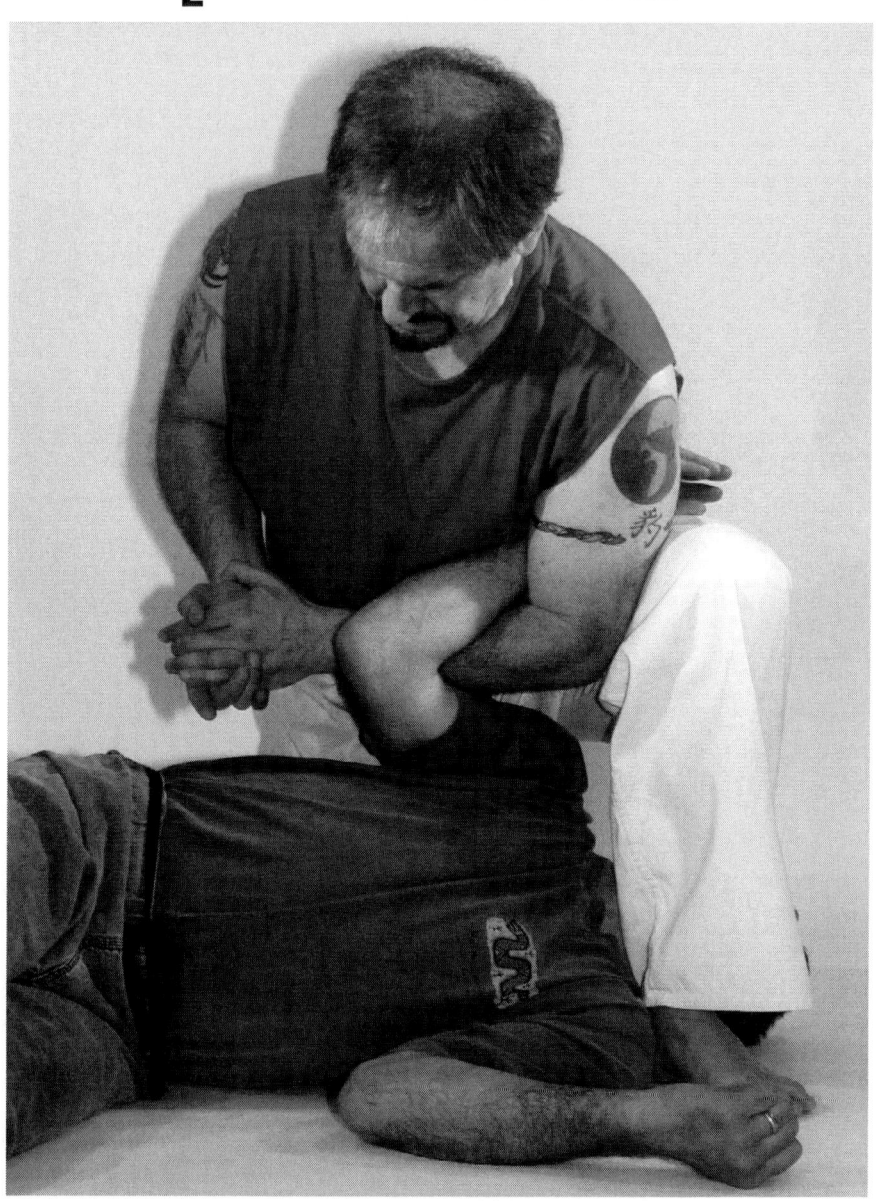

2. Drop your right knee next to his back. Your right knee and left foot are pressed tightly against his body to prevent his escape and create a base for the crank. Clasp hands.

SHOULDER TECHNIQUES

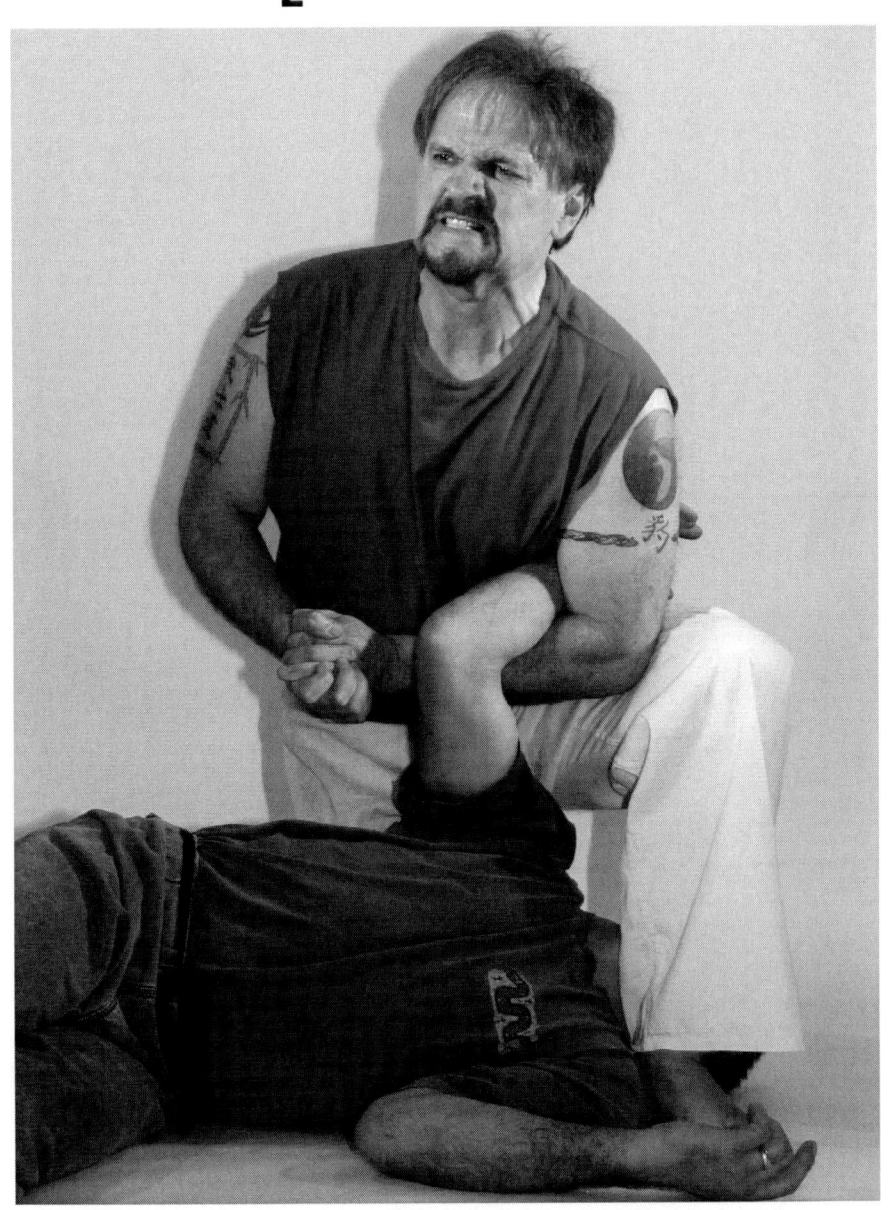

3. Keep your back as straight as possible, as your right hand pushes your left hand outward. If justified, push your left hand outward with great force.

CHAPTER 5
neck techniques

For years I thought that a broken neck meant instant death. Maybe it was from watching too many movies where the hero sneaks up behind a sentry, grabs the guard's head with both hands, and makes a quick, twisting move—complete with crunching sound—and the man crumples to the ground in a dead pile. The truth is that people survive broken necks all the time. It's no picnic, and for a while the injured party might wish that he was dead, but a broken neck is survivable.

Most police departments, if not all, have either stopped using chokes and sleeper holds or have elevated them to the same level of force as batons and firearms because of public pressure after suspects died from these holds. Interestingly, according to the most recent research I could find, no deaths in judo have occurred since it was founded by Professor Jigoro Kano in 1882 in Japan. So what's going on?

I've rendered people unconscious in training using a neck hold, and I've rendered lots of people unconscious on the street with it. There is clearly a difference in venues.

- In jujitsu and other grappling arts, fighters

EXTREME JOINT LOCKING AND BREAKING

THE NECK AS A TARGET

The neck is made up of seven individual small bones known as the cervical spine. They are those bony prominences you feel at the back of your neck. The neck bones are supported by strong ligaments and strong muscles because they have to carry around, on average, a 14-pound head all day. Small openings in the bones are pathways for vital nerves to connect to the muscles and the skin of your neck, the back of your head, and your arms.

Sprained Neck

The ligaments that hold the vertebrae together can be sprained or stretched when the head is snapped or forced backward.

Whiplash

A whiplash occurs when there is a combination of muscle and ligament strain to the neck as the result of a sudden, violent movement.

Concussion

A concussion is any loss of consciousness, even for a second or two, or any sense of disorientation after the head has been struck or slammed hard on the ground.

Broken Neck

A head-on blow with the ground can cause a compression fracture of the neck in which the force to the top of the head compresses and shatters one or more of the cervical vertebrae, the top portion of the spine. This may only chip the vertebrae, or it might compress or sever the spinal cord. The latter can cause quadriplegia or even death, depending on where in the spinal column the injury occurs.

    are taught to "choke" properly under relatively sterile and safe conditions.
- Fighters also know from experience what it feels like to be choked and know when to tap out or yield to it before they become unconscious.

- Teachers and referees recognize when a hold is applied effectively and can stop the action if it begins to look unsafe.

All these factors help make the hold fairly safe in training. Although trained, police officers must fight and subdue violent—sometimes extremely violent—suspects who are under the influence of heroin, PCP, cocaine, or alcohol—and sometimes all four. This makes the task more difficult for various reasons.

- These people often have a high tolerance to pain, which makes it enormously difficult to restrain them.
- Most teachers would agree that a correctly applied hold is a somewhat safe hold. But half the fight for an officer is getting to a place where the technique can be put on correctly. Therein lies the potential for injury.
- When the suspect does lose consciousness, it can be difficult to know if he is out because of drugs or the restraint hold.

The same issues are true for neck-crank techniques. Although they are somewhat safer in training, where experienced fighters know how to apply them and when to tap out when they are on the receiving end, an intoxicated attacker is likely to fight against the technique and inadvertently injure himself. Even in practice you must exercise great caution so that you can immediately release the hold if it doesn't feel right to you or an inexperienced opponent resists in such a way that could cause him injury.

The neck is a highly vulnerable target in the hitting and grappling arts. One doctor said, in effect, that knee injuries might end careers, but neck injuries might end lives or cause paralysis. Clearly, both training partners must use care in practice.

Likewise, it's important to stay in control of yourself on the street since your anger, fear, and adrenaline rush can result in unintended consequences.

EXTREME JOINT LOCKING AND BREAKING

That said, there remains an old saying among martial arts teachers: "I don't want you to fight, but if you have to it's nice to know how." Therefore, I am going to show you five neck techniques that inflict tremendous pain and have the potential to cause serious injury and even death. Use caution in training and be justified to use these on the street.

TECHNIQUE 1: DOUBLE-ARM-HOLD NECK CRANK

There are many responses to a tackle: techniques you can do when the attacker is moving into range; when he is almost touching you; when his arms first encircle your midsection, hips, or legs; and techniques you can do as and after he takes you down. In the following scenario you have pushed your attacker down, and you're on one or both knees. You're able to react to a small window of opportunity.

1. Your attacker shoots in to encircle your hips.

⌊NECK TECHNIQUES⌉

2. To prevent getting bowled over, make a 90-degree turn either left or right and press his head or upper back to drive him to the ground. If needed, spread your legs for stability. Reach over the top of his head and hook your right arm under his left arm.

EXTREME JOINT LOCKING AND BREAKING

3. Insert your left arm under his right. If needed, grab his clothing for added support.

▙ NECK TECHNIQUES ▜

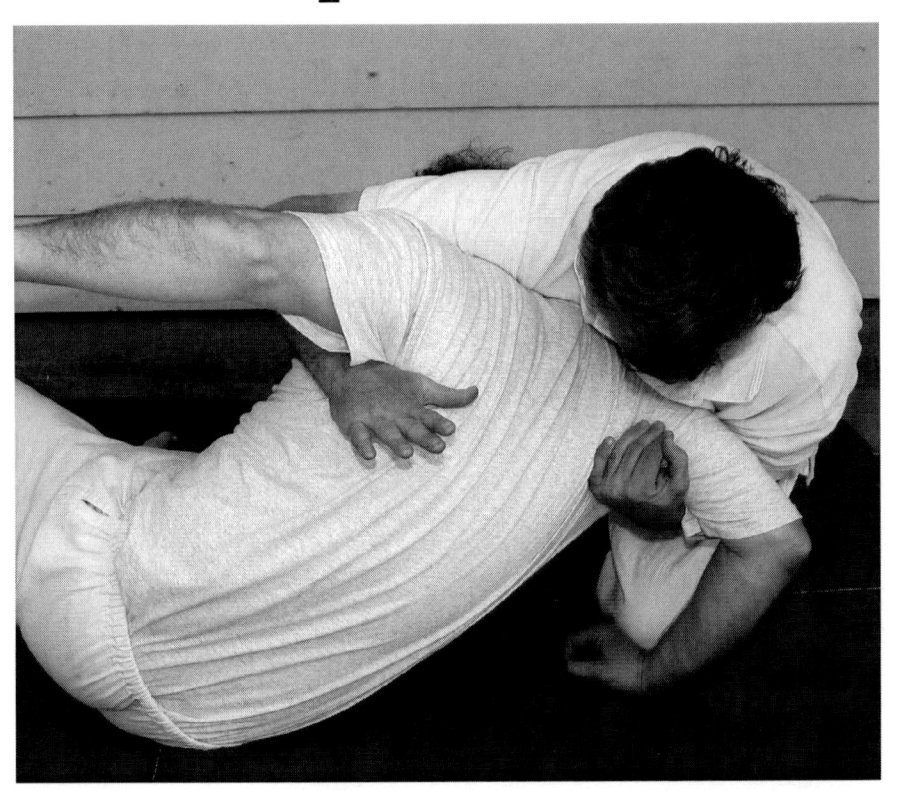

4. Roll him to your left onto his back, moving in a tight circle so he can't resist.

EXTREME JOINT LOCKING AND BREAKING

5. Sit through with your right leg and lean back to apply pressure on his neck.

Go slowly with step 4 in practice because it's difficult to feel how much pressure you're applying to your opponent's neck. Many opponents will tap out in pain before you even sit through with your leg. On the street, however, let the situation dictate the force you use. If you slam yourself back hard, it's likely that you will cause severe injury, maybe even a broken neck. Be justified.

TECHNIQUE 2: HEAD-TUCK NECK CRANK

This is a painful neck lock that gets even more painful when your attacker attempts to get out of it. It can be applied in any number of scenarios.

⌐ NECK TECHNIQUES ¬

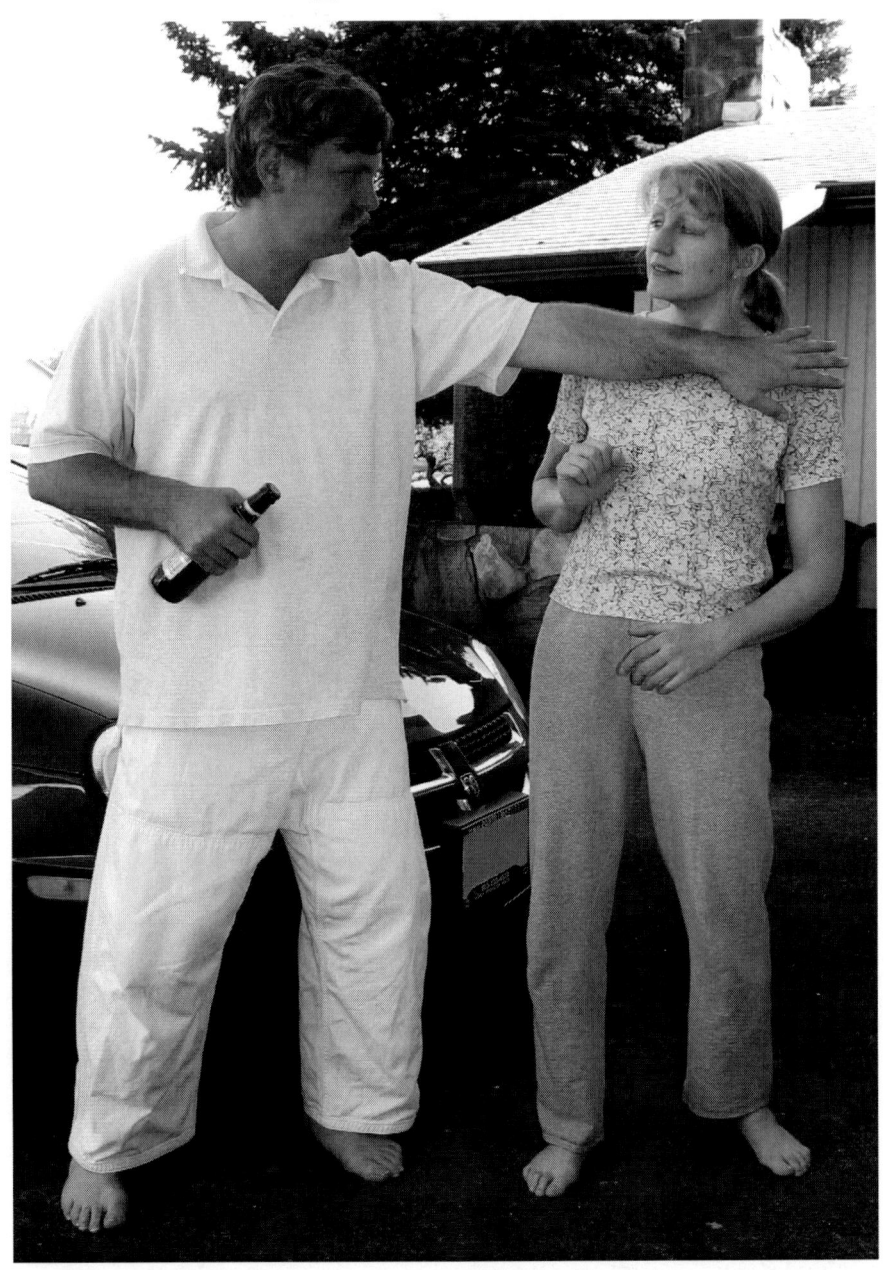

1. The attacker stops you from passing and threatens you with his bottle.

EXTREME JOINT LOCKING AND BREAKING

2. Immediately smack him in the throat.

└NECK TECHNIQUES┘

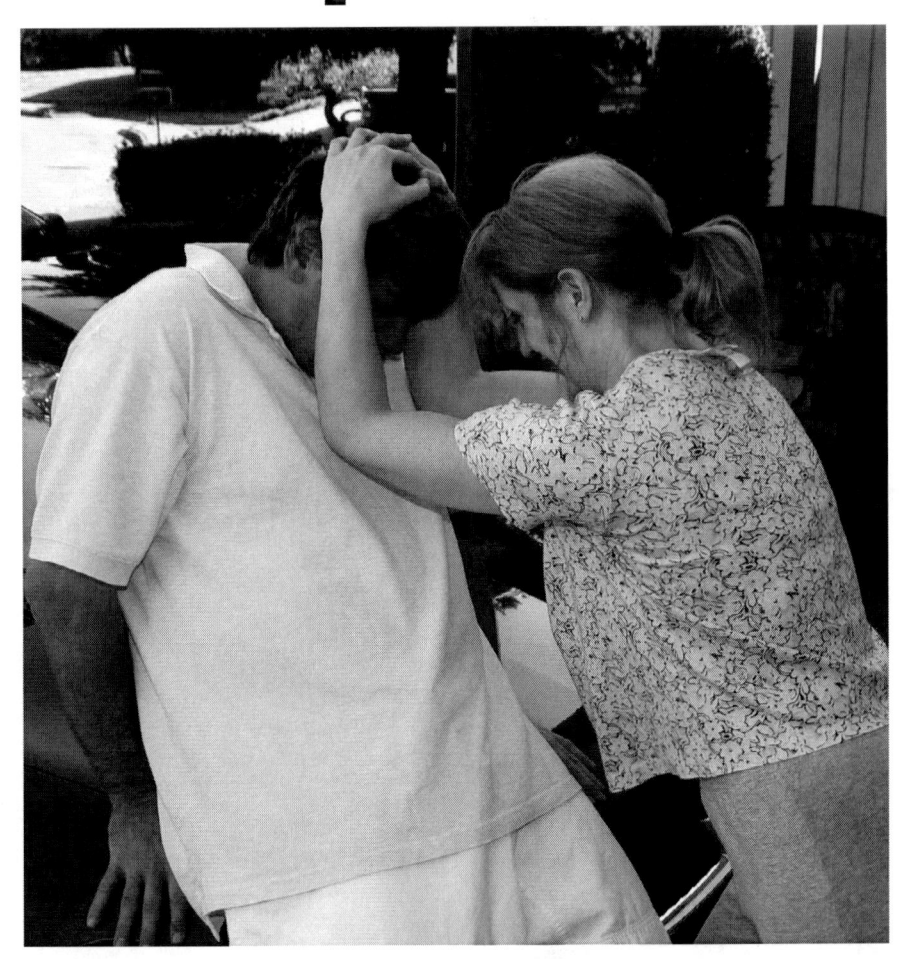

3. Clasp your hands behind his head with your elbows pointing down, and pull his head down toward his chest. Push him back just enough to weaken his position and make it difficult for him to grab you. If he still has the bottle and tries to hit you with it, you have the option of jerking his head down with great force, likely causing internal damage in his neck.

⌐EXTREME JOINT LOCKING AND BREAKING⌐

TECHNIQUE 3: HEAD-PUSHDOWN NECK CRANK

In the last technique you stretched your attacker's neck by pulling downward. With this technique, you maneuver yourself behind him to push down on his head. The potential for injury is high since you can easily put your body weight behind the technique. Use control or be justified if you deliberately push hard. Here is one of many ways to get behind an attacker.

1. The attacker kicks at you You knock aside the kick with enough force to spin him.

⌞NECK TECHNIQUES⌝

2. If he turns all the way around, great. If he doesn't, you need to step the rest of the way around. Grab his shoulders with both hands. It's critical that you keep your elbows pointing down as you jerk him down and back. Step back a little so he has room to fall.

EXTREME JOINT LOCKING AND BREAKING

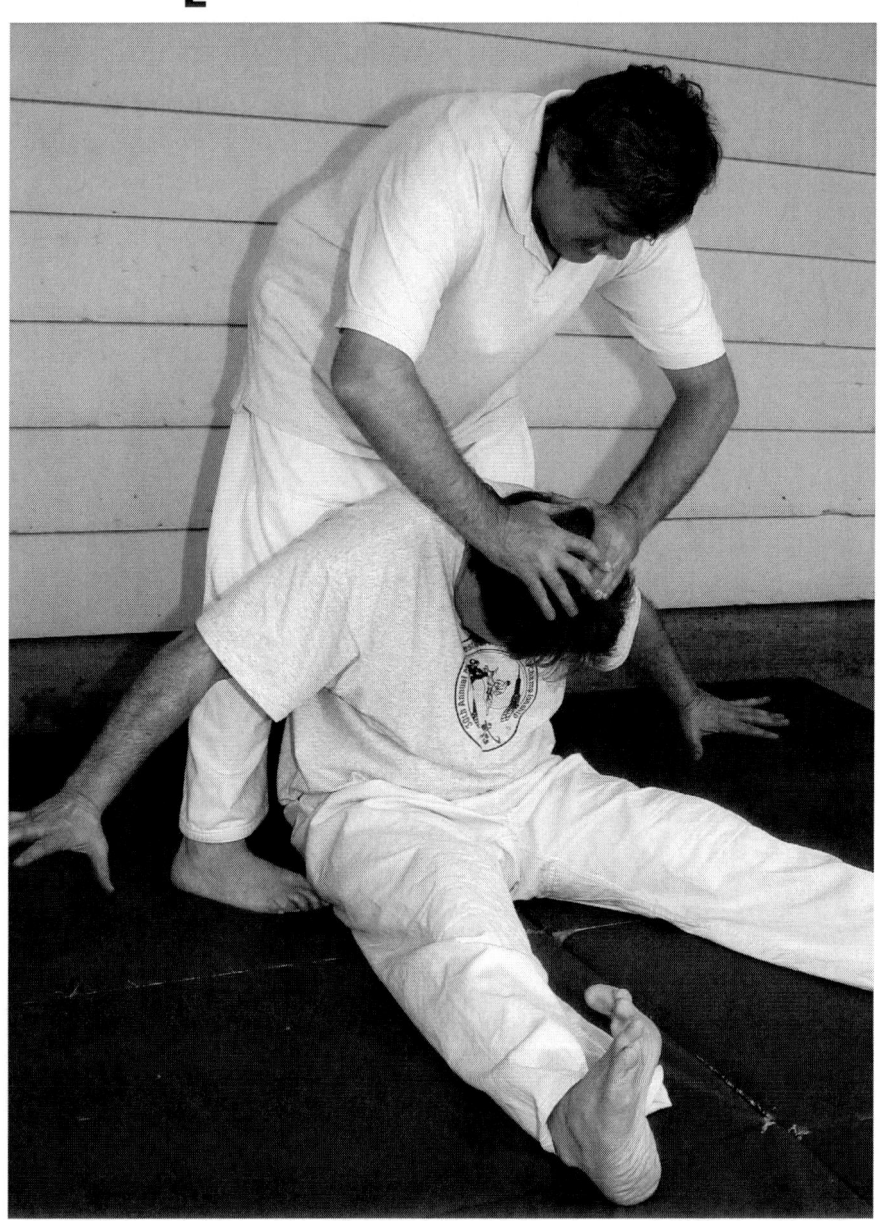

3. Jab your feet, which are turned inward slightly, under his butt, and pin his body with your knees. Press down on the back of his head.

⌊NECK TECHNIQUES⌉

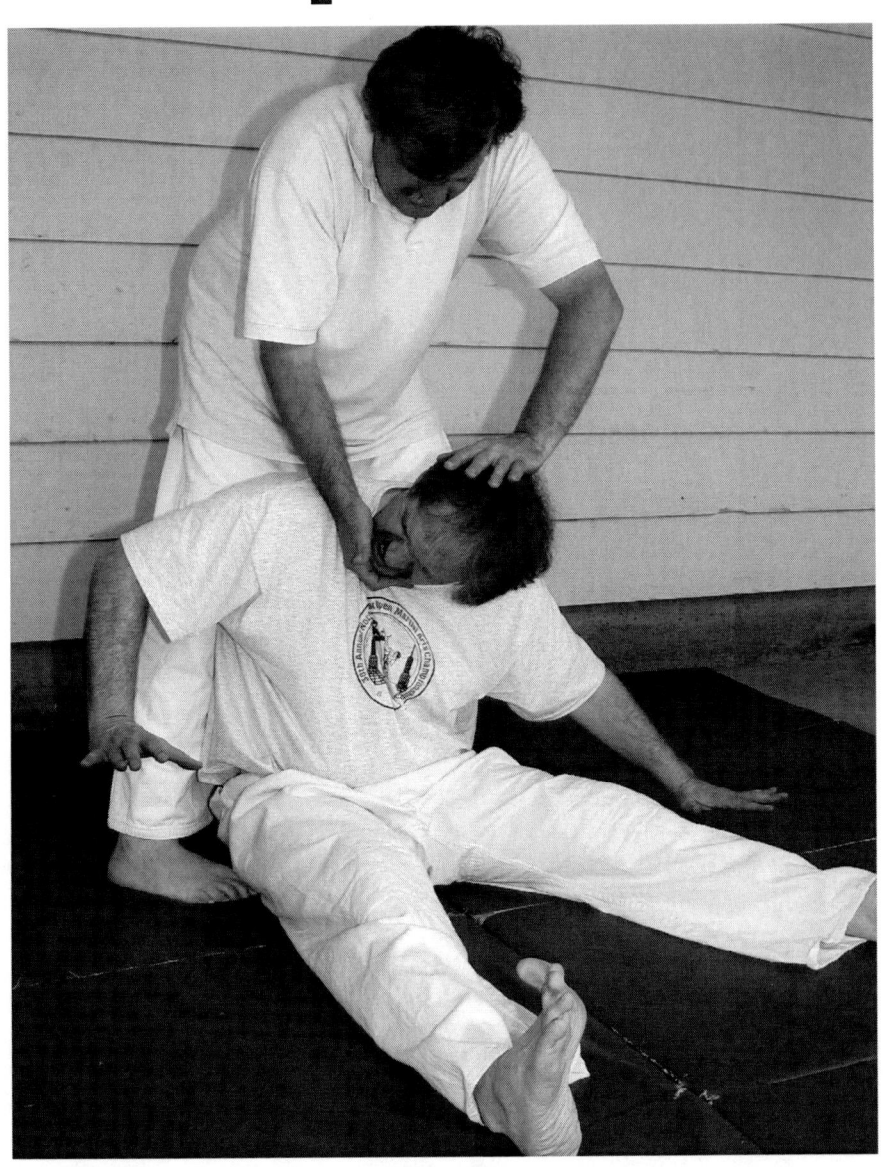

Variation 1
1. Beginning from step 4, push down on your attacker's head with one hand and pull his chin around in a twisting motion with your other hand. This stretches and twists his neck, doubling the grief.

⌐EXTREME JOINT LOCKING AND BREAKING⌐
TECHNIQUE 4: NECK PILE DRIVER

This technique can easily stun your attacker or, with a slight adjustment, potentially devastate his cervical vertebrae. It's most effective when you lunge forward hard and fast after blocking or evading the attacker's punch or kick. You can slam your forearm into his upper chest or, if the situation justifies greater force, into the front of his neck. The idea is to upset his balance so that he leans backward.

1. Your attacker throws a big, arcing haymaker, which you block.

⌐NECK TECHNIQUES⌐

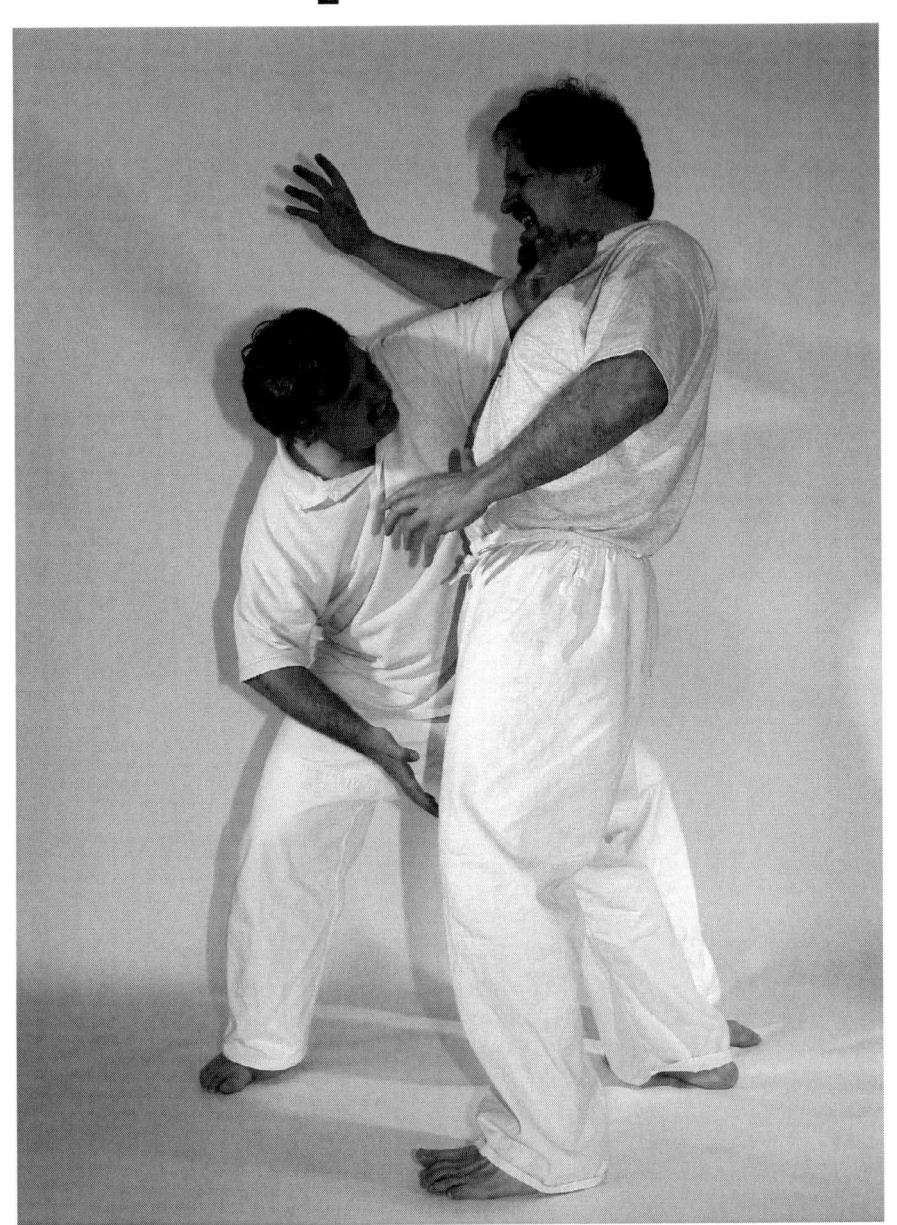

2. Shift your weight forward, thrust your blocking forearm into his chest or neck, and begin to reach between his legs.

EXTREME JOINT LOCKING AND BREAKING

3. Continue pushing upward as you reach deeper. If possible, grab his belt where it encircles his lower back. Press your face against his stomach to keep your face from getting punched.

⌐NECK TECHNIQUES¬

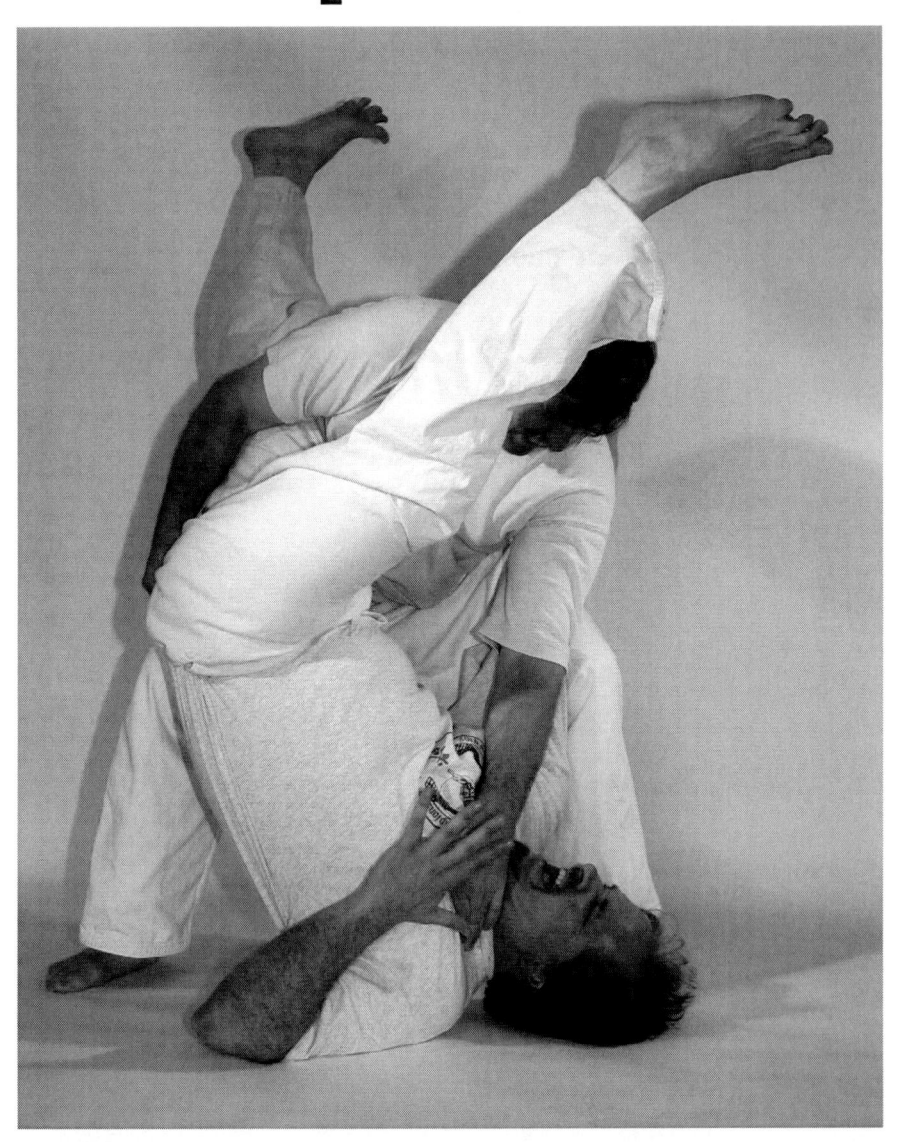

4. Lift his lower body with your right hand as you push with your left. If he lands on his shoulders and neck, he will probably be stunned. If the situation warrants extreme force, push harder on his neck and lift higher with your right hand to force him to land on his head, which will likely cause severe trauma to his neck.

EXTREME JOINT LOCKING AND BREAKING

TECHNIQUE 5: ELBOW LOCK AND NECK TWIST

This is arguably more painful and dangerous to the neck than it is to his elbow, but you need his arm to limit his resistance and reinforce the head push.

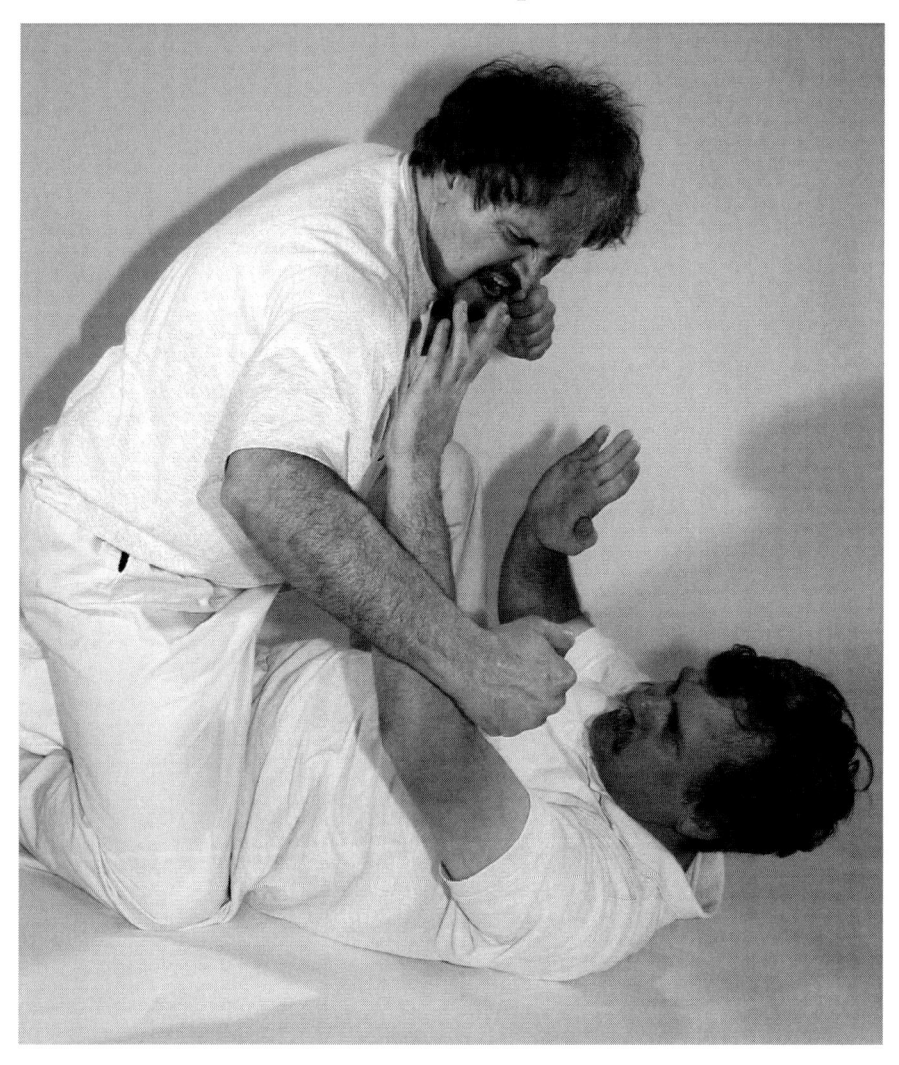

1. You're on your back with your attacker lying on top of or next to you. He punches at you with his right hand. Block it.

⌊NECK TECHNIQUES⌉

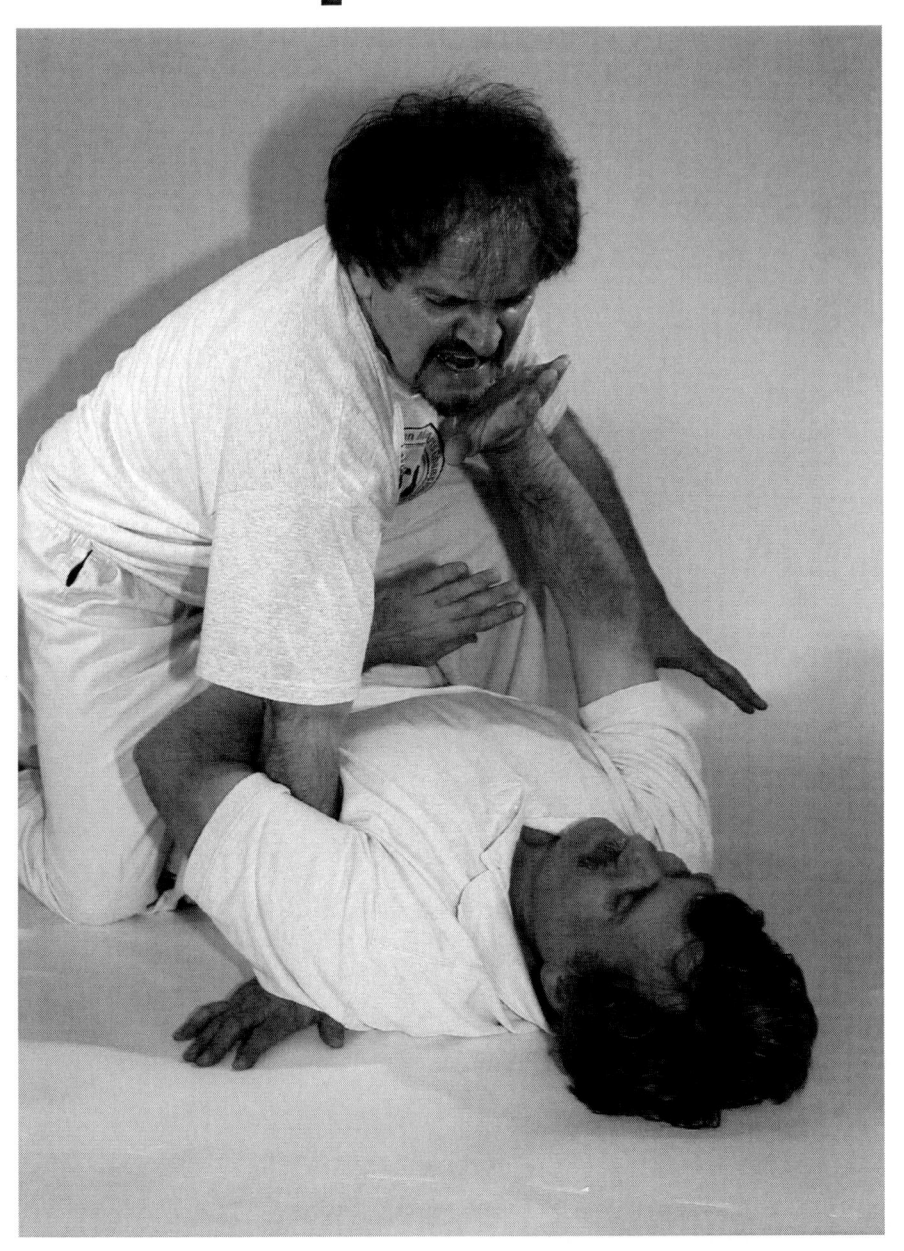

2. Pull his right arm down so that his hand is braced on the floor. Wrap your left arm around his elbow.

EXTREME JOINT LOCKING AND BREAKING

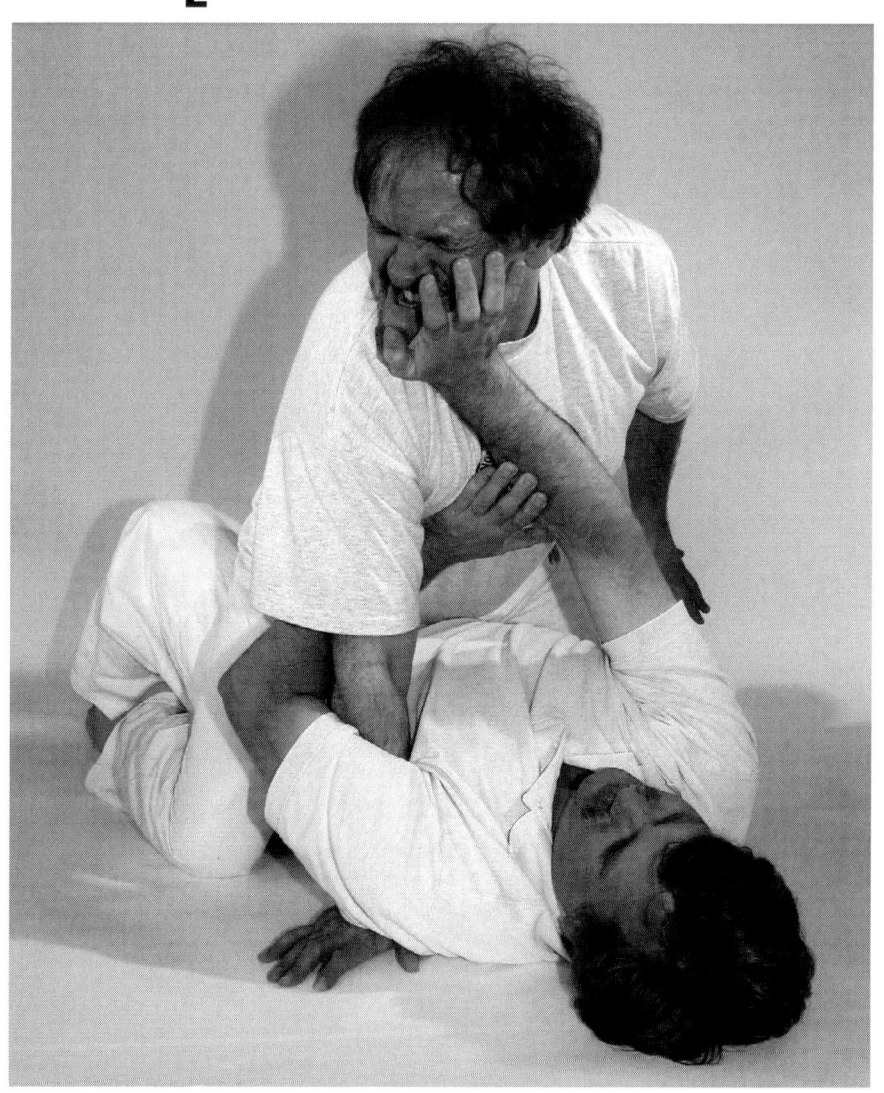

3. Slam your right palm against his face to turn his head and then secure your right forearm with your left hand. Your forearm hyperextends his elbow joint and keeps him from lifting his arm, while your left hand pushes your right arm to add strength to the head push.

If the situation warrants it, twist his head hard and far.

CHAPTER 6
back techniques

A back injury is an instant age accelerator. One moment life is good and all is sunny, and the next moment you're bent over painfully, struggling to breathe and move. It hurts to stand up, sit down, move left or right, and stand still. Your whole world is about your pain and the inability to do even the smallest task. Here are some ways to bring that world of hurt to your attacker.

TECHNIQUE 1: BACK BEND

Pro wrestlers enjoy this technique because it looks dramatic and the recipient can ham it up as he writhes, screeches, and slaps the canvas. Actually, he might not be faking it that much because, unless the recipient is extraordinarily flexible, even a little bend hurts. A lot of bend can cause serious injury.

THE BACK AS A TARGET

Your back is complex. It consists of the vertebrae, which are solid bones with attachments for muscle tendons; discs, which are jelly-filled sacs between the vertebrae that allow movement and absorb shock; muscles and the tendons that connect them to the vertebrae; and the spinal cord, which connects the brain to the rest of the body and runs down through the vertebrae between the discs and the muscles.

Back pain might be dull, sharp, constant, intermittent, burning, tingling, or debilitating. It can send hot, shooting pain into your hips, buttocks, or legs. It might be caused by joint sprain, muscle strain, or a ruptured disk stemming from a specific incident, such as a fall, twist, torque, or flex.

Muscle Spasm

Unlike the muscles in your legs, which are long, your back is composed of short extensor muscles that bridge from vertebra to vertebra. These are shorter and therefore more prone to spasm, a sometimes painful tightening of the muscles.

Coccyx Injury

In rare cases, back pain can originate in the coccyx, the small section of fused bones at the base of the spine. This pain usually results from a direct fall onto the buttocks.

Disc Injury

Each disc has a gel-like center called the nucleus. A disc can rupture from a fall or heavy strain, which causes the nucleus to break through its wall and place pressure on the nerves that branch off from the spinal cord.

Fracture

A hard fall or severe jolt to the spine can crack or fracture vertebrae. Cracked vertebrae can put the delicate spinal cord at risk.

⌐BACK TECHNIQUES⌐

1. Shoot in low and yank your attacker's knees forward as you ram your head into his midsection.

EXTREME JOINT LOCKING AND BREAKING

2. As he lands, catch his legs and trap them under your armpits. The calf muscles are quite tender, and just the sharp edges of your forearms pressing into them are enough to make your attacker yelp. But the worst is yet to come.

BACK TECHNIQUES

3. Turn him to the right and step over him as he rolls onto his stomach. Bend your knees and lean backward (do this slowly with your training partner) and listen to your attacker curse. Lean back forcefully to produce internal damage in his lower back.

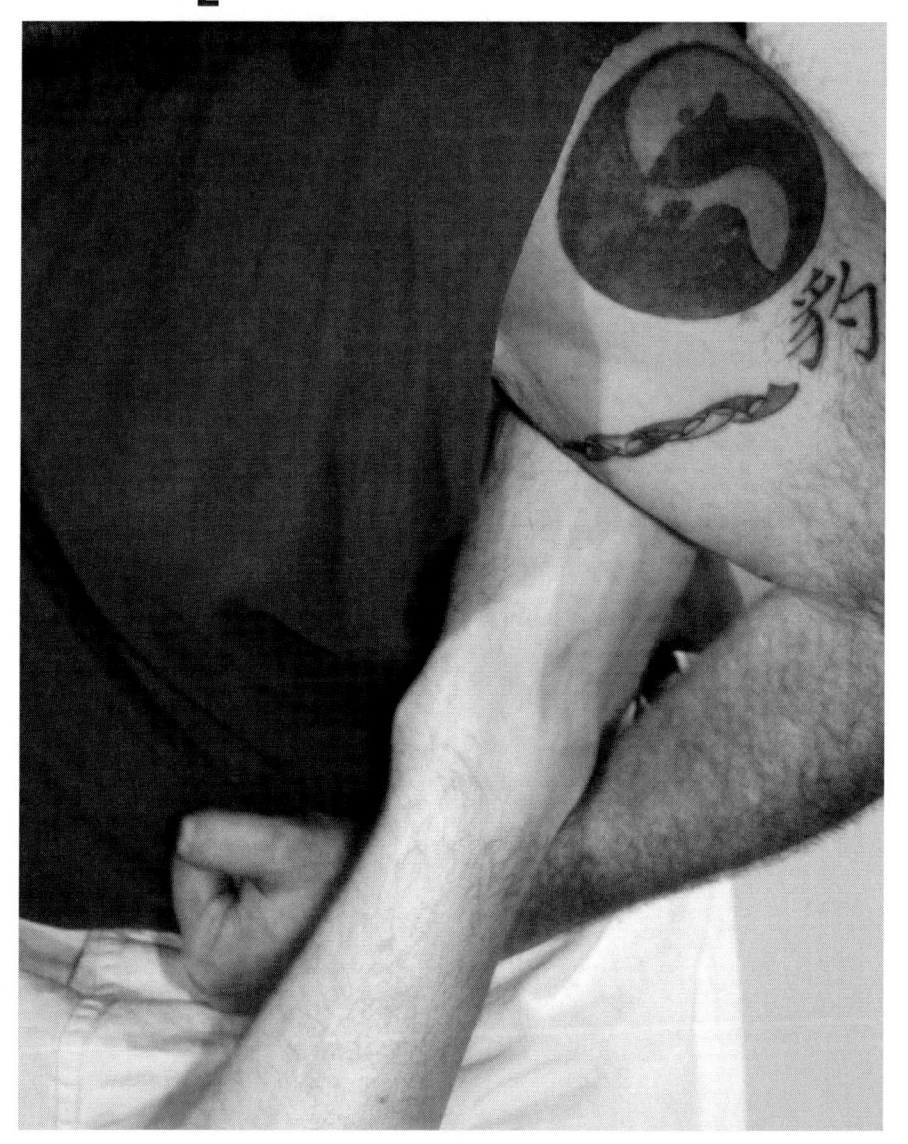

Variation 1
After you have taken the attacker down, do the following:

1. Secure his right foot tightly under your armpit; make sure his foot is bent downward. Use the edge of your wrist to apply intense pressure against his Achilles tendon.

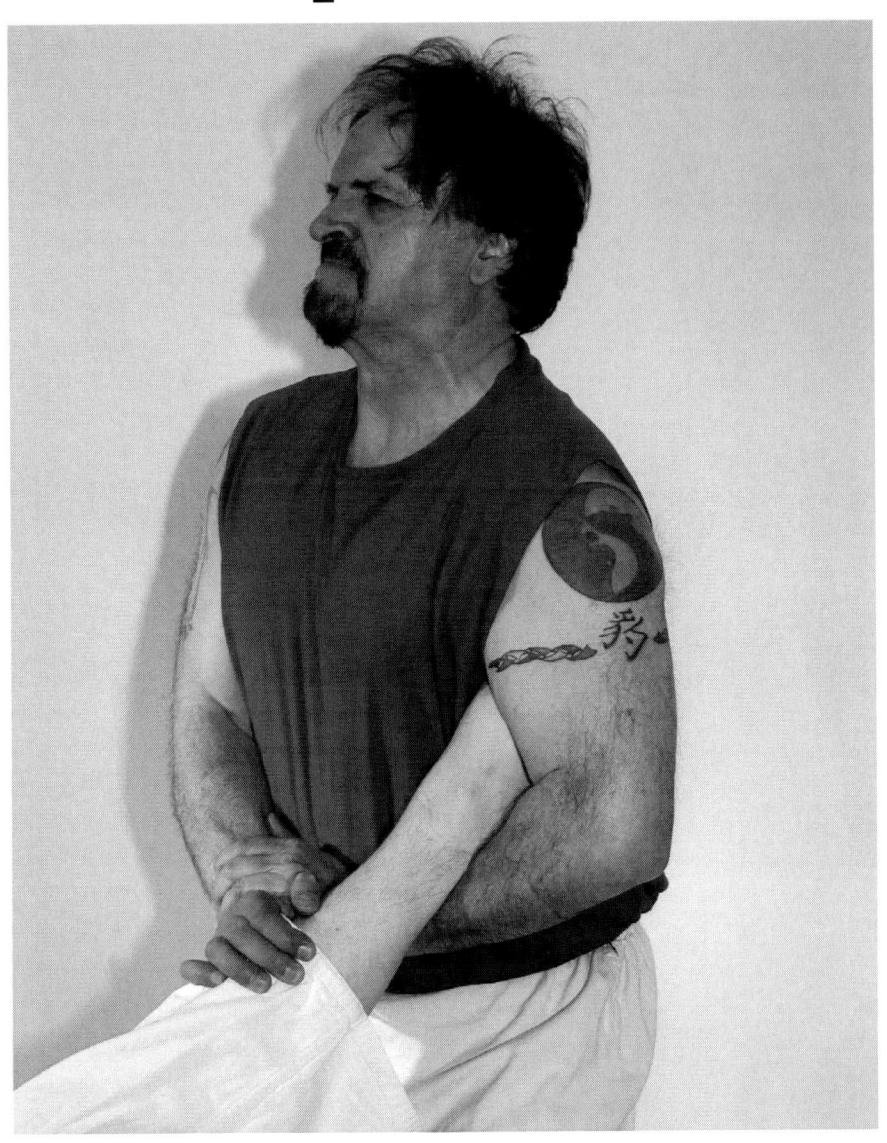

BACK TECHNIQUES

2. Grab your right wrist with your left hand and begin to arch your back. This places painful pressure against his Achilles tendon and ankle.

EXTREME JOINT LOCKING AND BREAKING

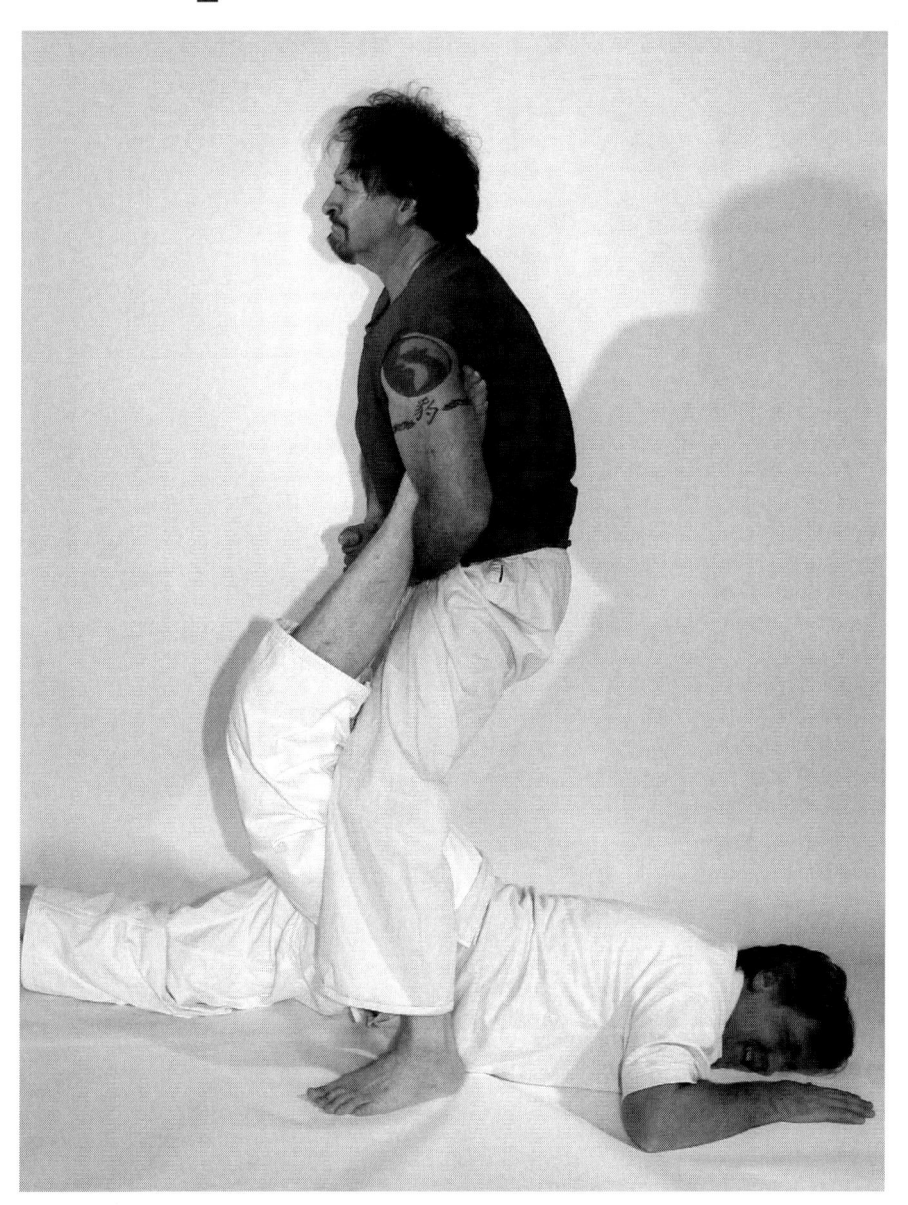

3. Flip him to your right onto his chest. Thrust your hips forward as you lift him by his Achilles tendon. He will feel this in his lower back, right hip, Achilles tendon, and foot.

BACK TECHNIQUES

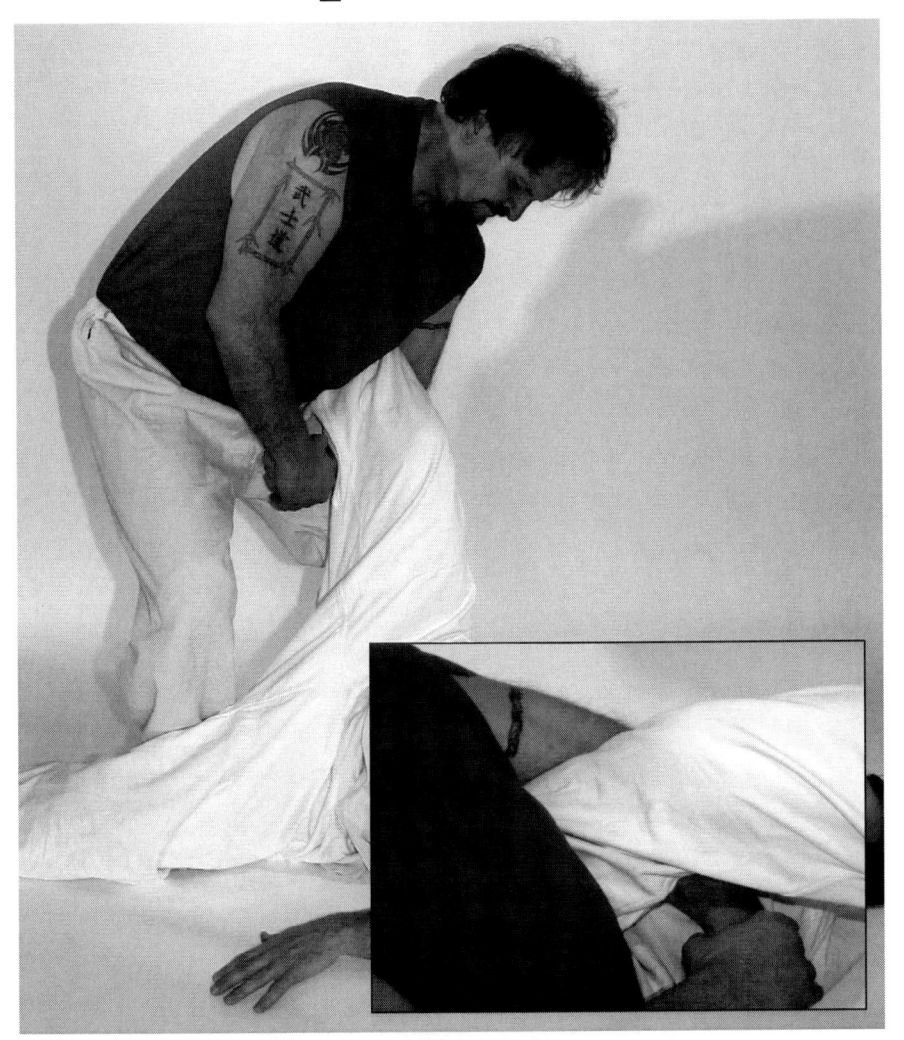

Variation 2

Some people like this variation of the one-leg hold because they feel they have a better grip on the leg than in variation 1. After you have taken your attacker down, do the following:

1. Wrap your arm under the attacker's right knee and grab your left forearm. Lift him by arching your back.

EXTREME JOINT LOCKING AND BREAKING

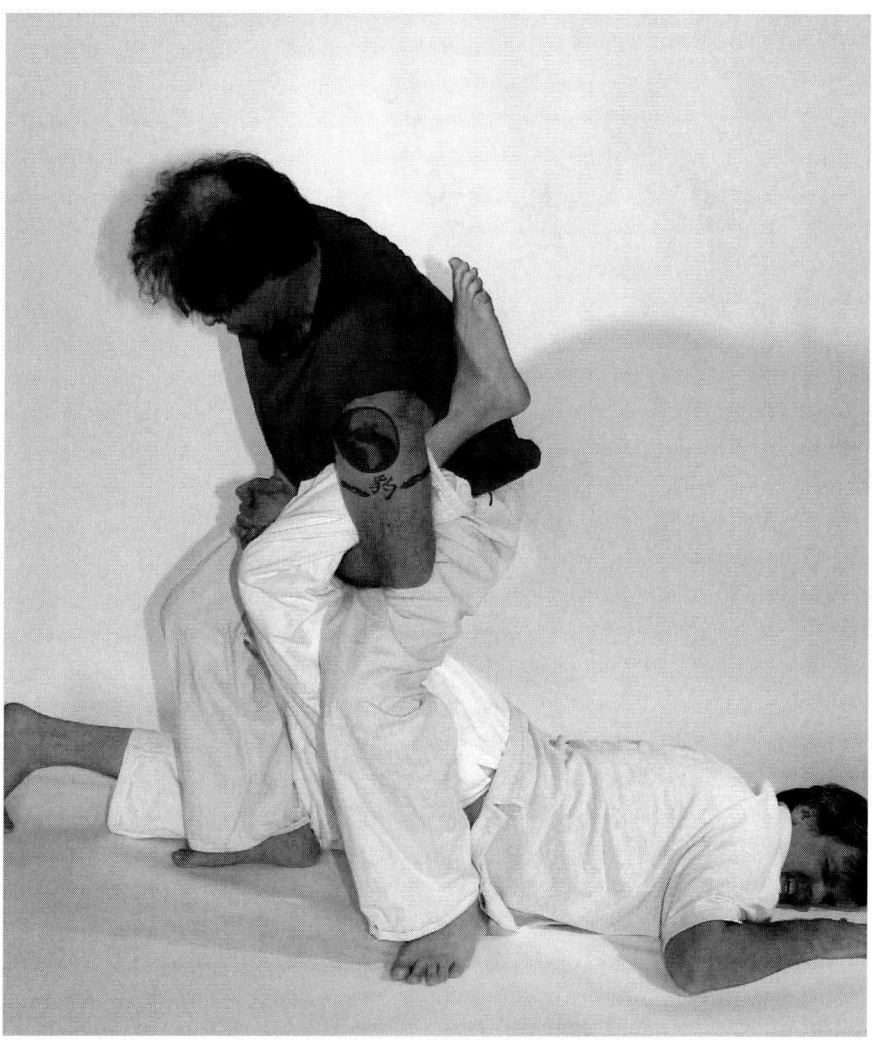

2. Roll him to the right by cranking his knee to the right. Arch your back to put pressure on his lower back.

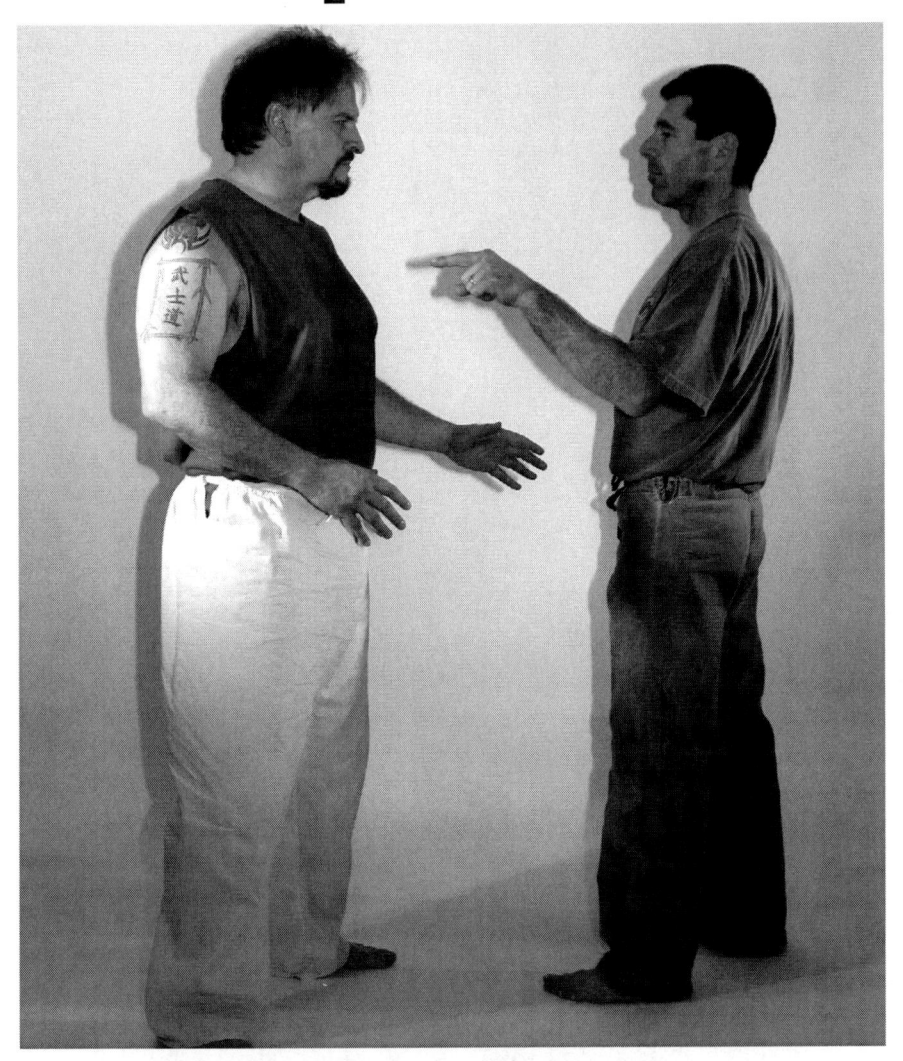

⌐BACK TECHNIQUES⌐

TECHNIQUE 2: BACK PRESS, CHIN LIFT

This is a fast and devastating technique that hits the attacker's back and neck. Don't do this one fast in practice, or you will twist your partner's head around like Linda Blair spun hers in *The Exorcist*.

1. The attacker is barking in your face like a junkyard dog.

EXTREME JOINT LOCKING AND BREAKING

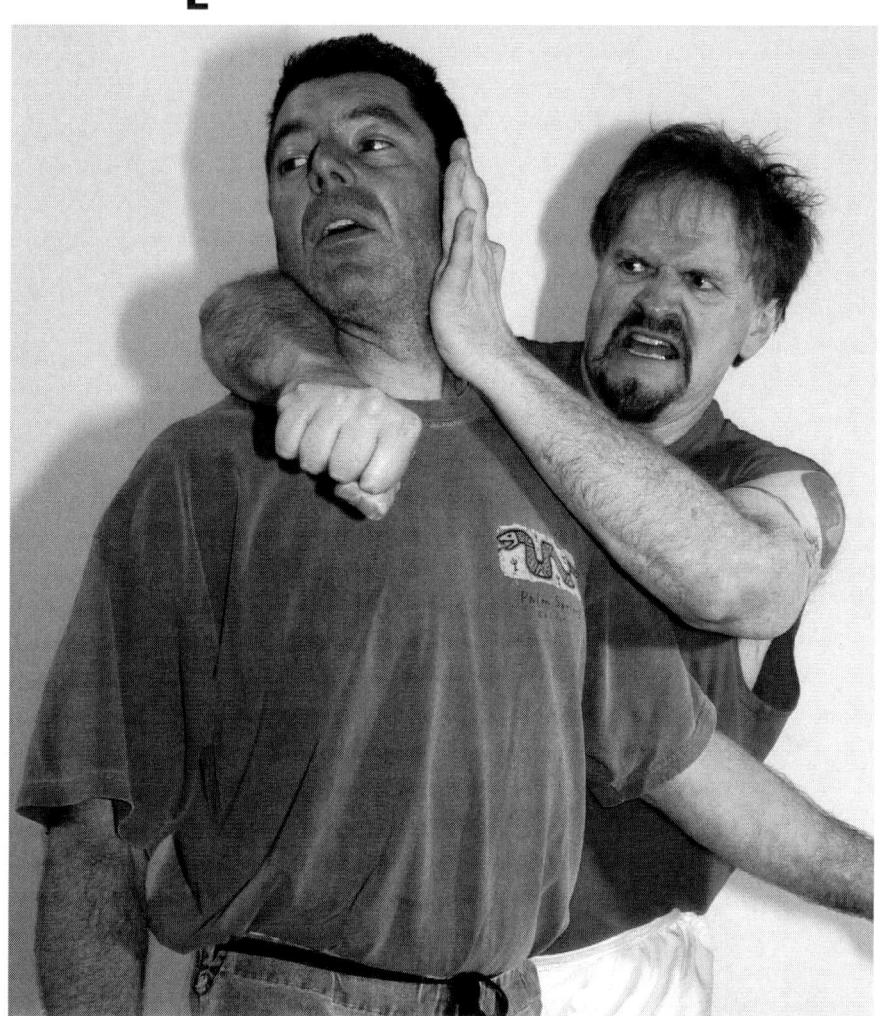

2. He threatens and then turns to his right to joke with a buddy or grab a weapon. (Camera angle changed for better viewing.) Slap your left palm against the left side of his face to prevent his head from moving and ensure that it absorbs all the impact of your forearm hook into the right side of his neck. Depending on your position, you might be able to hit your left and right simultaneously. If not, your forearm hook should follow no more than a half second after your slap.

┗BACK TECHNIQUES┛

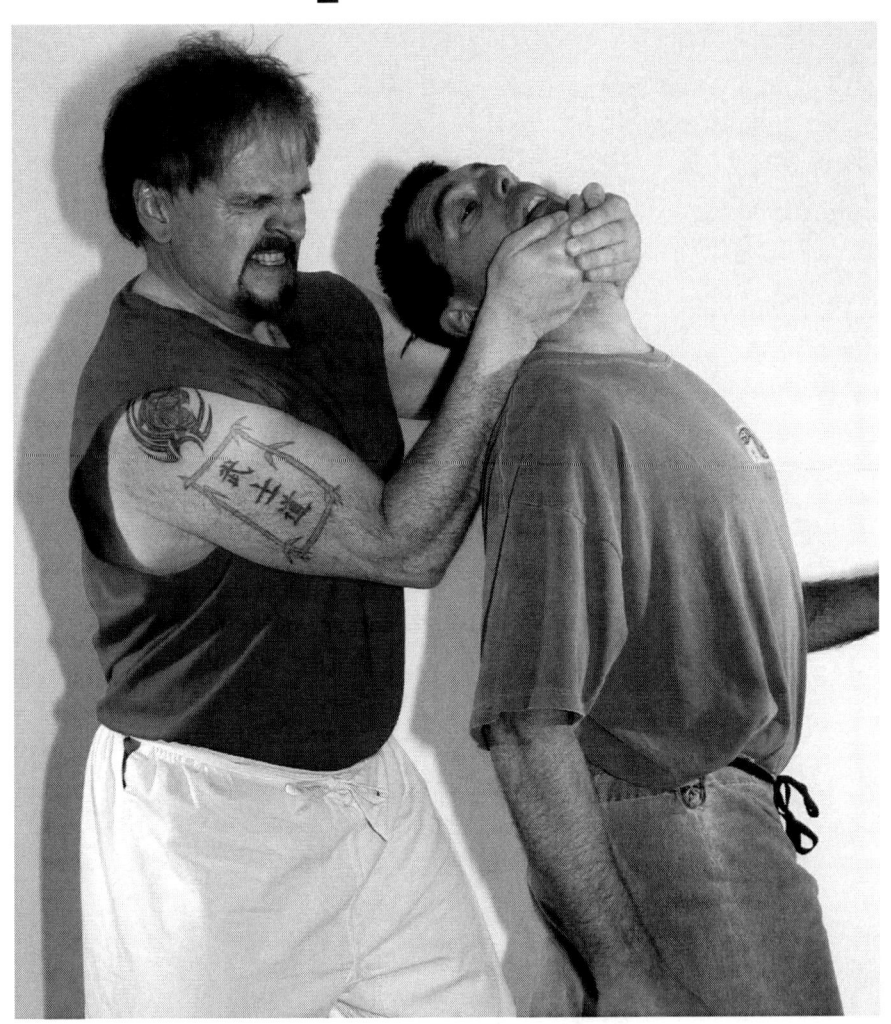

3. (Camera angle changed for better viewing.) Grab under his chin with both hands, push with your left, and pull with your right to spin him around. Your right elbow is pressed against his back and pointing downward for good leverage and to prevent him from spinning out.

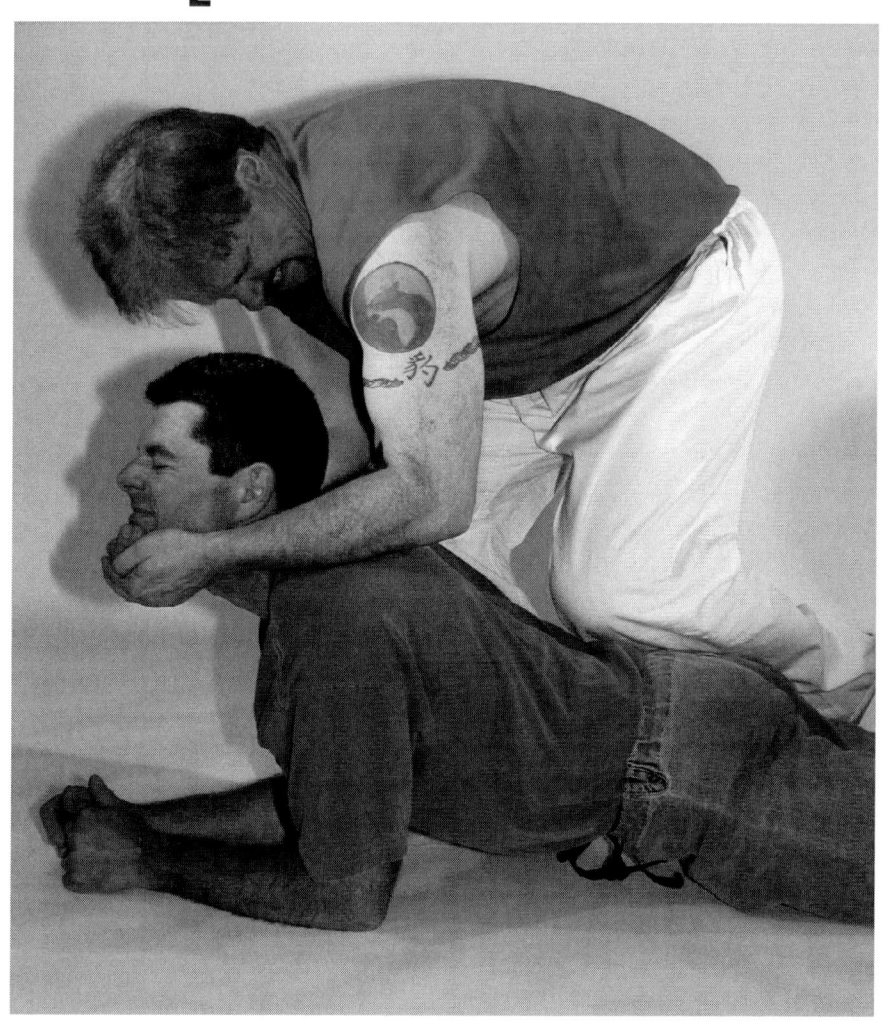

4. Turn your body to the right and spiral him to the floor. If he lands on his side, just keep turning his head and add a knee nudge to encourage him over onto his belly. If he lands on his belly, he saved you a step. To add more pain to his neck, possibly knock the wind out of him, and get him onto his belly even faster, ram your knee into his lower back and ride him down as he drops to the ground.

⌐BACK TECHNIQUES⌐

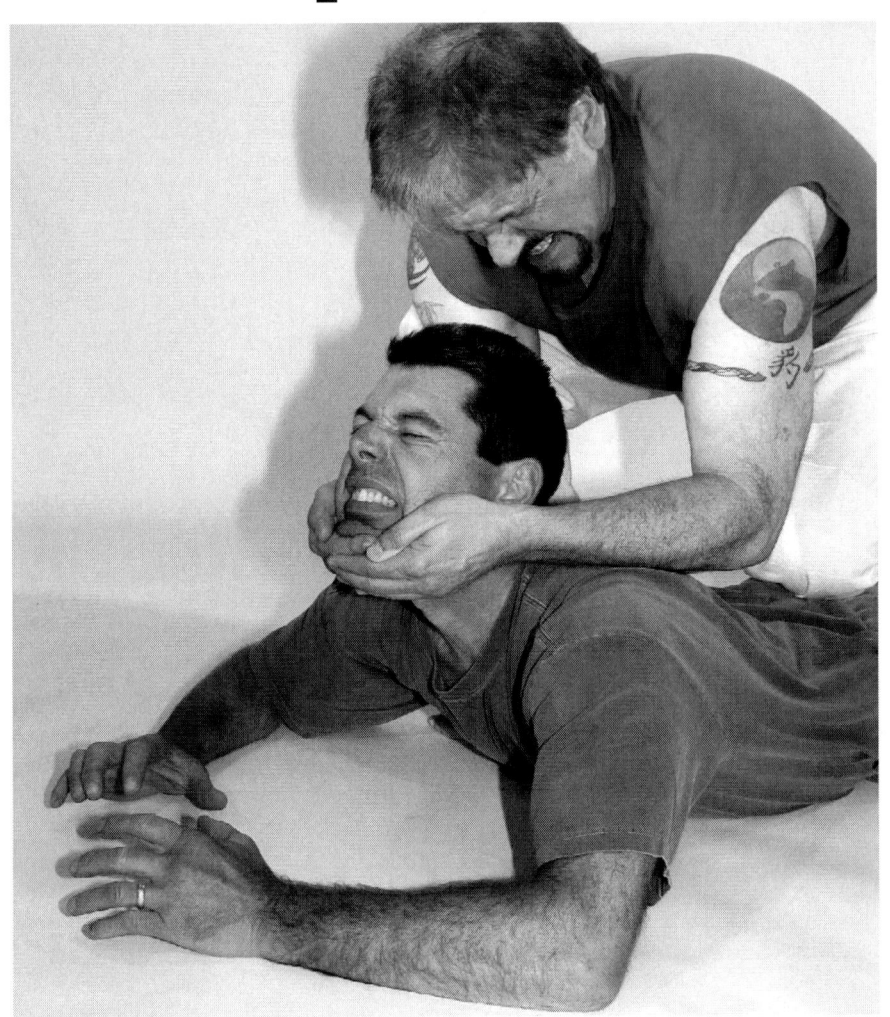

5. With your knee on his lower spine near his butt, press your elbows into his back and pull his chin up and back. If your elbows lose contact, the technique becomes a muscle move, which isn't good if he is stronger than you.

CHAPTER 7
knee techniques

On the "pain-o-meter" a broken knee comes in second only to having a finger rammed into your eye all the way to the last knuckle and then swirled about like a cocktail stir. I can attest to that. My kneecap was once torn away from where it's supposed to be and ended up near the back of my leg, destroying everything in its path.

Typically, when a knee blows there is a feeling of a void, as if the leg were suddenly not there. Then a wave of screaming pain and nausea washes over you, and up comes the meal you had an hour earlier. One moment you're enjoying your training, and the next moment your entire world morphs into one in which the only thing that exists is white-hot, debilitating pain. That is what makes the knee a good target in a self-defense situation.

Even untrained people have strong legs because these muscles are the largest in the body. So when you get a window of opportunity to target them, move quickly before your attacker can resist. If your attacker does resist, hit him. Remember, hitting is good.

EXTREME JOINT LOCKING AND BREAKING

THE KNEE AS A TARGET

The knee joint consists of the thighbone (femur), shinbone (tibia), and kneecap (patella). The thighbone connects the hip to the knee, the shinbone connects the knee to the ankle, and the kneecap protects the front of the knee. The fibula is a shorter, thinner bone running parallel to the shinbone on its outside. The joint acts like a hinge but with a little rotation. The muscles on the front of your thigh—specifically, the quadriceps tendon—insert into the top of the kneecap. The patellar tendon at the bottom attaches to the shinbone.

Strain
A knee strain occurs when you've partially or completely torn a muscle or tendon.

Sprain
You've sprained your knee when you have stretched or torn one of its ligaments.

Fracture
A fracture occurs when your thighbone, kneecap, or shinbone cracks, breaks, or shatters.

TECHNIQUE 1: FIGURE FOUR WITH SHOULDER PULL

Go easy in training with this technique because it doesn't take much pressure to send your opponent into a mat-slapping frenzy. It's easy to produce pain and dislocation with this one because to you it doesn't feel like you're doing anything.

KNEE TECHNIQUES

1. Catch your attacker's right kick and pull on the underside of his knee to turn him around.

EXTREME JOINT LOCKING AND BREAKING

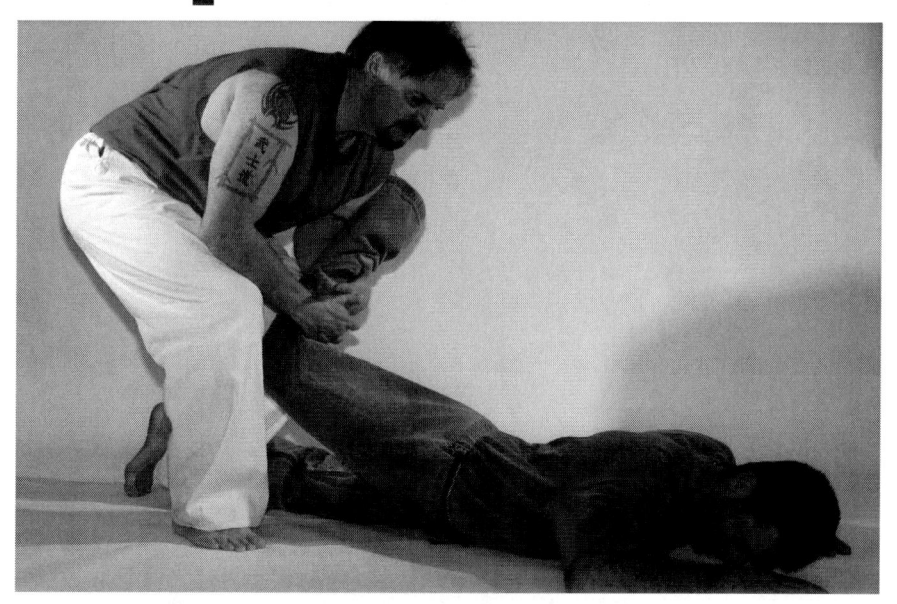

2. Drive him to the ground on his stomach.

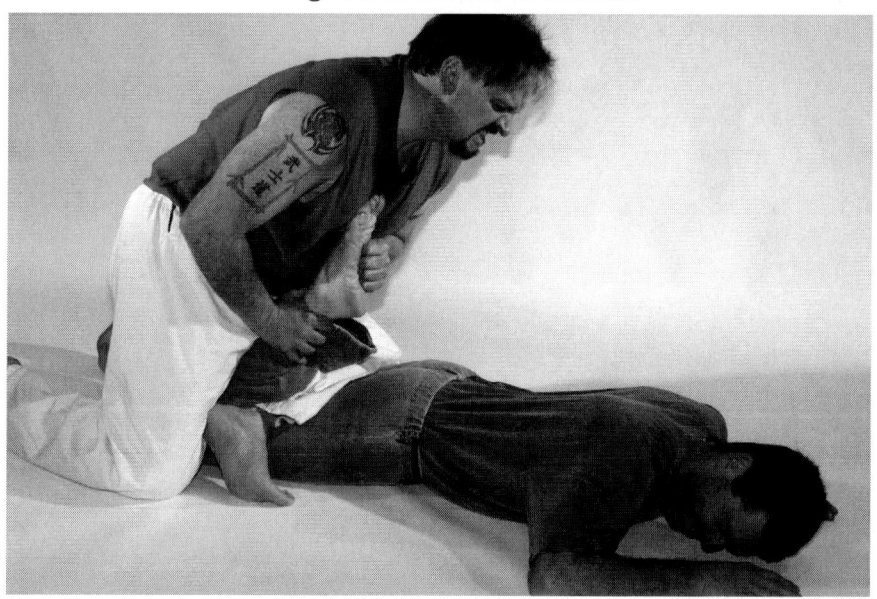

3. Step over his right leg with your left and draw your leg in tightly behind his knee. Drop your knee to the side as you lean forward.

KNEE TECHNIQUES

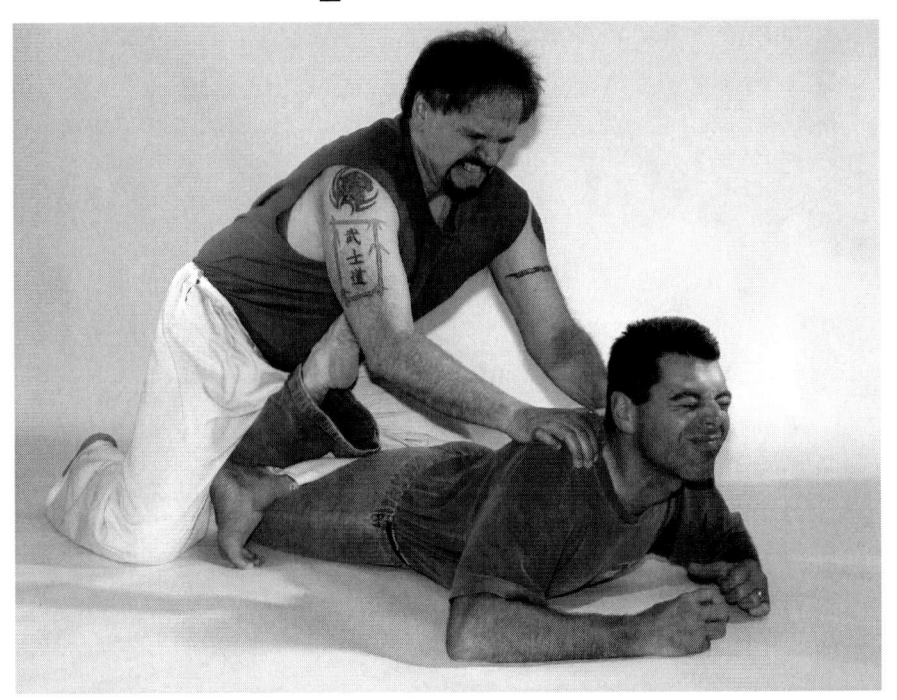

4. Grab your attacker's shoulders to pull you in more deeply and cause greater pain. If you pull and lean with great force, you will likely cause knee damage. Be justified.

EXTREME JOINT LOCKING AND BREAKING

TECHNIQUE 2: HEADLOCK TO KNEE BRACE

This is one of those techniques that you probably wouldn't deliberately seek out. But if it becomes available to you in the course of the fight and it's the best option at the moment, grab it. It can inflict tremendous pain, including breaking the joint.

1. You just crashed to the floor with your attacker, and you have him in a headlock. It's not the best technique in the world, but sometimes you've got to take what you can get. As he starts to pull his head free of your hold, smack him in the face to inflict distracting pain and slow his resistance.

⌐KNEE TECHNIQUES⌐

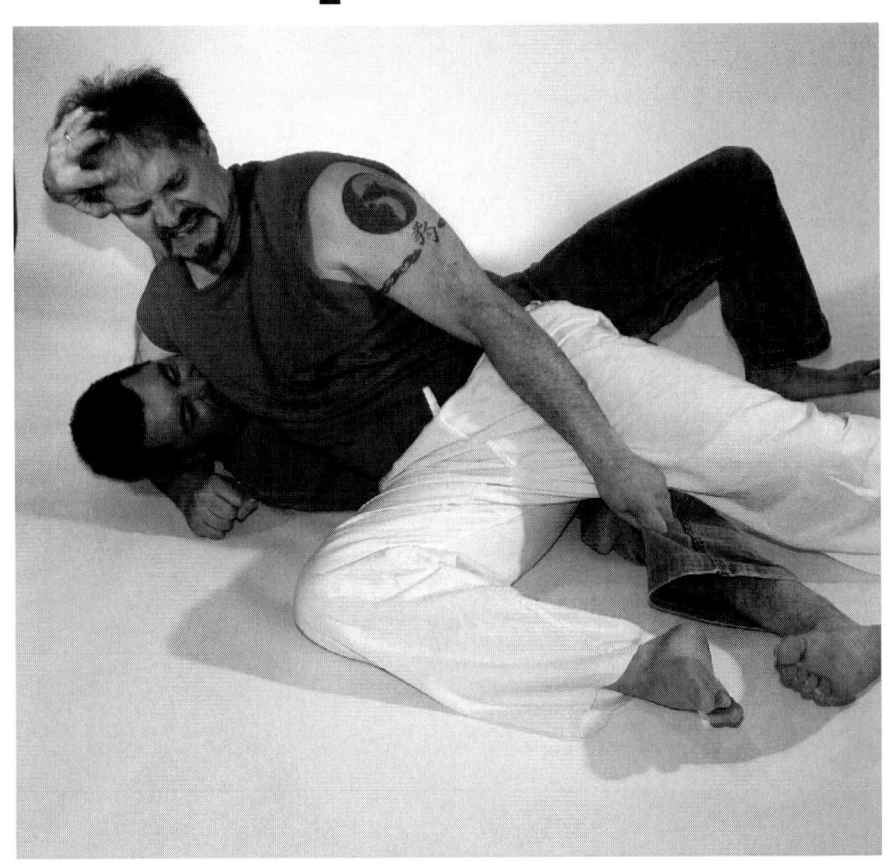

2. Grab his closer leg (the one he's trying to kick you with) and pull it between yours. Push your butt back against his hips.

EXTREME JOINT LOCKING AND BREAKING

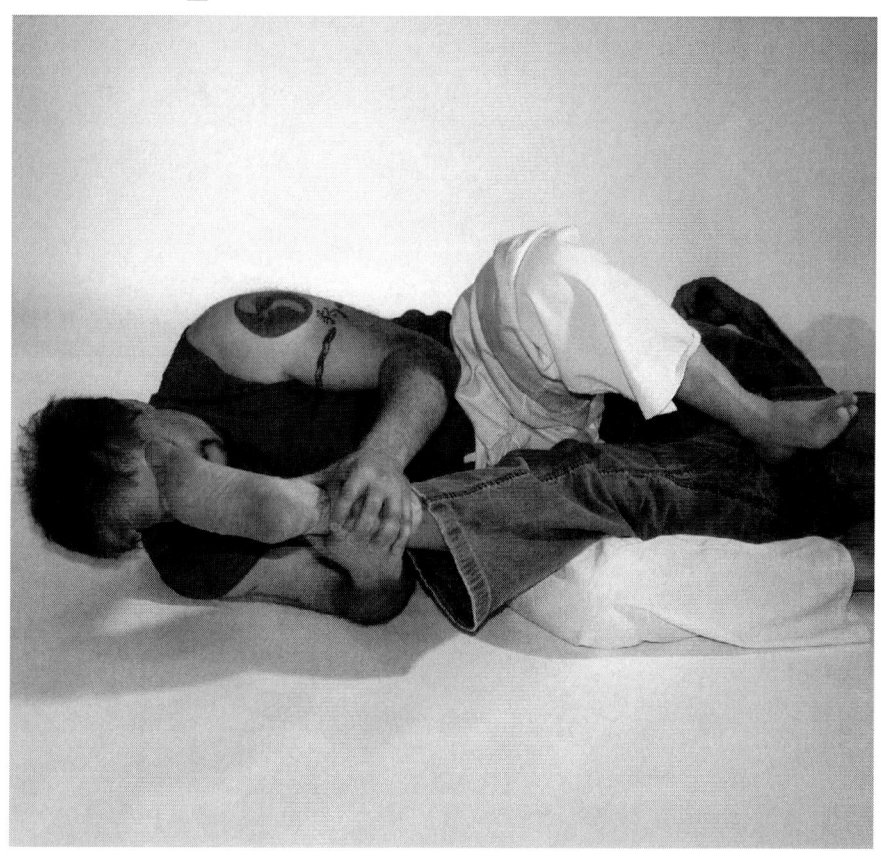

3. If you think he has another kick in him, back-kick his groin a couple of times.

KNEE TECHNIQUES

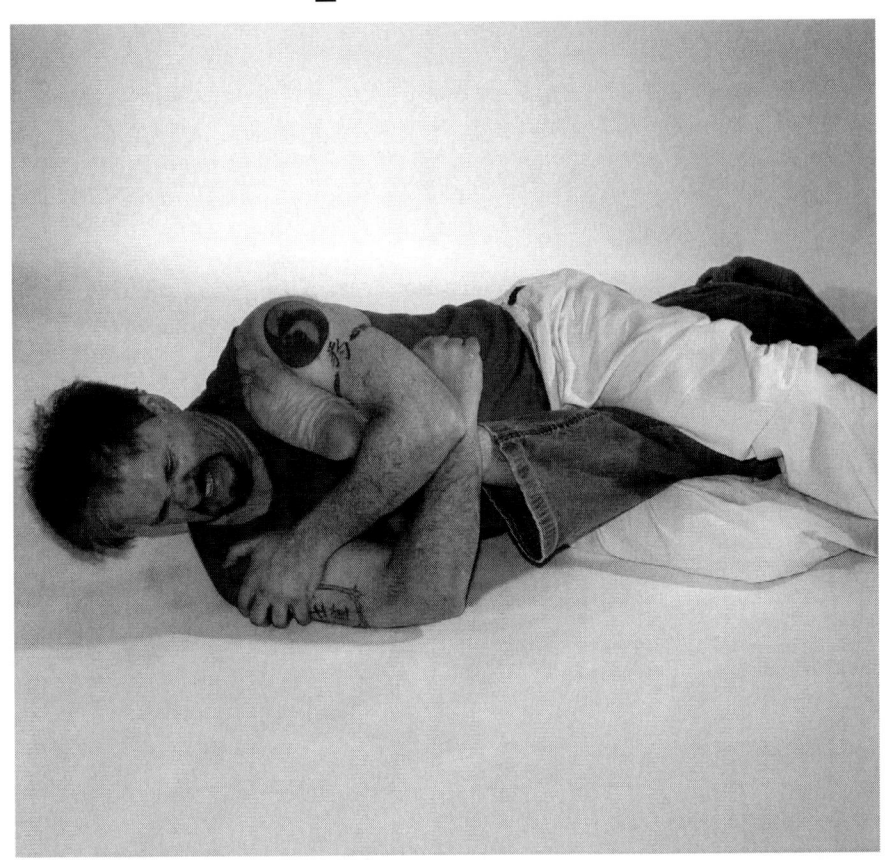

4. Hug his lower leg as you cross your ankles and press your knees together. Arch your back to apply pressure against the knee joint with your hips. Do it hard if you're justified to injure his knee.

EXTREME JOINT LOCKING AND BREAKING

TECHNIQUE 3: FIGURE FOUR LEG BRACE

This is a nifty response when your attacker attempts to kick you immediately after you have dumped him on his back. It's quick, easy, and painful.

1. Sweep aside the attacker's punch with your left palm and begin to shoot your right hand toward his shoulder.

KNEE TECHNIQUES

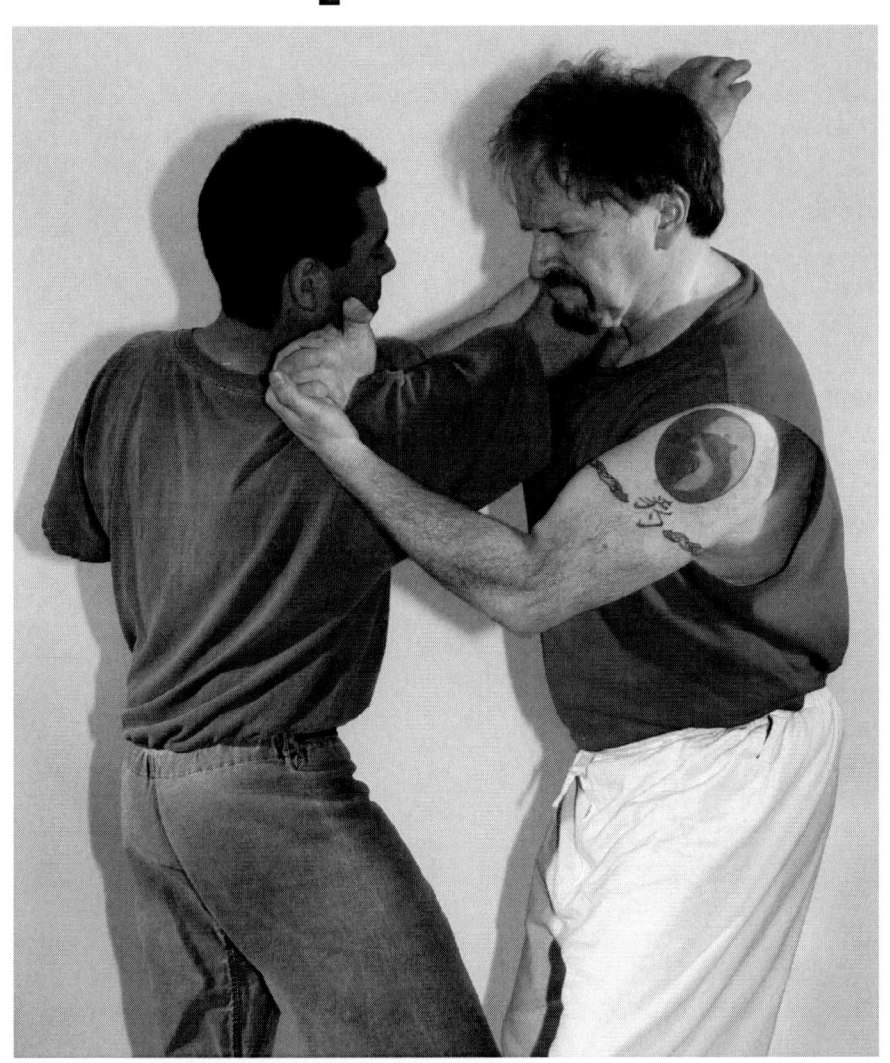

2. Press your right bladed hand into the indentation on the top of his shoulder and clasp it with your left. Press down and slightly back to dump him to the ground.

EXTREME JOINT LOCKING AND BREAKING

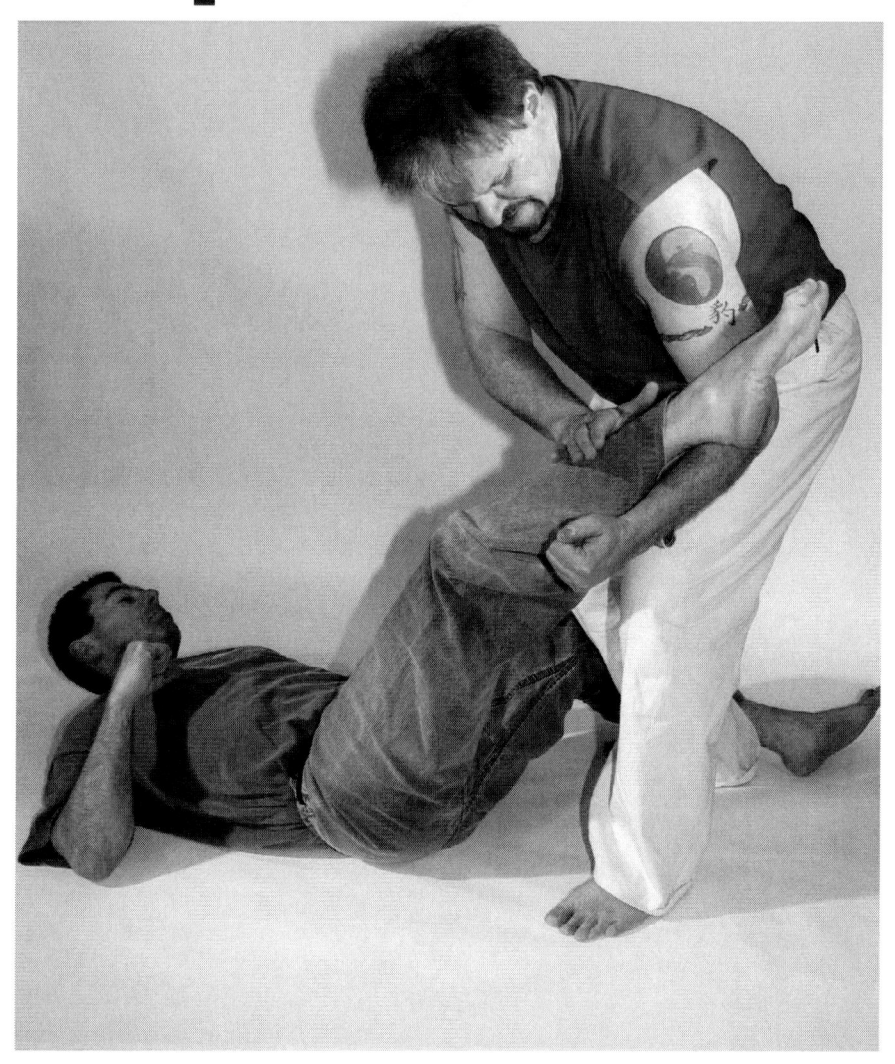

3. Catch his right leg when he kicks at you.

KNEE TECHNIQUES

4. Step over his leg and pin it between yours (see step 5).

EXTREME JOINT LOCKING AND BREAKING

5. Drop onto your back as you cross your left ankle behind your right calf and pull his locked leg across your thigh. If he has strong legs, cross your forearms across his shin and pull.

Speed is of the essence. If he bends his leg before you apply the hold, you lose your window of opportunity. A kick to the head and a groin stomp will take the fight out of him and facilitate a good lock on his knee.

CHAPTER 8
ankle techniques

Most people don't think about their ankles except when pulling up their droopy socks. But when they have an ankle that is twisted, sprained, or broken, that is all they think about—which is what makes the ankle a good target in a self-defense situation.

A sharp kick to the ankle is quite painful, especially when that protruding bone on either side is struck. A blow to the highly vulnerable Achilles tendon can be excruciating. When grappling the ankle, the effect of a severe lock or a violent twist can range from overwhelming agony to a debilitating sprain or break, which might be necessary to prevent the attacker from pursuing when you flee.

I'm guessing that most fighters don't set out to attack their opponent's ankles, but rather seize the opportunity when it's presented to them. Usually this happens when they catch, block, or jam a kick from their attacker.

CAUTION: When training, you and your partner should tap out the instant the ankle lock is applied. Wait a moment too long and the injured party will walk with a limp for a couple of days—or a crutch for two months.

THE ANKLE AS A TARGET

The top part of the ankle is composed of three bones: the tibia (the inner and larger bone extending from the knee to the ankle, also called the shinbone), the fibula (the outer and narrower bone extending from the knee to the ankle), and the talus (the bone that articulates with the tibia and fibula to form the ankle joint, also called the anklebone). The leg bones form a scooped pocket at the top of the anklebone so that the foot can bend up and down. The other joint below the ankle is called the subtalar, where the anklebone connects to the calcaneus (heel bone). This joint allows the foot to rock from side to side.

Sprain

Three ligaments over the outside of the ankle connect the bones and support the joint. A sprain occurs when the ankle is suddenly twisted or forced sideways and the ligaments are stretched farther than normal; some might tear.

Break

For our purposes, know that an ankle break occurs most often in the tibia, fibula, or both, and can take many forms. For example, one end of the bone might pierce the skin (compound or open fracture); a traumatized muscle or ligament can pull a portion of the bone away from where it was attached; or the ends of the broken bone can drive into each other.

TECHNIQUE 1: ANKLE AND FOOT STANDING CRANK

You can apply this against any leg attack, but it's easiest to learn on a front kick since the foot is in a perfect position, ready for you to crank it with prejudice.

ANKLE TECHNIQUES

1. Your opponent launches a left front kick at your midsection. Block and catch it, and then pop him in the face to get his energy moving backward.

2. Sweep his support leg to take him down.

ANKLE TECHNIQUES

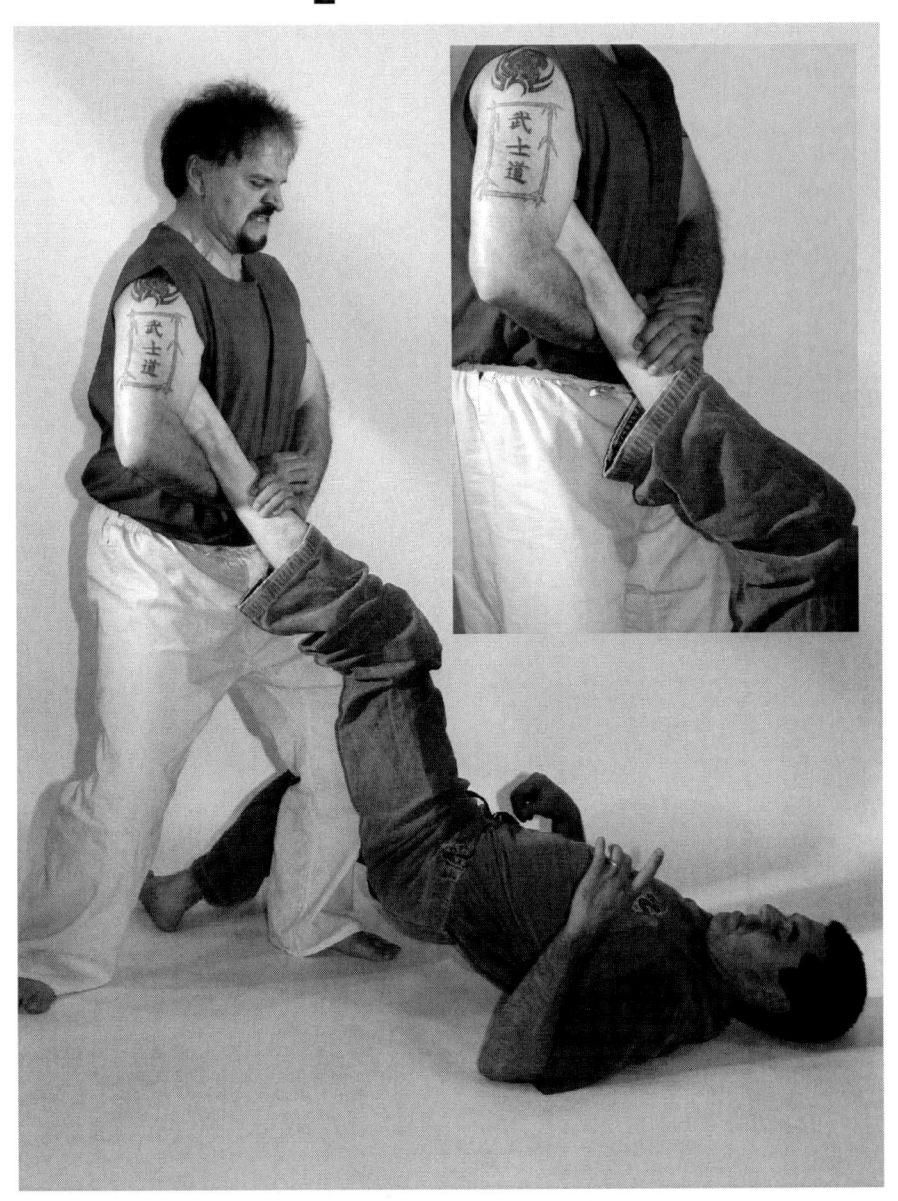

3. Wrap your right arm around his ankle and support it with a figure-four lock. Lean back a little to underscore the pain in the ankle and Achilles tendon areas. Use your hard wrist tendon to dig into his Achilles tendon.

EXTREME JOINT LOCKING AND BREAKING

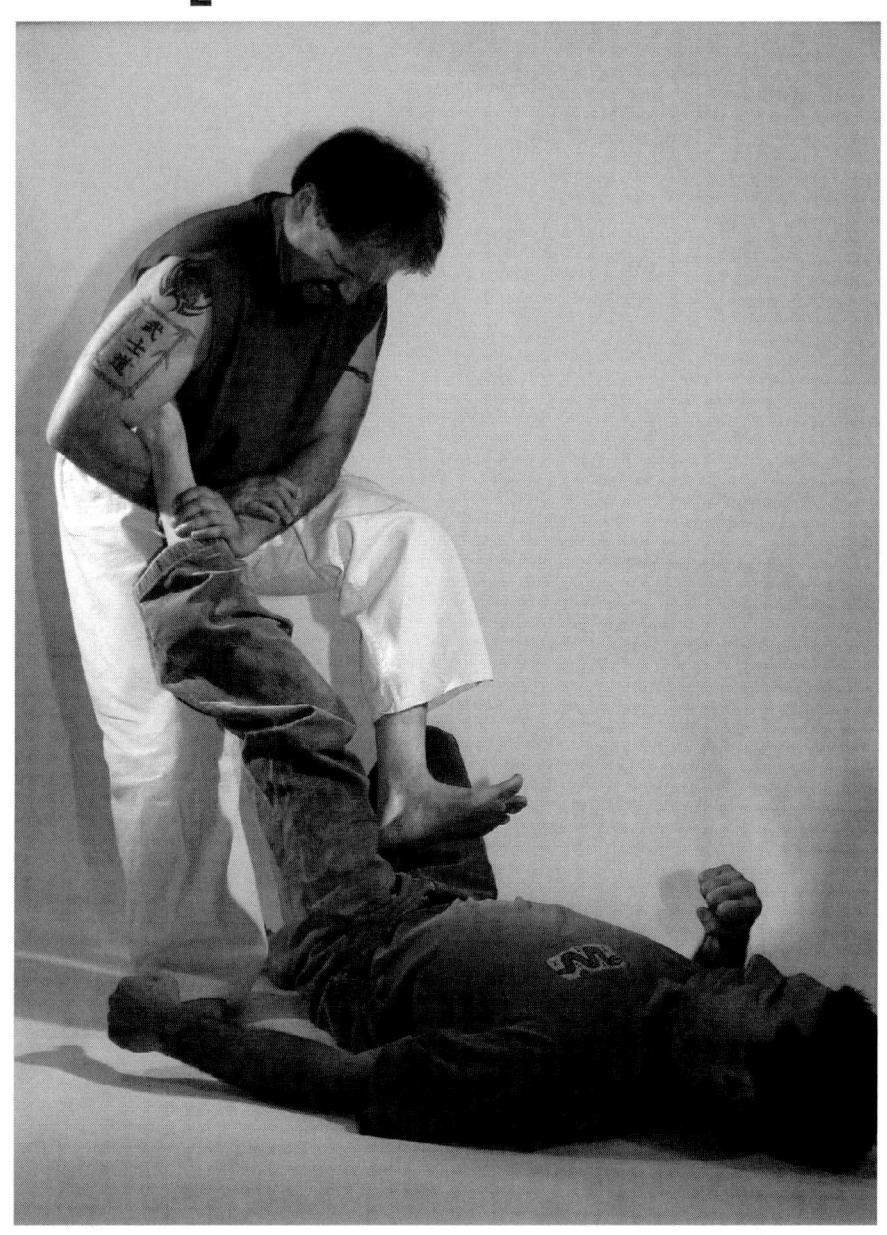

4. If you need an extra moment to better secure the hold, you're in a perfect position to do a quick stomp to his groin.

ANKLE TECHNIQUES

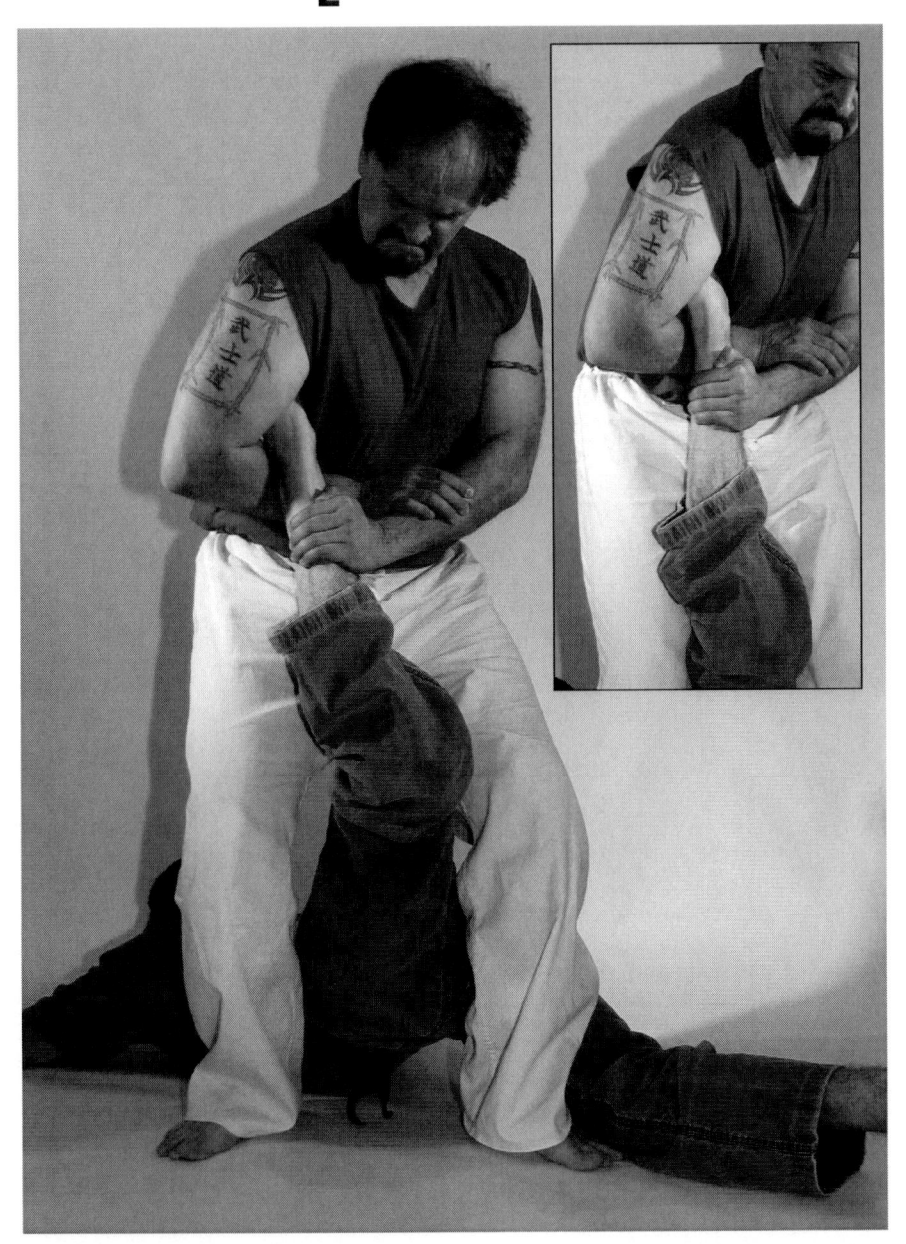

5. Should he roll over, follow without changing your hand position and increase the pressure. This places tremendous pressure on his ankle.

EXTREME JOINT LOCKING AND BREAKING

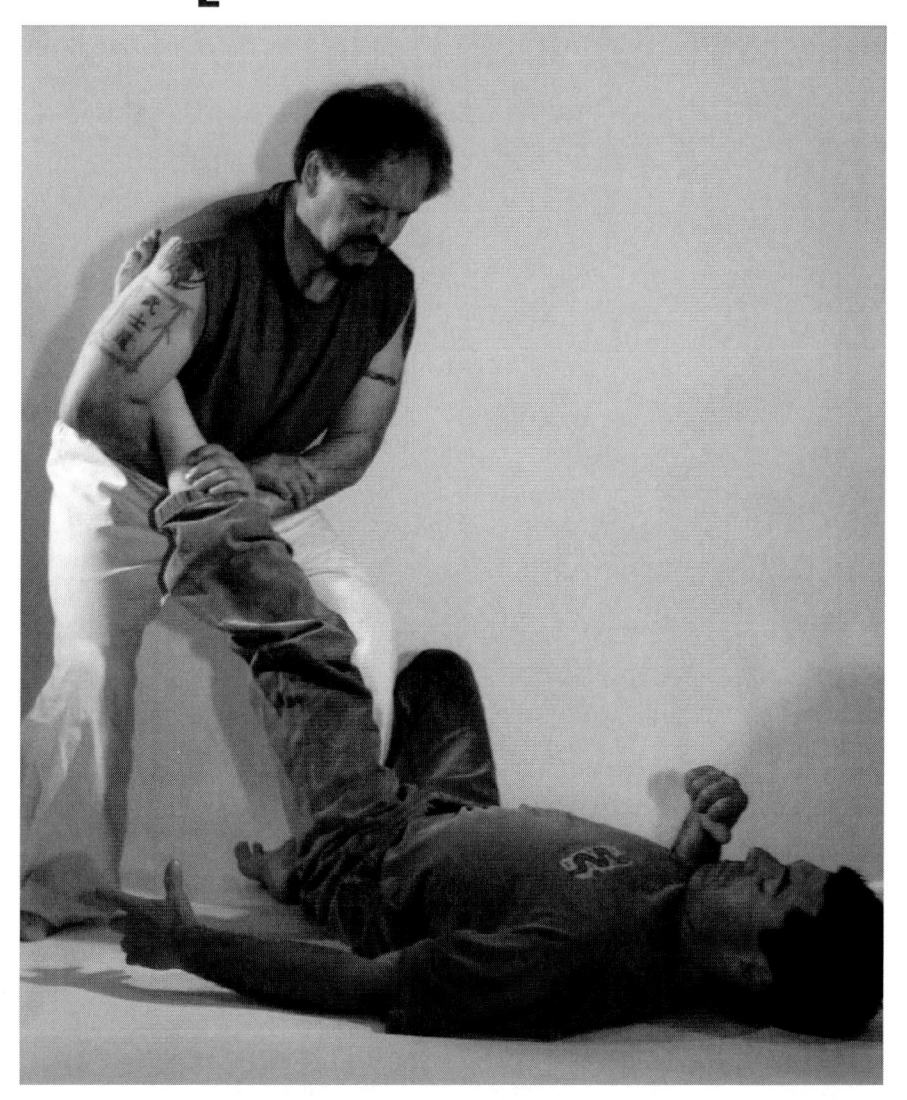

This technique is excruciatingly painful for most people. Should your opponent continue to twist and attempt to defeat the hold, it's quite possible he will suffer a broken ankle.

Variation 1
1. Start with the block and catch as before and then assume a figure-four armlock.

ANKLE TECHNIQUES

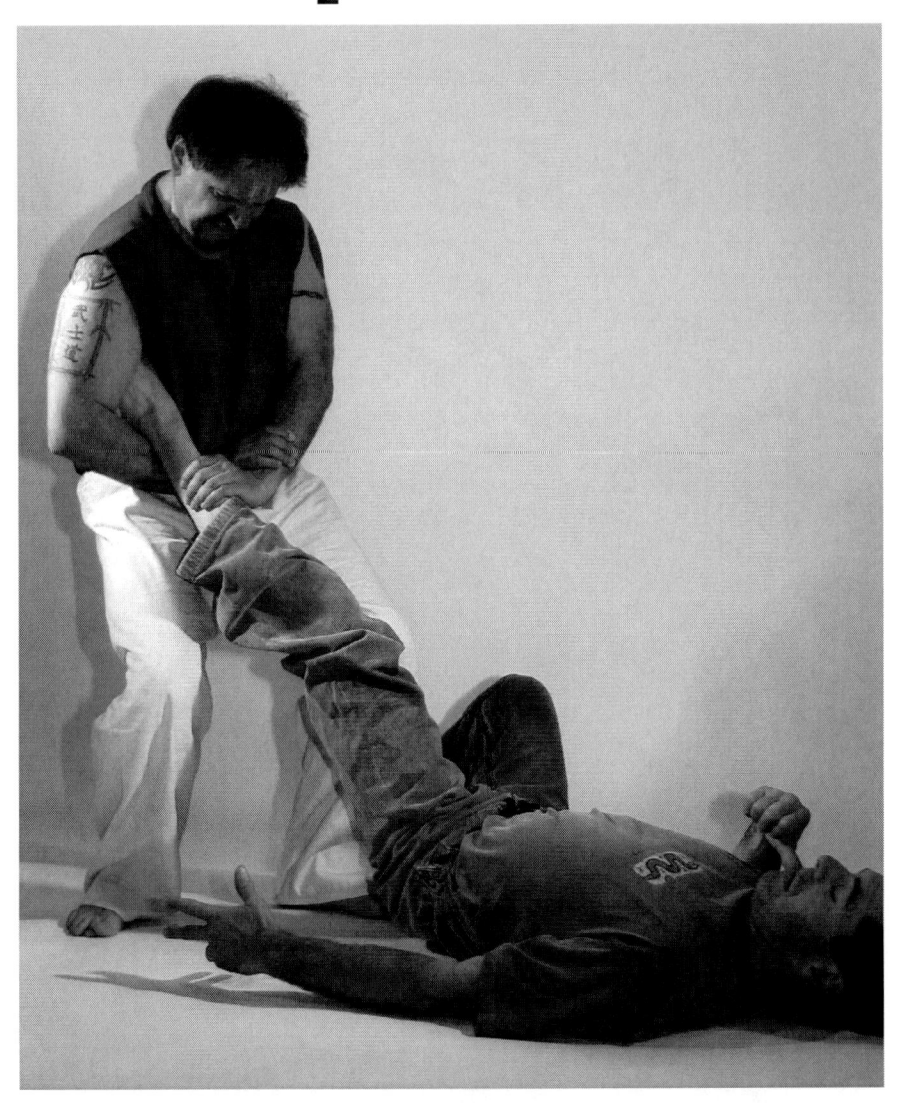

2. Move back a little so that his leg slides through your arms until you have caught his foot around his ankle. Be sure to bend his foot down with your armpit as you dig your wrist into his Achilles tendon.

EXTREME JOINT LOCKING AND BREAKING

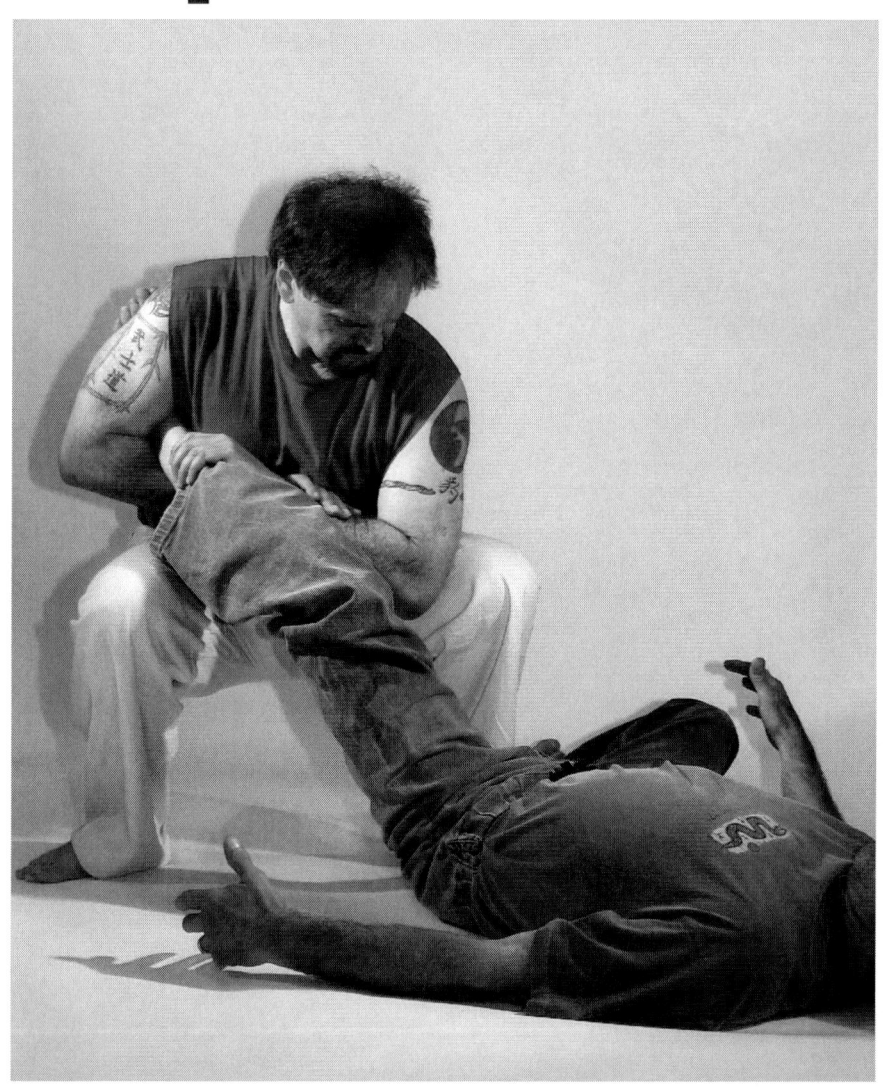

3. Squat down.

ANKLE TECHNIQUES

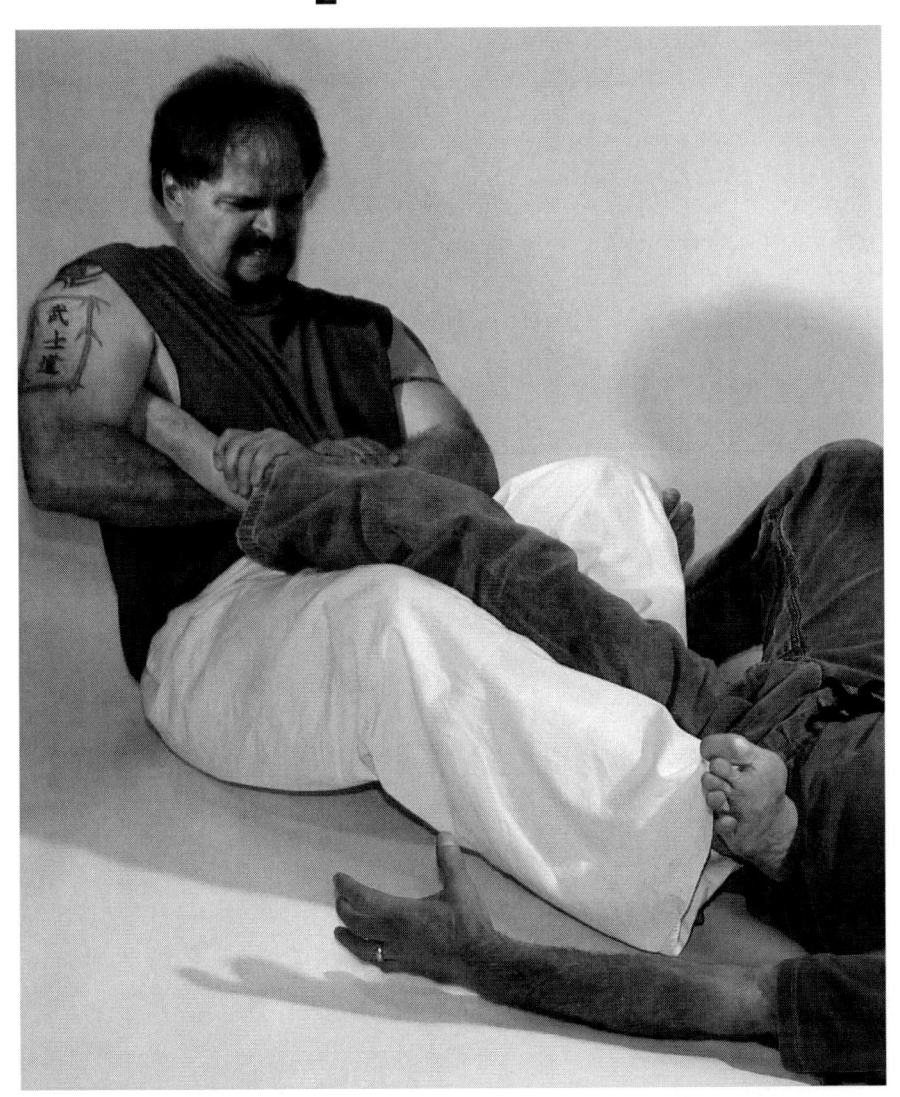

4. Sit down. Keep your left leg between his legs and extend your right leg. Use your heel to push against his rib cage if he tries to sit up. Arch your back to inflict pain; arch it hard if the situation requires that you damage his ankle.

EXTREME JOINT LOCKING AND BREAKING

TECHNIQUE 2: UPSIDE DOWN ANKLE LOCK

Imagine that you have taken your attacker down and he is trying to crawl away from you, but you don't want him to go quite yet. Let's begin with a takedown.

1. Trap your attacker's knees with your palms and ram his butt with your shoulder.

ANKLE TECHNIQUES

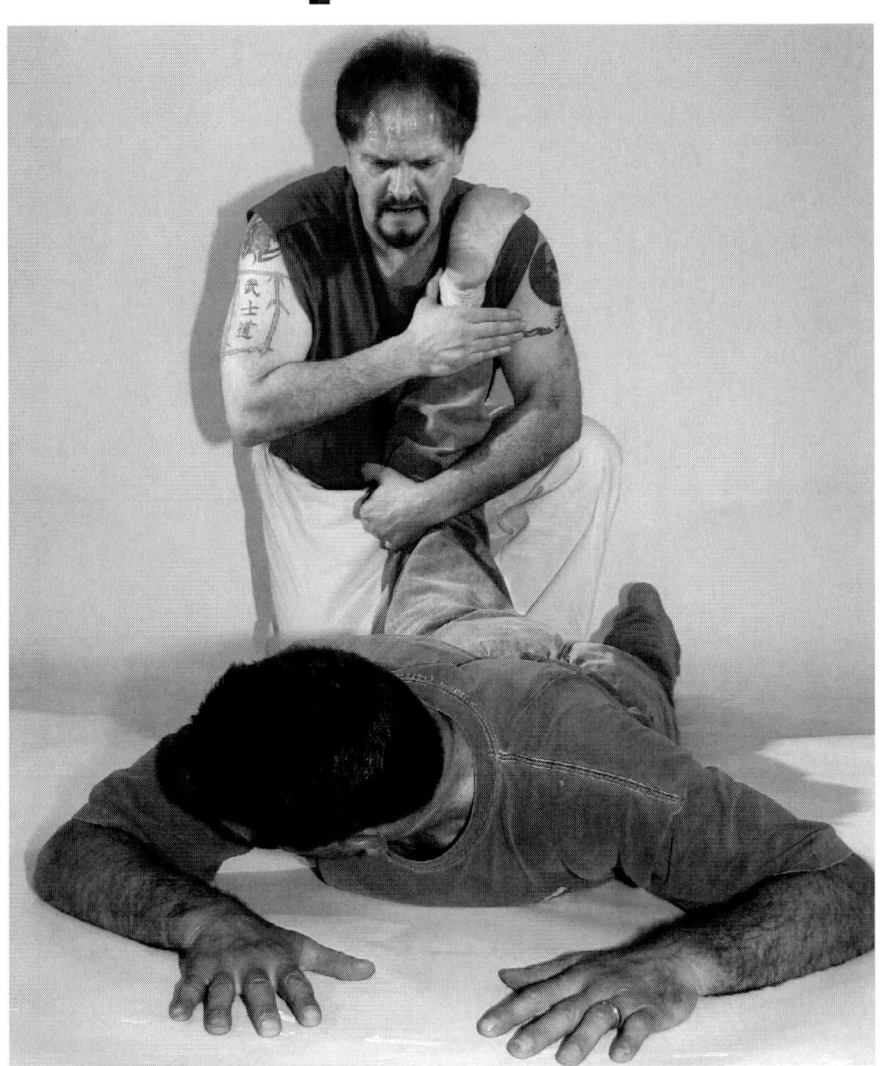

2. When he tries to scoot away, hook his right leg at the knee with your left forearm and use your right hand to push his instep against your left shoulder and upper chest.

EXTREME JOINT LOCKING AND BREAKING

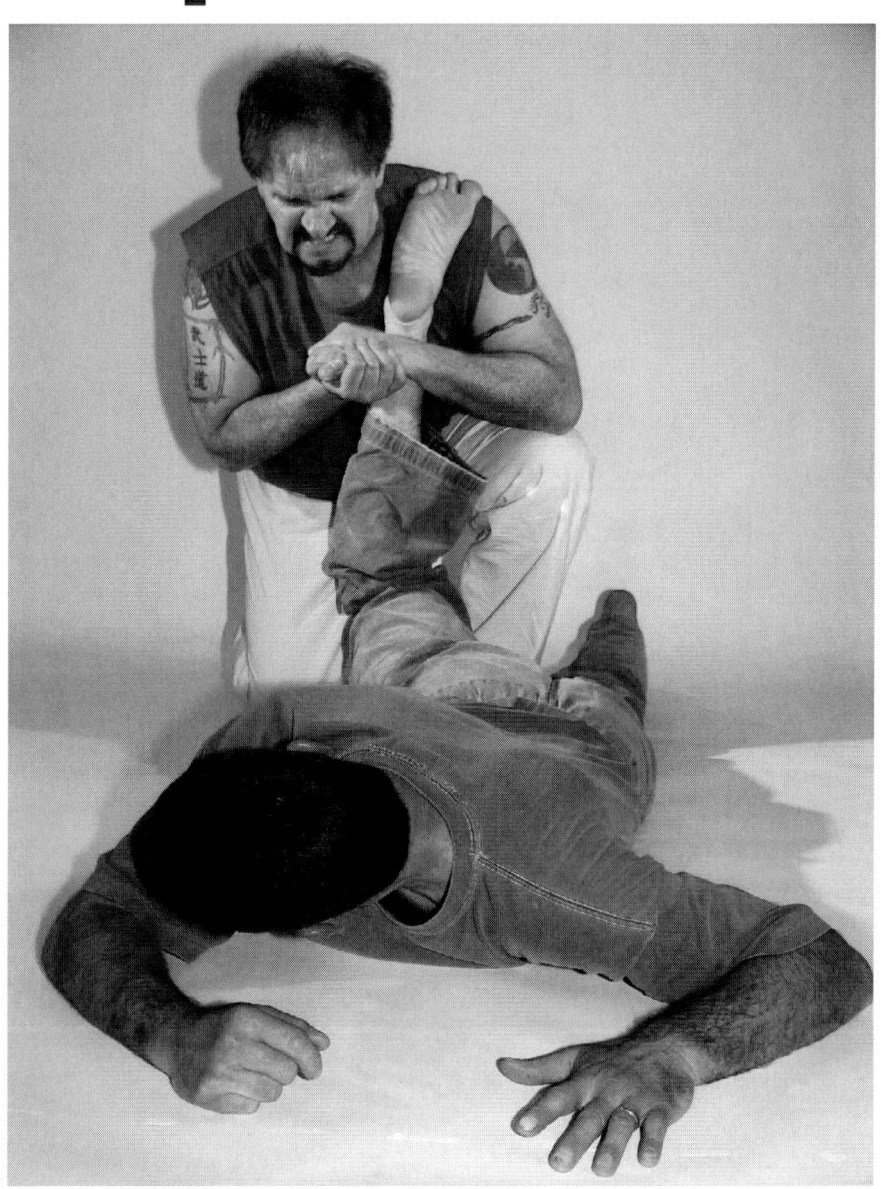

3. Clasp your hands and use the radial (thumb) side of your wrist to grind into his Achilles tendon. Lean your left shoulder forward a little to add extra torque on his ankle.

ANKLE TECHNIQUES

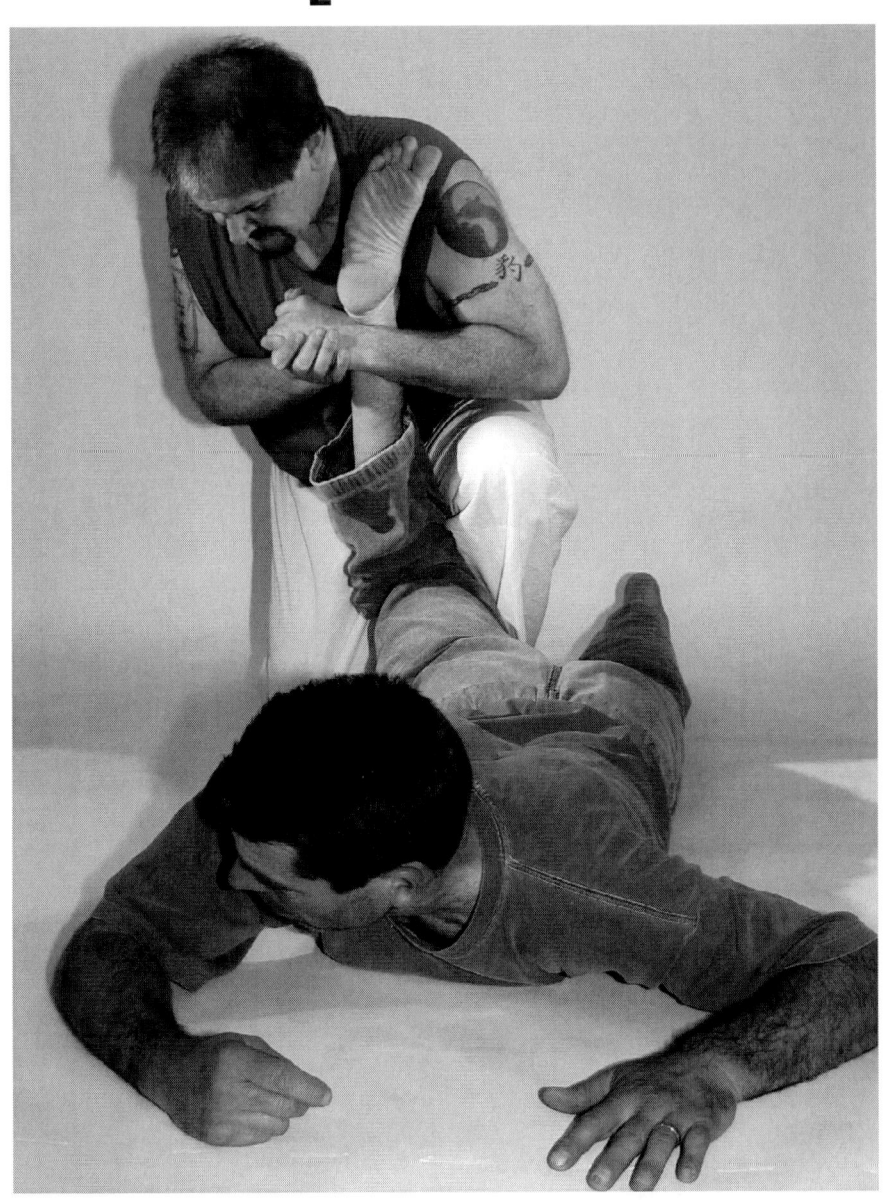

4. To simultaneously inflict pain on his knee, turn your upper body to the right. Do it with force, and you will likely cause internal damage to the knee joint.

EXTREME JOINT LOCKING AND BREAKING

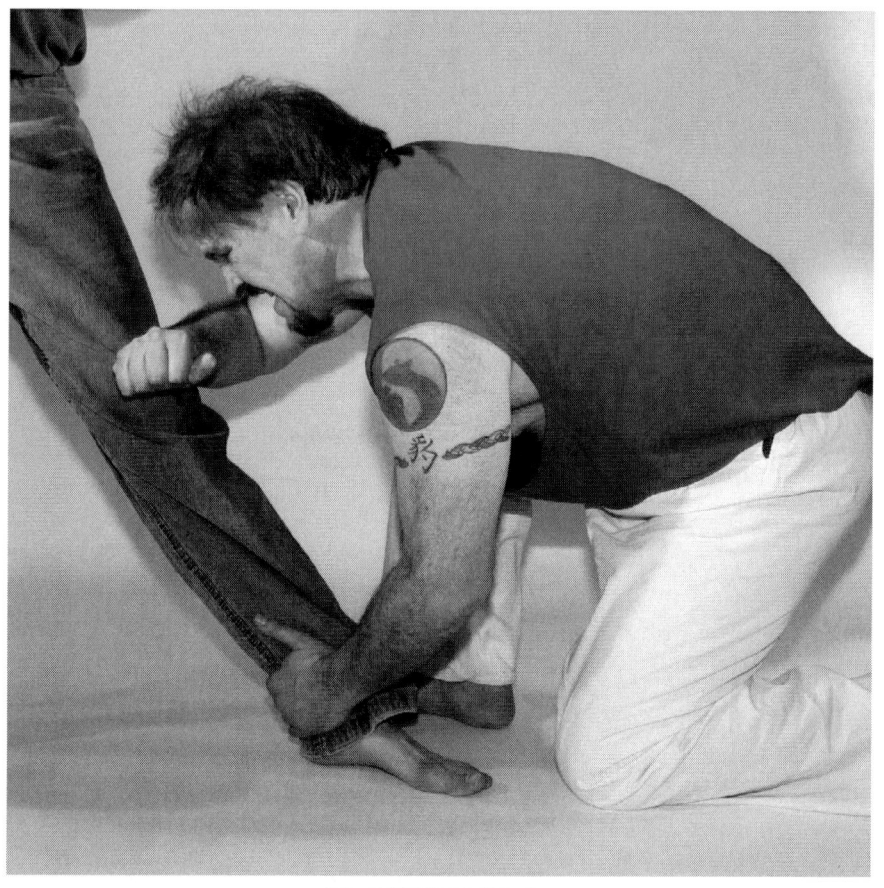

TECHNIQUE 3:
FIGURE FOUR KNEE BRACE WITH ANKLE CRANK

Apply this ankle crank when you have your attacker's leg trapped with a knee brace. Although this hurts, it probably won't damage the joint. It *will* immobilize and distract the attacker so you can apply a strong crank on his ankle, one that will cause damage if you slam it on with great force.

1. The attacker steps in range after you have slipped or been knocked to your knees. Quickly pull his closer ankle with one hand as you press just above his knee with your forearm to take him down.

ANKLE TECHNIQUES

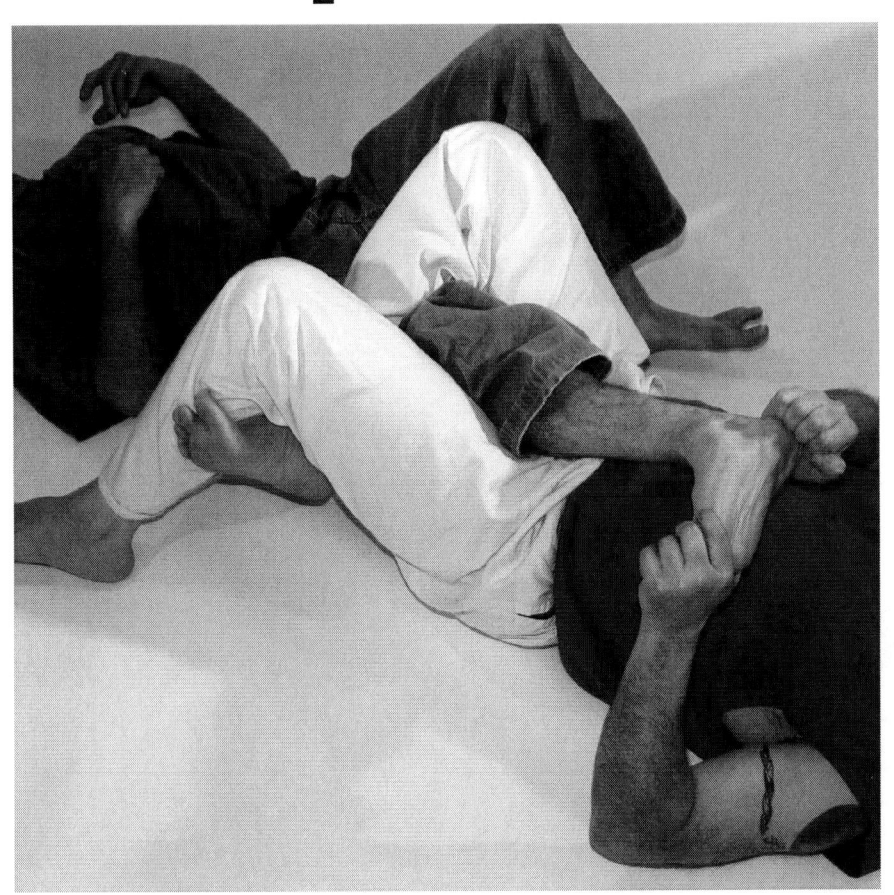

2. Scoot your legs into the attacker and wrap your right leg over his closer leg (the right one in this case), crossing it just above his knee. Your left thigh is positioned under his leg to create a foundation against which your attacker's leg is braced.

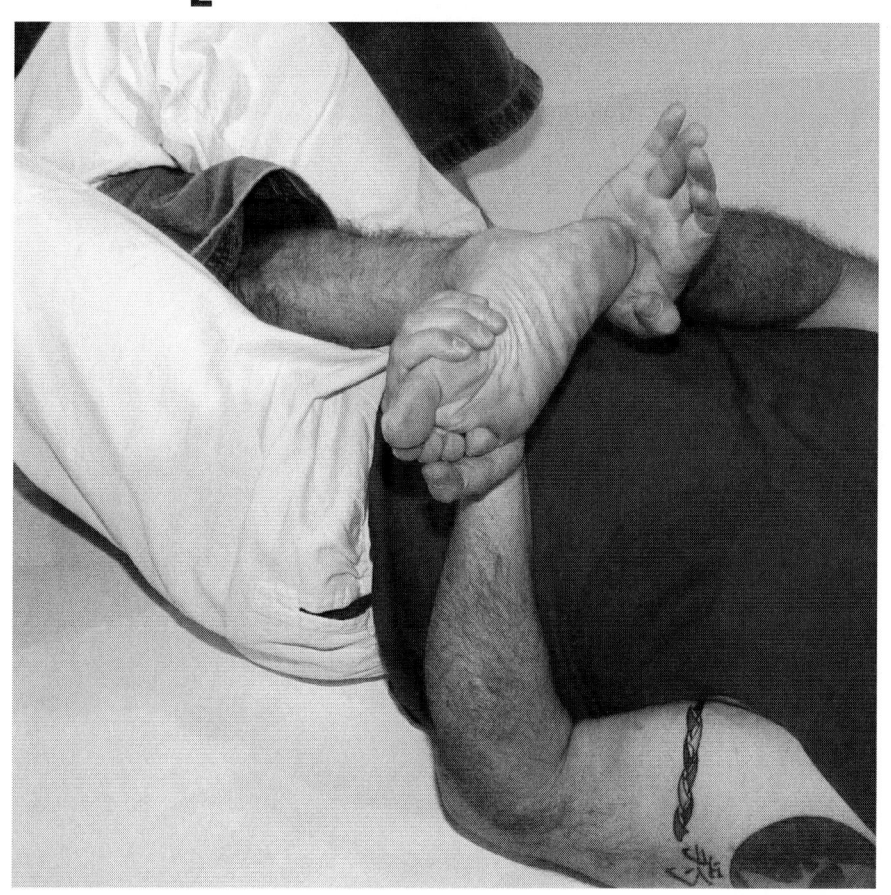

3. Secure each end of his foot in your hands and turn it counterclockwise until your attacker writhes. If needed, crank his foot with great force. Should he tighten his foot to resist, slam pressure on his knee to distract him.

ANKLE TECHNIQUES

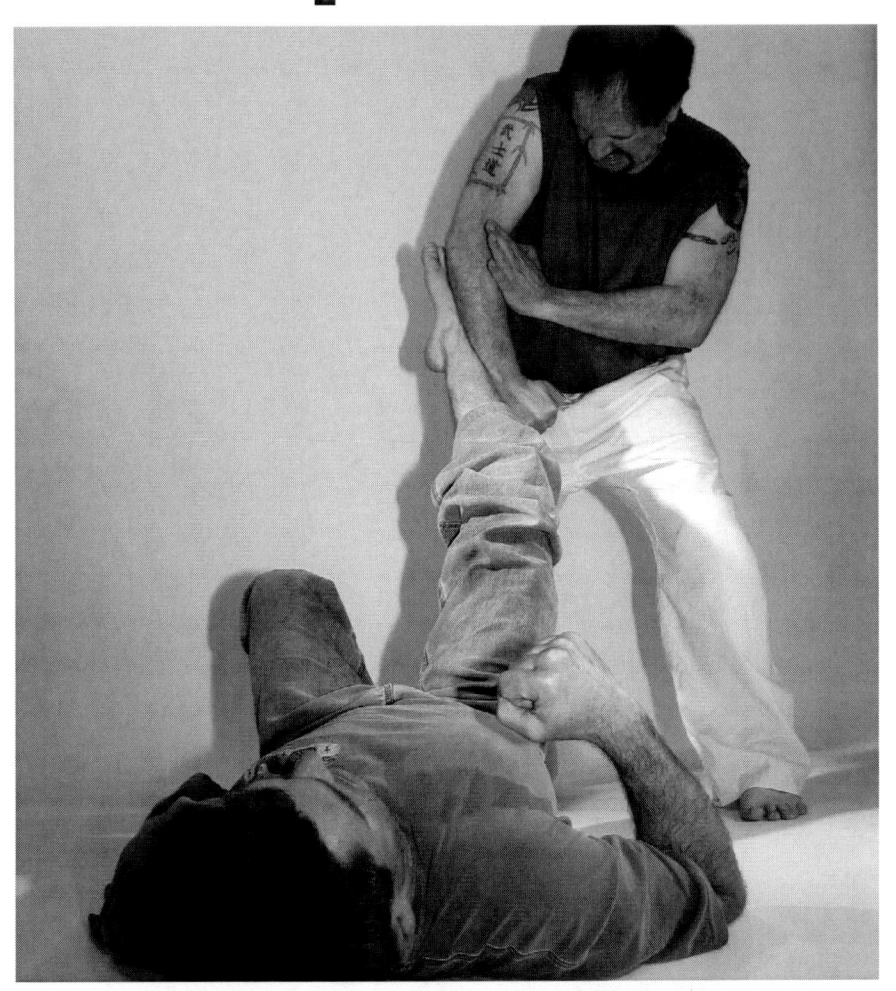

TECHNIQUE 4: FIGURE FOUR ANKLE LOCK

This is an easy-to-apply hold to use when your attacker kicks at you after being dumped onto his back or when you're on the ground next to him. The figure four allows you to apply tremendous force on his ankle with minimum exertion by you.

1. After you dump your attacker, he kicks at you with his right leg, which you block.

EXTREME JOINT LOCKING AND BREAKING

2. Quickly place your right arm under his ankle and heel.

ANKLE TECHNIQUES

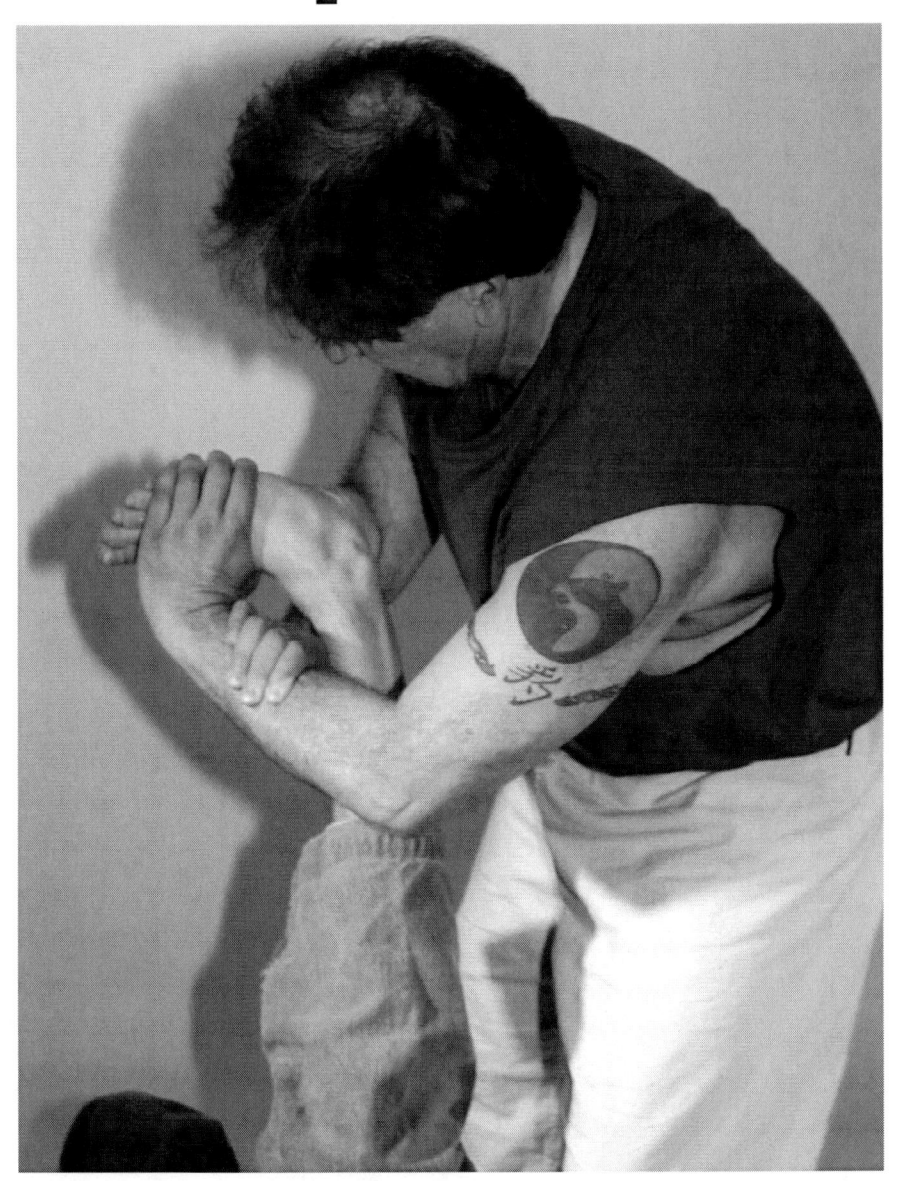

3. Grab his toe area with your left hand and your left wrist with your right hand to make a figure four. Apply pain by pulling down on the toe area while pushing his heel up with your right forearm. If you slam it home, you will break or sprain the ankle.

EXTREME JOINT LOCKING AND BREAKING

Variation 1
1. Apply the same figure four lock when you're on the floor with the attacker. This is riskier because his hands are

ANKLE TECHNIQUES

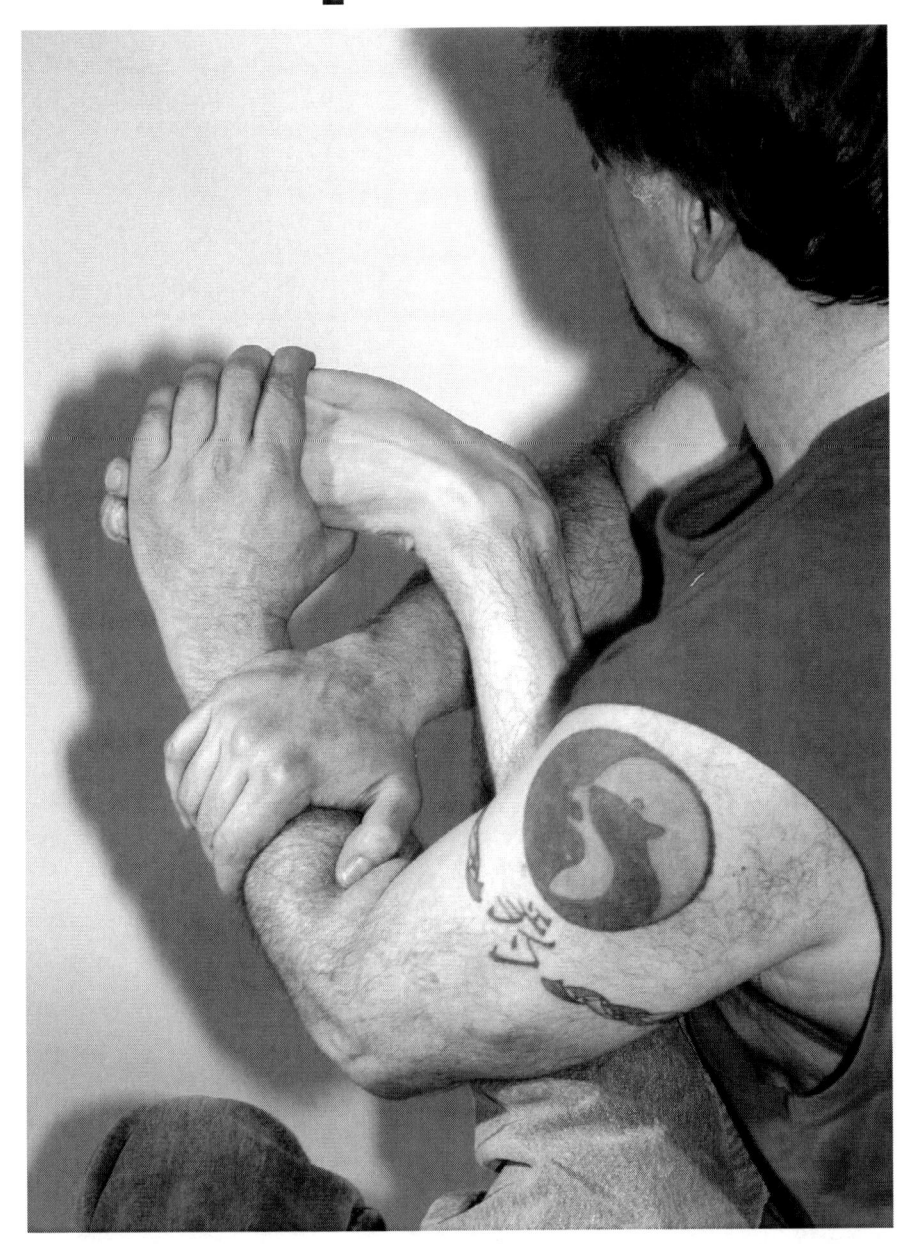

free and you are close to his other leg. Consider stunning him with head, throat, or groin blows first.

CHAPTER 9
toe techniques

Okay, most people don't run around barefoot, but I learned quickly as a cop that you can't discount anything in a fight. You might find yourself facing the proverbial sand-kicking bully at the beach, at the pool, or in the locker room, or the bully may lose his shoe during the course of the fight. In any of these cases, you have access to his toes.

In some cases, a toe might be all you have. Say your ankle hold begins to fail. Since there is almost always a brief moment of weakness when transitioning from one technique to another, you can distract your attacker with a quick and acutely painful toe technique. Be sure that you are justified to break and tear the toes.

THE TOES AS A TARGET

The toes consist of phalanges. The big toe has two joints: a proximal and a distal phalanx for the great toe. The other four toes have three joints: proximal (closest to the foot), middle, and distal (farthest from the foot) phalanges.

Break

There are two categories of toe breaks: traumatic fractures and stress fractures. A traumatic fracture is caused by sustaining a direct blow or having the toe pushed beyond its flexibility. A stress fracture is usually caused by repetitive movement and therefore isn't of concern for our purposes.

TECHNIQUE 1: TOE RIP

This is the same action as "finger rip" in Chapter 1.

TOE TECHNIQUES

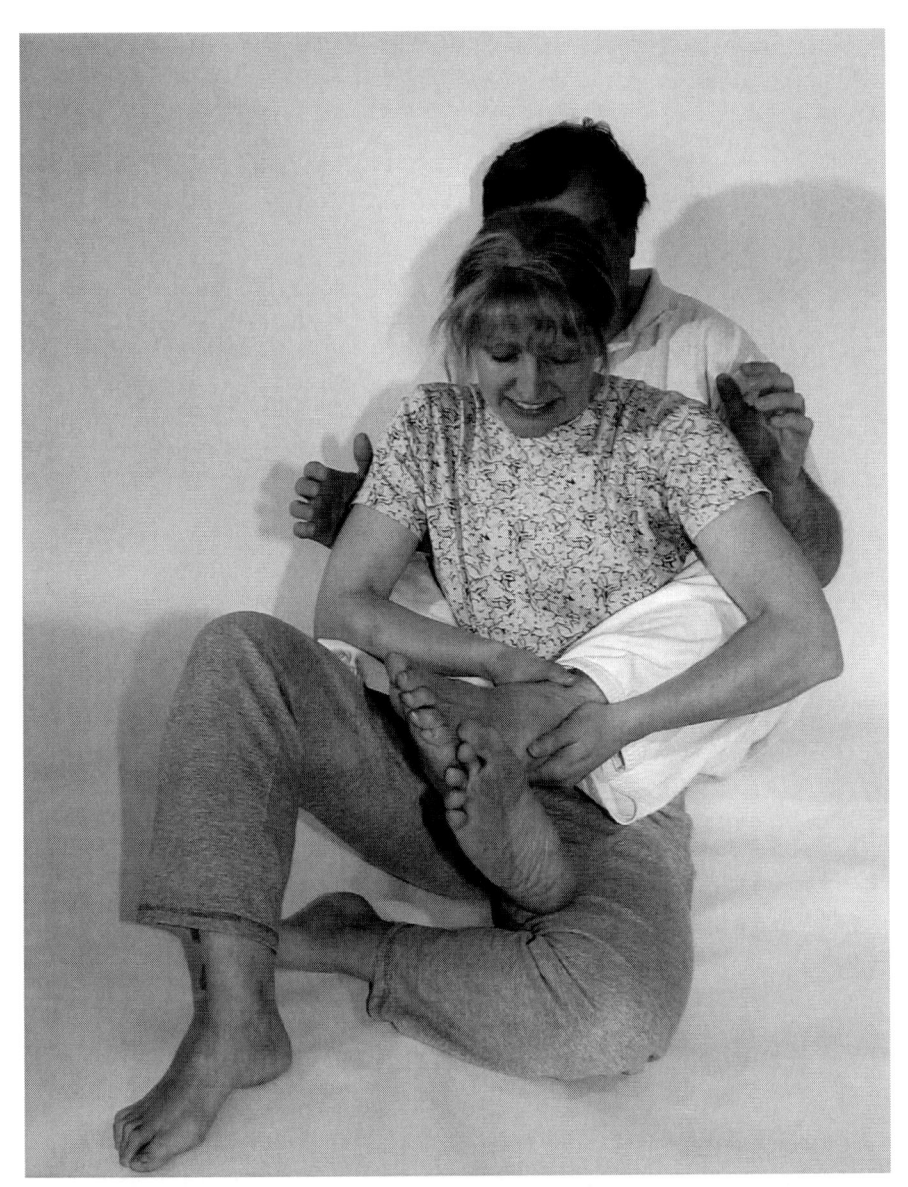

1. During the course of a ground struggle, your attacker wraps his legs around your waist. Since there are lots of nasty things he can do to you from here, you must react quickly.

EXTREME JOINT LOCKING AND BREAKING

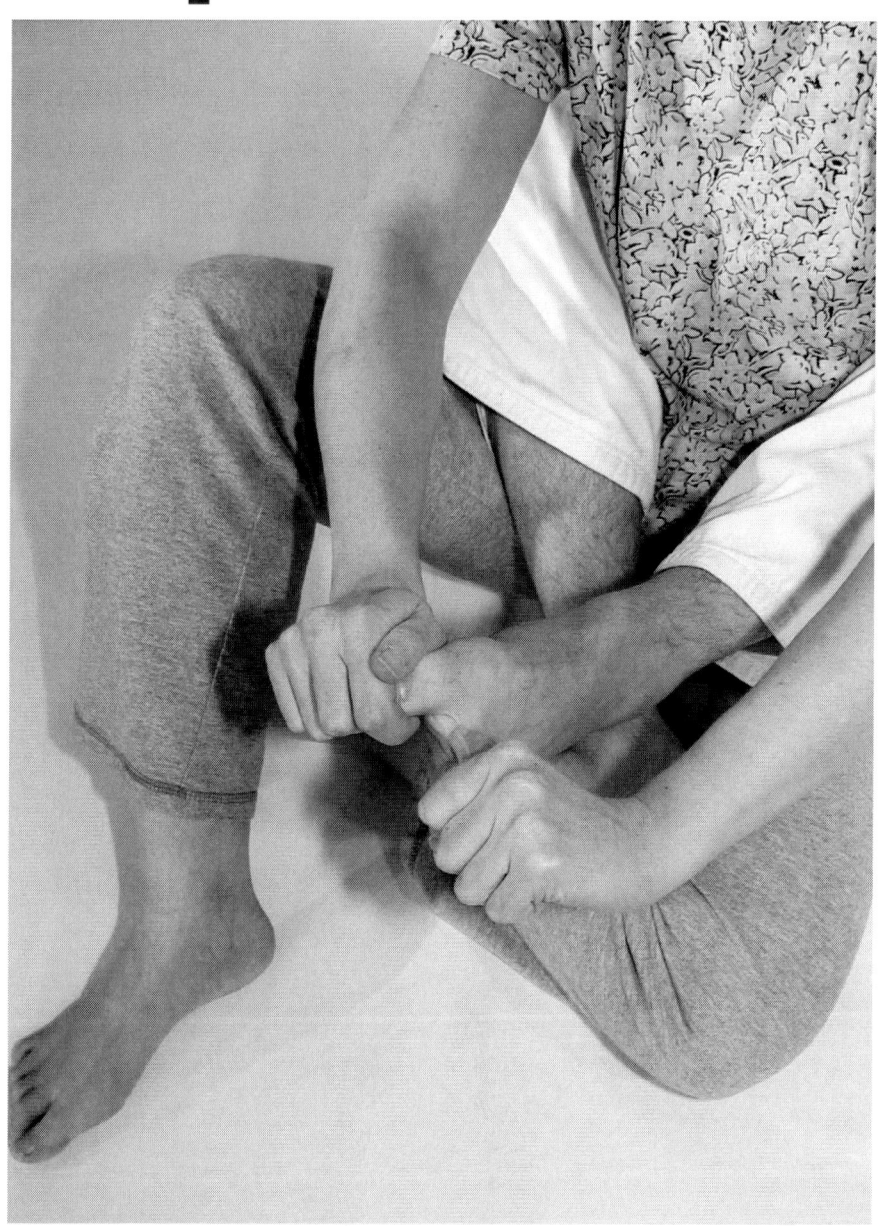

2. Grasp a toe in each hand and rip in opposite directions. As he screams in agony, the window is open for you to switch to another technique.

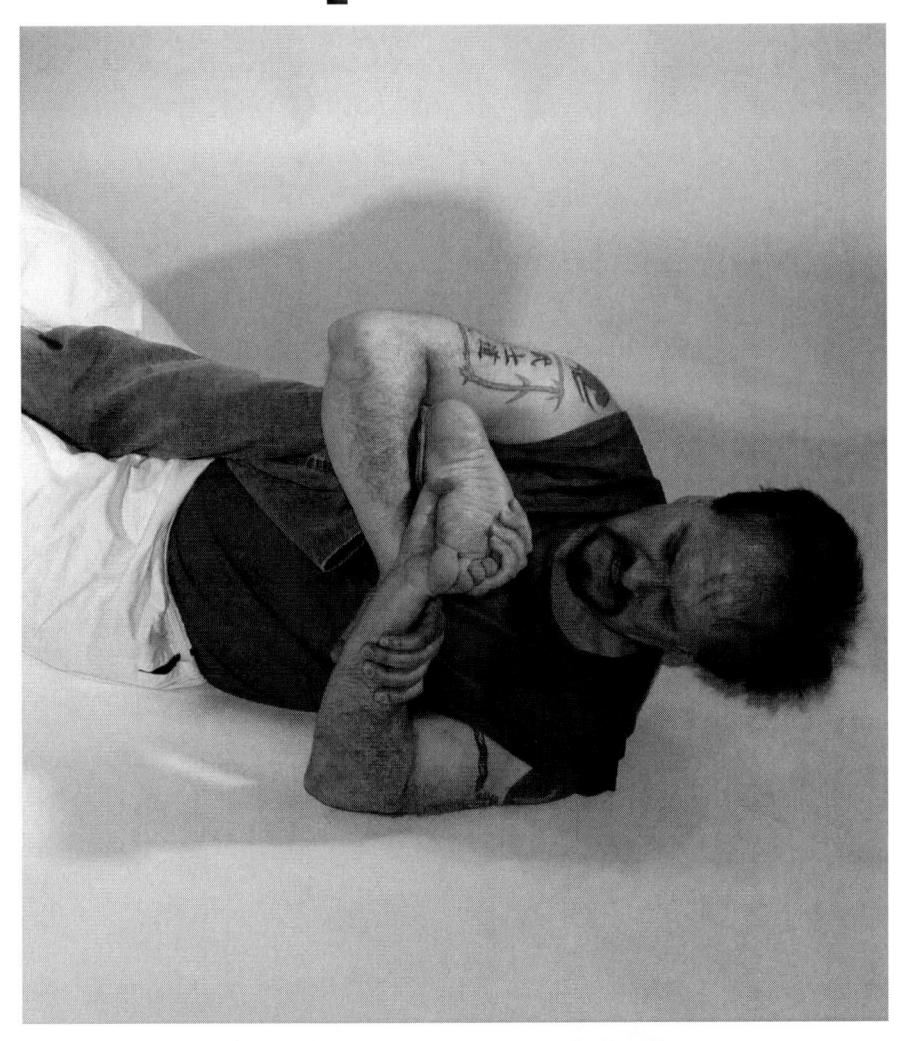

⌐ TOE TECHNIQUES ¬

TECHNIQUE 2: TOE STRETCH

This works well when your attacker is barefoot or wearing a light, flexible running-type shoe.

1. During the ground struggle, you trap your attacker's leg across your upper thigh. But before you can get him in the precise position to lock his knee, he starts to wriggle out of the hold.

EXTREME JOINT LOCKING AND BREAKING

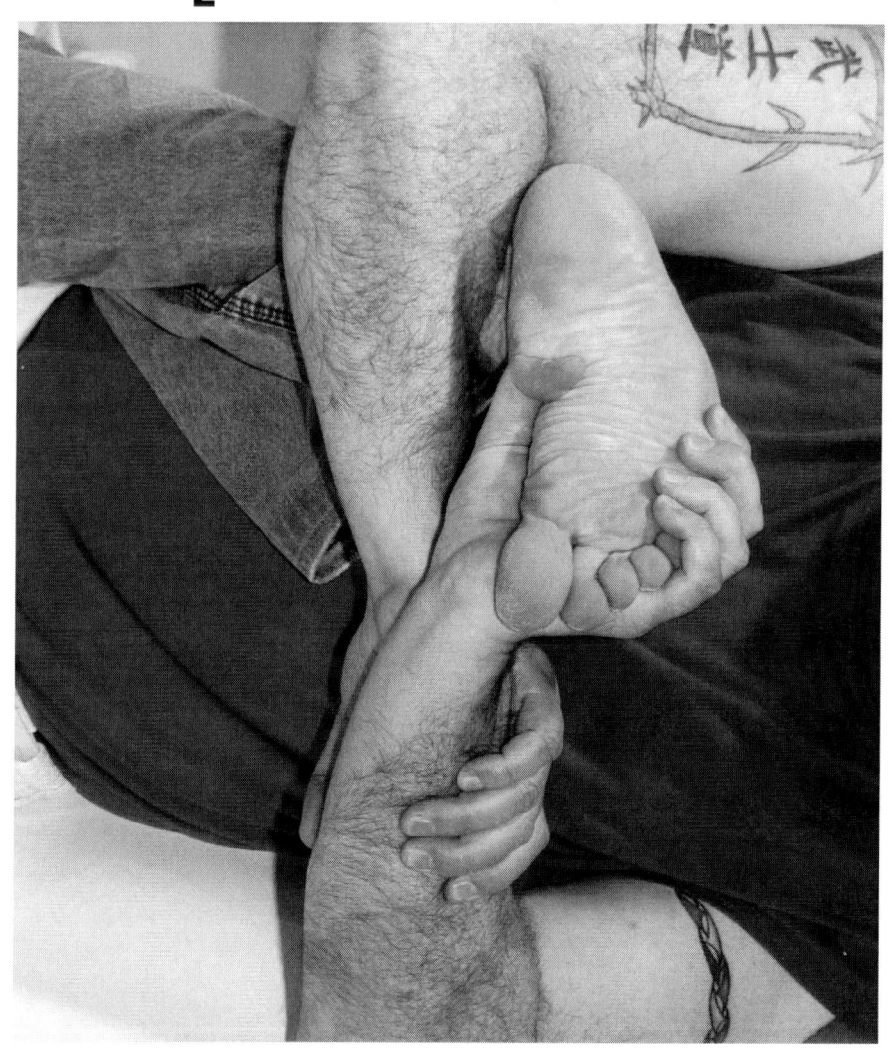

2. Since your hand is on his foot, seize the opportunity to hyperextend his toes by pushing them down toward the bottom of his foot or pulling them back toward the top, whichever way makes him scream the loudest. He will try to escape the pain by moving his leg away, allowing you the opportunity to get his leg where you want it. If it appears that he is wriggling away to reach for a weapon, ram his toes to break them.

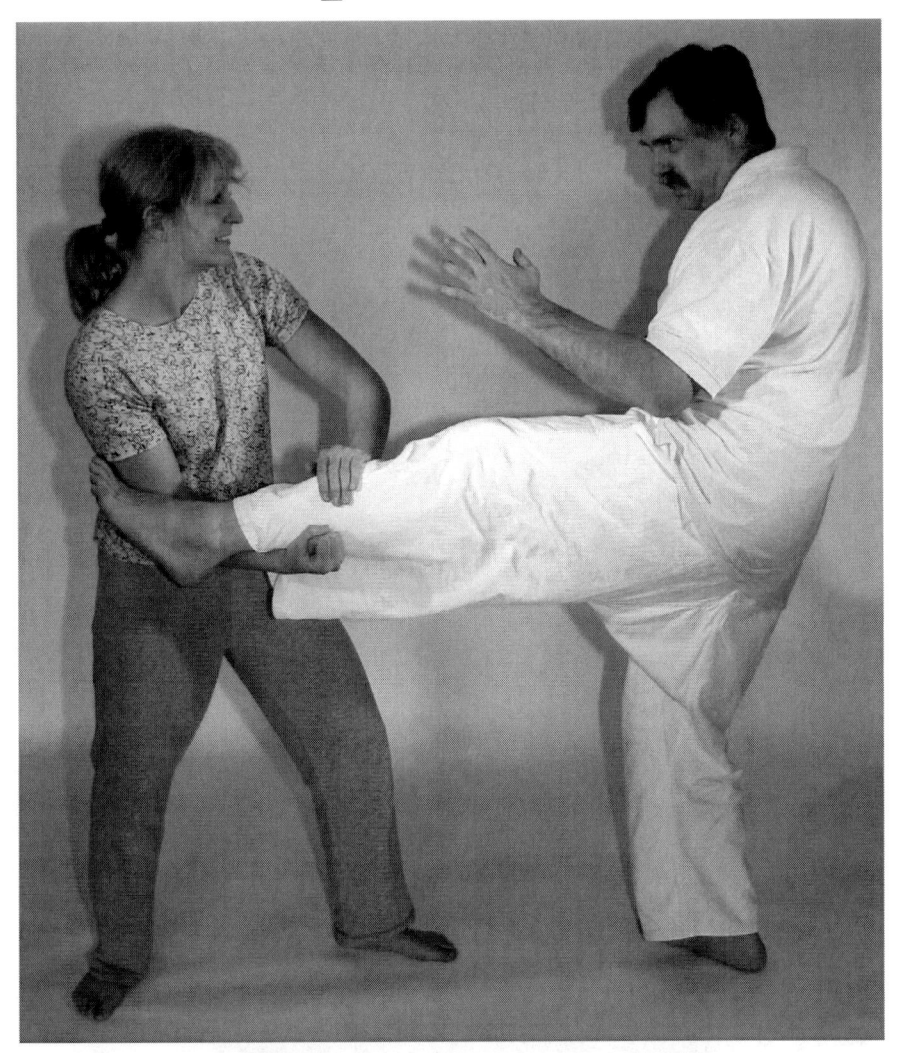

TOE TECHNIQUES

TECHNIQUE 3: CATCHING A KICK

You need to act quickly because you are grabbing a small target as your attacker fights against your catch.

1. Catch the attacker's front kick in the crook of your arm.

EXTREME JOINT LOCKING AND BREAKING

2. Before he can hop forward, step back to stretch his leg.

contents

Introduction 1

Chapter 1: **Finger Techniques** 5

Chapter 2: **Wrist Techniques** 25

Chapter 3: **Elbow Techniques** 51

Chapter 4: **Shoulder Techniques** . . 75

Chapter 5: **Neck Techniques** . . . 105

Chapter 6: **Back Techniques** . . . 127

Chapter 7: **Knee Techniques** . . . 143

Chapter 8: **Ankle Techniques** . . .157

Chapter 9: **Toe Techniques** 181

v

*But when the blast of war blows in our ears,
Then imitate the action of the tiger:
Stiffen the sinews, summon up the blood.*

—Shakespeare, *King Henry V*

warning

This book presents techniques designed to control and restrain through the application of pain. These techniques also have the potential to cause extreme injury, including damage to tendons, ligaments, and joints. In some cases permanent injury or even death could result.

It is the reader's responsibility to research and comply with all laws regarding self-defense, justified use of force in defense of one's life, and related areas. The author, publisher, and distributors of this book disclaim any liability from any damage or injuries of any type that a reader or user of information contained in this book may incur from its use or misuse. This book is presented *for academic study only*.

acknowledgments

I offer a respectful bow to my friend Professor Tim Delgman, a 9th-degree black belt, for appearing in many of the photos and advising on the techniques. Thanks also go to black belt student and friend Mark Whited; my daughter Amy; her husband, Jace Widmer; and my love, Lisa Place, for sharing their time posing for photos. And an especially big hug goes to Lisa for her work behind the camera and for putting up with my crankiness.

The following fellow martial artists offered suggestions, techniques, and critiques during the writing of this book:

Tim Delgman
Wim Demeere
Josh Bell
Amy Christensen
Bernard Cornet
Rock Dehon
Chris Fisk

Ian Hogan
Paul Janulis
Lawrence Kane
Lisa Place
Gary Sussman
Mark Whited

preface

To make this an easy-to-read, easy-to-reference text, and to reduce the clutter in the chapters, here are a few definitions used in the book and a comment about my approach to applying grappling techniques in a street encounter.

Break or fracture: Both words mean the same thing. The definition of a fracture is "the act or process of breaking."

Sprains and strains: A sprain is an injury to a ligament; a strain is an injury to a muscle.

Hyperextend: A joint is hyperextended when it's stretched or pushed beyond its normal range.

WHEN IN DOUBT, HIT

It's been my experience that in a real fight it's easier to apply grappling techniques when I hit first and when I can take my attacker by surprise. Grappling works even better when using both tactics.

During my 29 years in law enforcement, I used mostly the element of surprise because it was against policy to hit unless the situation was a high-risk one. Those few times when I did lead with a blow, the follow-up grappling went more smoothly. You will find that many of the following photo sequences lead with a hit to set up the grappling technique, and sometimes there is a blow in the middle of a sequence to help with a transition.

Hitting is good. It just makes things easier.

introduction

Jujitsu—also spelled *ju-jitsu, jiu-jitsu,* and *jutsu*—is considered by many experts to be the oldest form of martial art, one that many of today's fighting systems can claim as their roots. Historians tell us that jujitsu began sometime between the 11th and 12th centuries and was originally a generic term for all the ancient Japanese fighting arts. It wasn't until the 1600s that jujitsu became its own entity in Japan.

Many warriors relied on the early form of jujitsu on the battlefield, including samurai when they lost their swords during a fight. But during the 19th century, when the samurai era began to decline, jujitsu changed from a means of survival on the battlefield to the study of a mental and physical discipline.

Most often, *ju* is translated as "gentle" and *jitsu* as "art" or "combat." (Gentle combat?) It has also been translated to something similar to "compliant fighting techniques." This means that jujitsu doesn't involve resistance against force, but rather *redirection* of force. It's my opinion that both definitions are a little off target, as there is nothing gentle about breaking a neck, dislocating a shoulder joint, or hyperex-

EXTREME JOINT LOCKING AND BREAKING

tending a person's spine. And I don't agree that it doesn't involve resistance against force because sometimes it does. Since it doesn't serve any purpose to nitpick at these definitions, let's just say that they are ideals.

Jujitsu was one of the first martial arts systems practiced by Westerners, most often by U.S. servicemen stationed in Japan and Okinawa. Over the years it has adapted a little to fit modern times and modern practitioners, though it mostly remains true to its original concepts. While the majority of martial arts systems today have been modified for competition, and in so doing have lost much of their true combat qualities, many hard-core jujitsu practitioners argue that their fighting system should never be regarded as a sport, but rather remain a true combat system. Police agencies and armed forces around the globe agree since they rely on combat jujitsu to control, maim, and even kill.

This book isn't about sport fighting, flashy techniques, or how to become a better person through the mental and physical discipline of a martial art. The purpose of this text is to provide today's modern warrior—the self-defense oriented martial artist, combat soldier, and law enforcement officer—with easy-to-apply but devastating techniques that, when taken to their maximum potential, will inflict severe physical injury. The simple techniques outlined in this text are for surviving extreme circumstances when all other means have been exhausted or made impossible.

I assume that the professional warrior understands when such force is applicable and is familiar with the laws and guidelines under which it can be applied. It's paramount that civilian readers also know the laws as these laws pertain to self-defense and use of force in their communities.

I began my study of karate, kung fu, arnis, and jujitsu in 1965. As a result of serving nearly three decades in law enforcement, I've focused my training, teaching, and writing primarily on reality-based techniques. Many of the jujitsu techniques I have used on the street appear in this text. I have also called on my martial arts friends in the United States, Europe, and Asia to gather specific grappling tech-

INTRODUCTION

niques they know from experience to be devastatingly effective. Those too are in this book.

This book of proven techniques follows a theme. Not only are the moves painful in the extreme, they can also be used to dislocate joints, break bones, and wreak havoc on tendons, ligaments, and other support tissues. The injury might happen as a result of the attacker's resistance to the technique or because you deem such a level of force necessary given the extreme nature of the fight. For example:

1. The only way to stop the attacker's violent assault on you is to break his wrist or elbow.
2. The only way to get him to release his deadly grip on his weapon is to dislocate or break his fingers.
3. The only way to prevent him from continuing to attack and pursue you is to break his knee or ankle.
4. The only way to stop the assailant's deadly attack is to inflict severe trauma to his neck.

Clearly, these are extreme measures to be used in situations in which no other options are available. Better read that sentence again because if you deliberately dislocate or break an attacker's bone, you're going to have to prove that there were no other options available to you. First, you're going to have to prove it to the responding police officers after they roll up on the scene and find you standing tall and strong over a writhing form on the sidewalk. Then you will have to prove it again in court, in a criminal prosecution, civil case, or both.

Bottom line: Be justified before using extreme force.

I've organized this book using a device I call "walking the body." I start by examining techniques for the fingers, wrists, elbows, shoulders, and neck. Then I descend the body, examining techniques for the back, knees, ankles, and toes.

The pragmatism of the techniques can't be debated; they work. So whether you like or dislike a technique depends on personal preference based on your skill level, physical ability, experience in training, and experience on the street. I suggest that you practice the techniques until you can flow easily into them and then see how many situations you can devise in which you can apply them, such as while standing, on the ground, or in a tight, crowded space. The more you practice the movements in a variety of situations and settings, the greater your understanding of them will be.

Perhaps you have other techniques you like for a particular joint or one or two that you like better than the ones presented here. Simply make a note of them on paper and slip it into the pages of the appropriate chapter. Your noted techniques, as well as those in this book, will provide you with quick references for your training or teaching.

Okay, warm up, and let's get started.

CHAPTER 1
finger techniques

I classify pain as either general or acute. While general pain (a punch to the chest, a kick to the leg) hurts, acute pain (such as a sprained finger joint) may hurt so intensely that the brain can think of little else. I found this working as a street cop with chronic alcoholics on skid row. Early in my tour when I applied a wristlock, most of the inebriants looked at me as if to wonder why I was holding their hands. But when I cranked a finger in a direction it wasn't meant to go, they would suddenly dance on their toes, yelp, and beg for mercy. The finger pain was more intense and thus able to bypass those parts of their brains numbed with alcohol.

PHALANX FALLACY 1

Is it a guarantee that your attacker will stop his evil ways if you wrench or break his finger? No. If he is drunk on alcohol, high on drugs, or cooking on adrenaline, he might not feel it at all. I once broke a knuckle in my little finger on a resisting suspect but didn't feel it until 20 minutes after the man was cuffed and stuffed in my police car. The fight had fol-

EXTREME JOINT LOCKING AND BREAKING

THE FINGER AS A TARGET

Each finger has three bones, or phalanges: the proximal (closest to the hand), the middle, and the distal (farthest from the hand). The thumb has only two because there is no middle phalanx.

Jammed Finger
This usually results from a direct blow to the tip of a finger. It can cause tendon or ligament damage, as well as a fracture or dislocation of the bones.

Dislocation
A dislocation is an injury to a joint that causes a bone to move out of its normal alignment with another bone. Usually dislocation causes damage to the surrounding ligaments, which remain stretched and injured even after the dislocation is put back in place.

Break
A break might be a crack in a bone, or it might be when a phalanx or joint is broken into several pieces. Most often this occurs when the finger has been pulled or twisted suddenly and forcefully.

lowed a high-speed car chase and then a foot pursuit. My adrenaline was so deep into the red zone that I could have been run over by a truck and not felt it. But my finger sure hurt later.

Break your attacker's finger if you're justified, but don't allow the sound of the breaking bone—*pop!*—to stop you from fighting because it might not slow him down at all. More on this in a moment.

PHALANX FALLACY 2

Many self-defense classes advocate grabbing an attacker's finger and bending it in some way. That, claims the instructor, will stop the attacker in his tracks so that he no longer wants to pursue his course. Oh, really? It's been my

FINGER TECHNIQUES

experience that most people, when grabbed, simply jerk their hands away. Sure, a student will writhe, screech, and slap his thigh as his instructor demonstrates before the class, but in the real world the receiver pulls his hand away. Why? Because it hurts, that's why. *And because he can.* So what is the solution? There are two.

First, use a finger technique only when you have another restraint hold on the attacker. Use the finger hold to deliver a shock of acute pain to distract him so you can change to another hold or improve the one you have. Second, if you don't have a restraint hold, use a finger technique only if you intend to break the bone. There is no tweaking your attacker's finger and trying to make him get down on the ground, as some self-defense classes want you to believe is possible. If the situation warrants it, grab his finger, break it, and then run away to call 911.

TECHNIQUE 1:
BEHIND THE BACK WRISTLOCK WITH FINGER JAM

This is a standing handcuffing position used by many police officers around the globe. When you pull on the back of the hand (pulling the attacker's palm toward his elbow), the action painfully stretches the tendons and ligaments in his wrist. This makes it a good "escort" technique for removing an unwanted person from a bar or party. However, some people under the influence of drugs or alcohol might not feel this—what I referred to earlier—"general pain" technique. No problem, because the attacker's fingers are right there, ready and waiting.

EXTREME JOINT LOCKING AND BREAKING

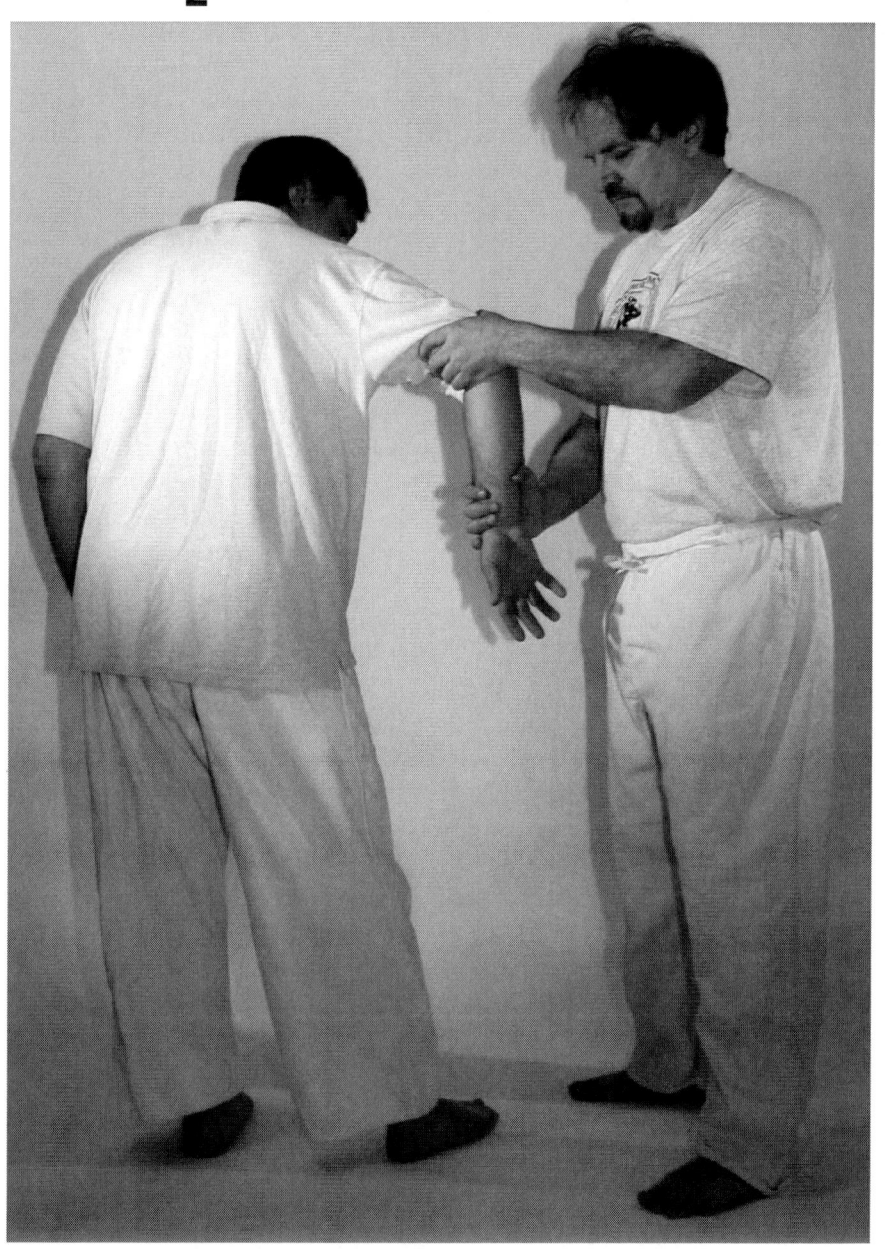

1. Grab your attacker's arm with both hands and begin to push it behind him. Start to rotate your right hand.

FINGER TECHNIQUES

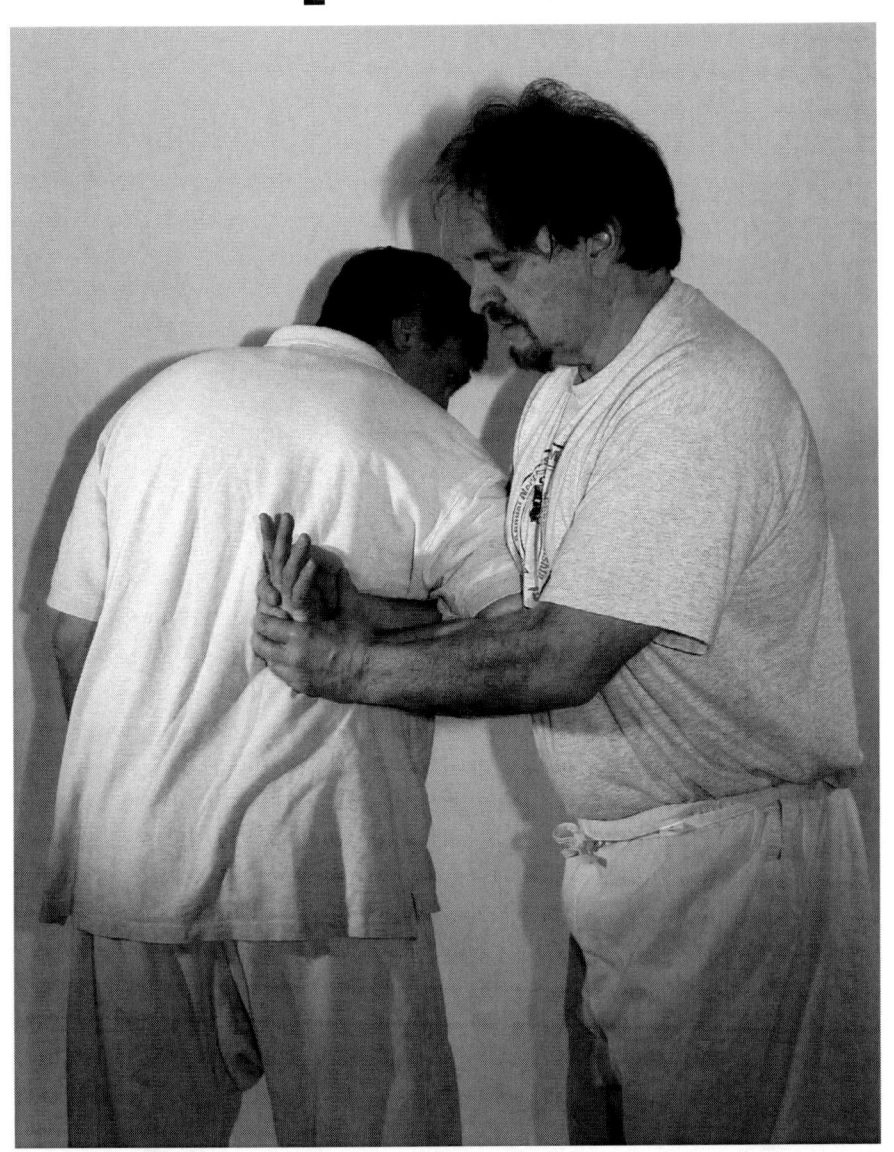

2. Step in close so that his elbow is against your side to provide a base for the wrist flex. Your hand is completely rotated now and pulling on the back of his hand. This is enough to elicit cooperation from most people, but let's say your person needs more.

⌞EXTREME JOINT LOCKING AND BREAKING⌝

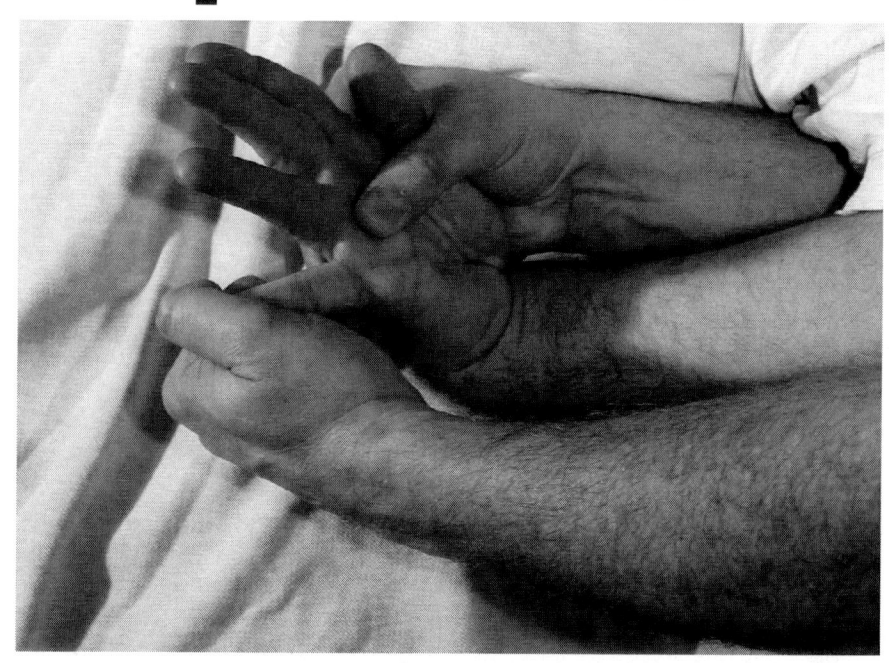

3. With your outside hand, grasp any finger and push it away from you. Push it back until his body jerks in pain.

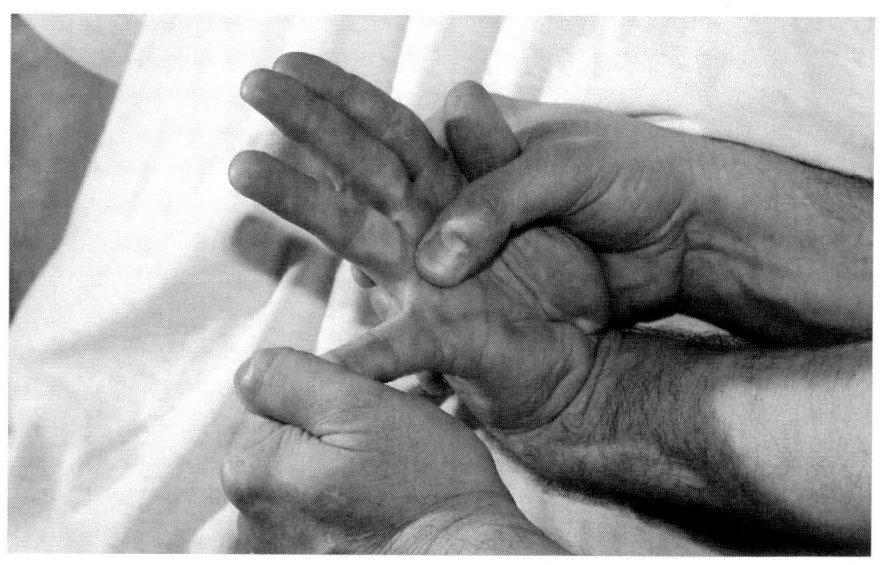

4. For added pain, push it off at an angle.

TOE TECHNIQUES

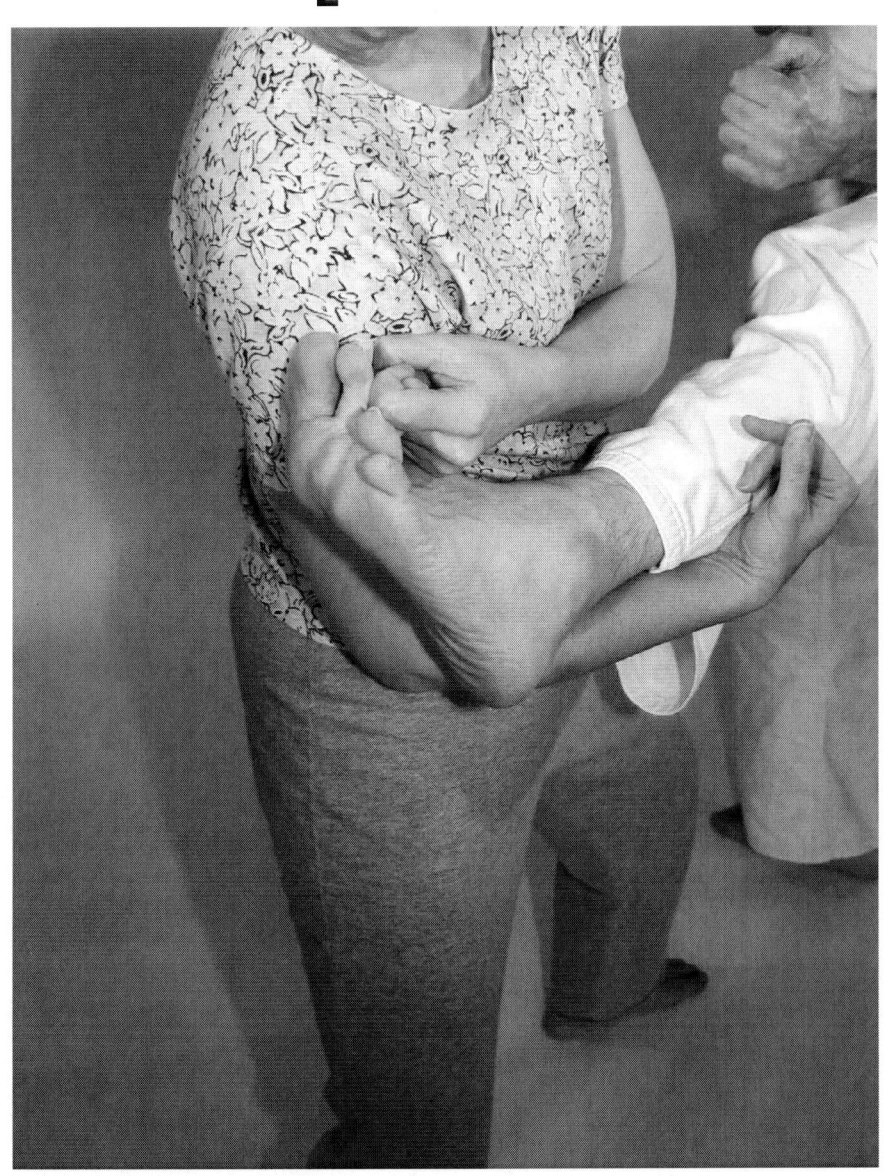

3. Then yank a toe back.